Evolutionary Psychology

Evolutionary Psychology

A Critical Introduction

Christopher Badcock

Polity

First published in 2000 by Polity Press
in association with Blackwell Publishers Ltd

Editorial office:
Polity Press
65 Bridge Street
Cambridge CB2 1UR, UK

Marketing and production:
Blackwell Publishers Ltd
108 Cowley Road
Oxford OX4 1JF, UK

Published in the USA by
Blackwell Publishers Inc.
350 Main Street
Malden, Massachusetts 02148, USA

ISBN 0–7456–2205–4
ISBN 0–7456–2206–2 (pbk)

A catalogue record for this book is available from the British Library.

Library of Congress Cataloging-in-Publication Data

Badcock, C. R.
    Evolutionary psychology : a critical introduction / Christopher Badcock.
        p.   cm.
    Includes bibliographical references and index.
    ISBN 0-7456-2205-4 (alk. paper) — ISBN 0-7456-2206-2 (pbk. : alk. paper)
        1. Genetic psychology.   2. Human evolution. I. Title.

BF701 .B235 2000
155.7—dc21   00-029126

Typeset in 10½ on 12 pt Sabon
by Ace Filmsetting Ltd, Frome, Somerset
Printed in Great Britain by T. J. International, Padstow, Cornwall

This book is printed on acid-free paper.

Contents

Figures

Boxes

Preface

In order to make this book as easy to read and to understand as possible, I have tried to make the text as straightforward and transparent as I can. I have assumed little or no existing knowledge of the subject in my readers, and developed the text out of many years' experience of teaching courses on evolution, psychoanalysis and sociology to university students studying for social science degrees. However, I have attempted to cover some difficult new material, and so I hope that readers who are knowledgeable in the field will not find the book without interest or value.

I must emphasize that this book is not intended to be a general critique of evolution or psychology. Because most evolutionary psychologists take the fundamental assumptions of modern Darwinism and genetics for granted, I have not spent much time discussing the many controversial questions that these subjects properly raise outside of evolutionary psychology. To do so would take us far from my main subject and would have resulted in a far longer book. However, where a fundamental issue of evolutionary interpretation does have pertinence to evolutionary psychology, I have discussed the difficulties that are relevant to it. A good example is the whole question of adaptation, which is discussed in the first chapter. Although I have space to do no more than allude to the considerable criticism that adaptationism in general has aroused, I do discuss the difficulties involved in the approach for evolutionary psychology in some detail.

Similar remarks apply to psychology: I have not discussed the problems posed, for example, by the modular or cognitive approaches to the mind in general, but do discuss them in some detail where they are relevant to evolutionary psychology. In general, I have not raised criti-

cal issues simply for the sake of being critical of evolutionary psychology, controversial though it may be. Instead, I have broached them
where they seemed in my judgement to be fundamental and significant
for a proper understanding of the subject.

This book is described as a critical introduction not because it is
critical of the fundamental claim that human psychology has evolved
– so much is indisputable – but because much criticism is warranted in
the application of that belief to particular aspects of psychology by
evolutionary psychologists. As a writer who adopted the term
PsychoDarwinism to distinguish his own view of evolved psychology
from that of others (Badcock 1994), I can be counted on to share the
overall aims and aspirations of evolutionary psychology, but to be
very critical of some of the particular forms that it usually takes. This,
I hope, has qualified me to be both sympathetic and objective in my
approach.

Essentially, there are two ways to write a book like this. One is to
make it as complete a survey as possible of the entire literature of the
subject. This provides coverage, but often at the cost of comprehension, because so much material has to be summarized so succinctly,
and because contradictions, discrepancies and disagreements in the
literature tend to be glossed over in the need to ensure equal representation to all points of view. By and large, this has not been my aim in
this book. Instead, I have adopted the alternative method of trying to
focus on key concepts, findings and arguments, and have attempted to
lay a secure conceptual foundation from which readers can venture
out into the literature on their own, confident that they grasp its fun-
damentals. To this extent, I hope that it will be as useful to readers
outside evolutionary psychology who wish simply to be informed about
its scope and claims as it will to those who are already well acquainted
with the field.

To date, most publications in evolutionary psychology have either
been technical papers published in journals and edited books, or popular
accounts, aimed at the general reader. This book is somewhere between the two, being intended for readers who may have little or no
existing knowledge of the field, but also being a critical review of published material. To this extent, you could see it as both an introduction to evolutionary psychology, and a commentary on some of the
existing literature. It attempts to get at the fundamental facts and theories of evolutionary psychology much more than the popular accounts
do, but also to take a wider, more critical view of the field than is
normally possible in a scientific paper. To this extent, I hope that it
will fill an important gap in the literature of the subject, and that it

will both equip and encourage readers to explore it further for themselves. Suggestions for further reading are given at the end of each chapter to help in this respect, and there is a full reference list of cited material at the end of the book.

Wherever possible, I avoid jargon and difficult language, but do try to carefully explain and define those technical terms that must be introduced. Definitions are also given in the glossary of technical terms at the end of the book. Boxes contain text that is additional or peripheral to the chapter in which it is embedded. Some of these feature examples of points made in the main text. Others add additional information or technical details. Some contain alternative material, or non-essential but still relevant additions to the central argument. Where the content of a box is relevant to the issue being discussed, it is indicated. The intention of having boxes is to keep the central argument of each chapter as simple and direct as possible, but not to rule out other relevant, illustrative or alternative material that may help with understanding it. Some boxes are relevant to more than one discussion, and where this is so, the reader's attention is drawn to them on each occasion.

Christopher Badcock

Acknowledgements

I have received the help of many different people in writing this book, and would particularly like to thank Peter Abell, Simon Baron-Cohen, Austin Burt, Charles Crawford, Timothy Crippen, Helen Fisher, Derek Freeman, Anthony Giddens, Simon Good, Oliver Goodenough, Valerie Grant, Edward Hagen, David Haig, the late William Hamilton, William Irons, Philip Johnson-Laird, Barry Keverne, Joan Kingsley, Joseph Lopreato, Benita Ludin, Robert Martin, David McFarland, Alex Monto, Fraser Muir, Randy Nesse, Kate Rigby, Antonio Santangelo, Rolf Schäppi, Jennifer Scott, Bill Shropshire, David Skuse, Joao de Sousa, Dan Sperber, Nigel Stead, Chris Stringer, Peter Sykora, Lili Tarkow-Reinisch, Andy Thompson, Robert Trivers, Eckart and Renate Voland, Andy Wells, George Williams, and Lewis Wolpert. The generous and untiring help of Robert Kruszynski of the Natural History Museum meant that this book is much better referenced and researched than it would have been otherwise. I am also indebted to my son, Louis, for finding some vital references and for drawing some of the figures. I must thank students following my courses at the London School of Economics during the academic year 1998–9, on whom much of what is here – and some of what is not – was tested. Finally, I am deeply indebted to Lynn Dunlop and John Thompson of Polity Press for invaluable editorial advice and guidance, and to Ann Bone for help with the preparation of the printed text and figures.

1
Selection and Adaptation

As far as we know, human beings are the only organisms in the universe who have evolved to the point where they are able to enquire about their own evolutionary origins. Today the claim that our bodies are the product of evolution is nothing like as widely contested as it once was. However, the proposition that not merely our anatomy and physiology but our psychology too might also have evolved is much more controversial. This is the subject matter of evolutionary psychology, and it is the aim of this book to introduce and explain the principles of the field to those with little or no existing knowledge of it.

The concept of evolution

Today the word *evolution* is strongly associated in people's minds with **Charles Darwin** (1809–1882) and his theory of natural selection. Yet Darwin himself only used the word once in the first edition of his *Origin of Species* (and only then at the very end, where the last word of the book is 'evolved'). In Darwin's day, 'to evolve' meant to unfold, roll out or unfurl (Pagel 1998). Darwin himself used the term 'transmutation' or the phrase 'descent with modification' rather than 'evolution' to suggest a slow, gradual change of one thing into another. Understood in the sense of continuous change, you could see evolution as contrasting with *revolution*, which means sudden, discontinuous change.

However, it was **Herbert Spencer** (1820–1903) who was mainly responsible for introducing the term 'evolution' to the English-speaking world. According to Spencer,

> Evolution . . . is a change from a less coherent form to a more coherent
> form. . . . Alike during the evolution of the Solar System, of a planet, of
> an organism, of a nation, there is progressive aggregation. . . . From the
> lowest living forms upwards, the degree of development is marked by
> the degree in which the several parts constitute a co-operative assem-
> blage . . . there are not several kinds of Evolution having certain traits
> in common, but one Evolution going on everywhere after the same
> manner. (Spencer 1884)

The antithesis of evolution for Spencer was not revolution, but disso-
lution. As this quotation shows, Spencer interpreted evolution as a
cosmic process of incremental aggregation and integration into increasingly more complex wholes that embraced the entire universe, organic
and inorganic, human and social. The culmination of this process at
the social level was human society, with the largest, most integrated
and complex societies representing its supreme expression. However,
science was also a product of the evolutionary imperative to combine
knowledge into larger and more integrated units, and here Spencer's
own work was evidently intended as the culmination of the trend: a
general philosophy based on the most general principle of all – Evolution.

Darwin took a different view

Despite the widespread assumption that evolution is inevitably progressive, Darwin himself confessed in a letter to a correspondent that
'After long reflection, I cannot avoid the conviction that no innate
tendency to development exists.' In *The Origin of Species* he added,
'The inhabitants of each successive period in the world's history have
beaten their predecessors in the race for life, and are, insofar, higher in
the scale of nature; and this may account for the vague, yet ill-defined
sentiment, felt by many palaeontologists, that organization on the whole
has progressed' (cited by S. J. Gould 1990: 257–8).

   To see what Darwin meant, suppose that you were standing on the
stage of a theatre. Outside there is a large crowd of people wanting to
get in to see some spectacle. Seats are allocated on a one-price, first-
come, first-served basis, and the doors are opened. What will happen?
Obviously, the first to get seats will want them at the front of the
stalls, normally the most expensive in a theatre. Once these are filled,
boxes and the centre and back stalls will begin to fill, as will the front
rows of the dress circle. When stalls, boxes and dress circle are filled,
higher circles will be filled, until eventually only the 'gods' – the high-

est seats, most distant from the stage – will remain. But are the gods the best seats, and would anyone with a free choice of any seat choose such a seat? Of course not. The gods only got filled because the rest of the theatre was full already.

This suggests an arresting parallel with evolution. The first-comers of organic evolution to the Earth found a completely open environment and filled the easiest and most accessible parts first – the equivalent of the stalls in my theatre analogy. These were the first, very simple unicellular organisms, descendants of which – bacteria – are still found in vast numbers everywhere on Earth. Later comers had to do a little more to survive, so they evolved separate nuclei in their cells, or became multi-cellular – the equivalent of those filling the circles in the theatre analogy. Eventually all these environments were filled and it was more likely than before that large, complex, 'higher' organisms would find new ways of exploiting what remained – often by preying on organisms 'lower' down the scale. Eventually, and very late in evolution in relation to the beginning, human beings, the 'highest' of all organisms, appeared – the 'gods' in my theatre simile.

The point of this analogy is that no one standing on the stage and watching such a theatre fill would make the mistake of thinking that higher seats were necessarily 'better' than lower ones. On the contrary, the evidence of their eyes would suggest the opposite: that it was the lower seats in the theatre, those nearer the stage, that were filled first, and the higher ones – including ultimately the gods – were only filled after all the lower ones were taken.

An objective view of organic evolution on Earth would take a similar view. Life evolved into increasingly complex and elaborated forms only because simpler and more fundamental ones had evolved first and had already colonized most of the available environments for such organisms, leaving newcomers to find new, 'more advanced' and usually more complicated ways of existing. There is no reason to presume that there is some universal law of progressive evolution apart from this as envisaged by Spencer – or at least, no reason to think so if the mechanism that drives evolution is the one discovered by Darwin.

Natural selection

Darwin's contribution to our understanding of evolution lay in his discovery of *natural selection* as a mechanism that could explain much evolutionary change. The inspiration for Darwin came in part from his interest in and astonishing knowledge of what by contrast we could call *artificial selection*. This term describes the human interference in animal and plant breeding that has resulted in the many domesticated species that we see around us today. Although all modern dogs are believed to be descended from a few wolf ancestors, they have been selectively bred by humans to be as different as a chihuahua or a Great Dane, a corgi or a greyhound. In each case, successive selection by human breeders for dogs with larger or smaller size, longer or shorter legs, has resulted in these and the many other different types of dog that exist today.

Darwin's great insight was to see that purely natural factors could have a similar result. For example, greyhounds have been bred to run fast and win races, giving them their characteristic long legs, deep chests, slender build and small heads. However, it is easy to see that natural factors could have selected for speed in a similar way, for instance in species of predators who engage in single-handed chases of fast-moving prey. Here the best example is the cheetah, which is even faster than the greyhound (and can reach speeds of 50 miles per hour for short periods). But just like the artificially selected greyhound, cheetahs too have very long legs, a light build, big lungs, and heads which are small in relation to the body. It is easy to see that success in catching prey may have selected these features in cheetahs in much the same way that success at winning races made breeders select them in greyhounds.

Artificial selection relies on the fact that traits like longer legs or bigger lungs may in large part be heritable, so that breeding from winners is likely to produce new winning greyhounds in the future. Similarly with natural selection: if long legs and the other features that make for speed in cheetahs were heritable, those cheetahs that possessed them the most would tend, not merely to be the best fed, but also to be those who would be most likely to hand them on to the greatest number of progeny, thanks to the contribution that food can make to reproductive success. Given long enough, natural selection for speed in the chase could produce results in a cat closely comparable to those which human breeders have achieved in a dog. Furthermore, the same principle could apply to any other heritable feature: natural selection could have exactly the same kinds of results that artificial selection is known to have had.

An important consideration – and one that was decisive for Darwin – was the realization that most species normally produce vastly more offspring than can ever survive, given the natural resources they need. Most plants, for example, produce large numbers of seeds, and many animals that lay eggs do so by the hundred, thousand or million. Clearly, rapid population growth is not just something of which human beings in the modern world are capable. Most species produce potential off-spring in staggering numbers, and could in principle expand exponentially (in other words, two original parents could have four offspring, who could produce eight grandchildren, sixteen great-grand-children, and so on). For Darwin, this meant that there was a constant and unremitting struggle for survival among the members of a species, both with each other and with other species that might compete for the same resources. Any natural factor that affected the survival and reproductive success of individuals in this struggle would effectively be playing a selective role – at least if it operated for long enough to affect the evolution of the species.

Another important assumption of the theory is that normally individuals in a species will vary slightly in many heritable traits. This variation is necessary to provide the differences that natural selection – just like artificial selection – might exploit. Common observation convinced Darwin that this was in fact the case and that in any population of plants or animals, such tendencies to variation always exist. He also found that new variations will sometimes appear that did not exist before, and to-day we would call these *mutations* (Darwin would have called them 'sports'). According to modern evolutionary theory, a mutation is a random, heritable variation in a population that arises spontaneously. Clearly, such mutations will add to the stock of variation in a species and provide further raw material on which selective forces can act.

Nevertheless, it is important to realize that evolution by natural selection doesn't claim that organisms are simply products of chance. On the contrary, its central concept is that they are the result of cumulative natural selection, which by definition is discriminating, and selects particular features that promote an organism's survival and/or reproductive success. Chance doesn't do any more than generate the variations and mutations from which natural selection selects. To this extent, it is quite true that Darwin's theory begins with chance factors, but the whole point of natural selection is that what is selected is not random, even though it may be selected from a random set. What is selected is selected because ultimately it confers better than average reproductive success on its possessors, and anything that departs from the average in a systematic way is by definition non-random.[1]

Most of the time, natural selection prevents evolution

A common error is to imagine that natural selection and evolution are synonymous, and that evolutionary change is continuously driven by natural selection to produce new forms. This is not necessarily true. To see why, consider the issue of mutation a little further.

Mutation can have three effects on an organism: it can improve its survival and/or reproductive success; it can damage its survival and/or reproductive success; or it can leave either or both unaffected. Because most living organisms are very complex, any random change – or mutation – in a given part or aspect of the organism is much more likely to damage it than it is to leave it unchanged, and it is even less likely to improve it. Imagine taking a watch to pieces, arbitrarily changing one part, then putting it back together again. You wouldn't be surprised if it worked less well – or not at all – afterwards. The same would happen with any complex, integrated whole; and living organisms are much more complex than watches.

This means that the vast majority of mutations will probably damage living organisms, rather than improve them. Because such mutations don't promote survival and reproductive success, natural selection will tend to eliminate them. Nevertheless, such mutations *are* evolutionary changes, and they occur constantly. Only very occasionally and exceptionally will a mutation promote the survival and/or reproductive success of an organism in which it finds itself, and only then will natural selection take a hand and perhaps preserve it.[2]

Survival of the fittest

'Survival of the fittest' was a phrase coined by Spencer to describe natural selection, and it is still widely used today, particularly in popular writing about evolution. As with Spencer's other term, 'evolution', Darwin himself was reluctant to adopt it, and with hindsight, it is easy to see why.

Survival is only a means to reproductive success   The first reason to be cautious about 'survival of the fittest' is that survival is not necessarily the key issue in evolution by natural selection. Although I linked survival and reproductive success together in my comments above about natural selection, a moment's thought reveals that they are not quite the same. As far as evolution understood as gradual change in a species is concerned, survival is only a means to the more important end of reproduction. This is because it is the number of descendants an organism has that determines its contribution to the evolution of the species. How long and how well an organism survives may often critically affect its ultimate reproductive success, but it is reproductive success and only reproductive success that ultimately matters where evolution is concerned.

Survival can cost reproductive success   Another reason why survival may only be a means to the end of reproductive success is that survival and reproductive success may imply trade-offs against each other: that is, more or better survival – less reproductive success, and vice versa. Because resources devoted to survival are often the same ones exploited for reproductive success (such as food), there usually is such a trade-off, so that an organism has the 'choice' of devoting those resources either to survival (say, laying down fat) or to reproduction (say, laying eggs). Clearly, an organism that was selected to divert all its resources to survival would lose out in the evolutionary competition with those that instead were selected to divert some or all of them to reproduction. Indeed, as box 1.1, 'Testosterone and fitness' points out, this is effectively what happens in human males, and explains their reduced life expectancy as compared to females.

The box on testosterone also illustrates another difficulty with 'survival of the fittest'. This is the tendency to interpret 'fitness' in terms of personal health and vigour. As the box explains, the very thing that promotes men's sporting success – testosterone – also significantly reduces their life expectancy and increases their vulnerability to death and disease from many causes. Once again, this is because personal health and vigour is a means to the end of reproductive success, rather than being an end in itself.

Because of such difficulties with the meaning of 'fitness', it is often modified in scientific literature with adjectives like 'Darwinian', 'true', 'heritable', 'genetic' and so on. As long as those using the term 'fitness' fully understand its meaning, no harm is done, but throughout this book I propose to avoid it wherever possible and substitute other terms, such as 'reproductive success', in part to escape the unfortunate associations brought to Spencer's slogan by Social Darwinism.

Errors about the meaning of 'fitness' underlie the worst excesses of some other nineteenth- and twentieth-century views of evolution. For instance, Spencer's concept of 'survival of the fittest' was applied to social inequality, suggesting that the powerful, wealthy and able-bodied members of society were products of a social equivalent of natural selection which determined that the 'fittest' should succeed and the less fit should fail. It was an inevitable consequence, according to this view, that those who were poor, ill, or disadvantaged in any way were not among the elect of evolution and were neither fit nor fitted to share the privileges enjoyed by those who had beaten them in the struggle for survival. Indeed, some argued that merely to support or to succour such evolutionary failures was perverse and worked against the grand plan of evolution: it would weaken the race and

Box 1.1

Testosterone and fitness

Men die more readily than women at all ages from all causes which can affect both sexes – an effect which is seen from conception to death and can only be reversed by castration. In early adulthood men are approximately 400% more likely to die from accidents, wounds and stress than are women, and remain at least 100% more prone to death from these causes up to age 75. Where violent death is concerned, a man is 20 times more likely to be murdered by another man than is a woman by another woman.

However, marked differential life expectancy can also be found between male and female members of celibate, non-violent and abstemious religious orders, and a similar finding is also reflected in heart disease, the leading cause of death for both sexes in the United States, where women again have only 30% the mortality of men between the ages of 35 and 54. Nevertheless, castrated tom-cats live longer than their intact male counterparts, and so do human castrates. Detailed comparisons standardized for age, intelligence and category of mental deficiency among castrated and intact inmates of a mental institution in Kansas demonstrated that the median age at death of intact men was 55.7 years, as compared to 69.3 years for castrates, and that the earlier the castration was performed, the more life expectancy increased. These data suggest that it is being male and being subject to the effects of male sex hormones – principally testosterone – that actually shorten male life-spans.

Such observations can't be explained as the consequence of social causes, because the greatest rate of male wastage occurs before birth, and in some societies male mortality is lowest when male and female sex roles are most differentiated in early adulthood. However, testosterone levels in males are ten times what they are in females, don't overlap significantly in their range, and are detectably different between the sexes from birth.

One known effect of testosterone is to raise the resting metabolic rate of males by approximately 5% as compared to females. Effectively, this means that the male biochemical 'engine' is running about one-twentieth faster all the time than is that of a woman, perhaps explaining why it wears out sooner. Again, a major factor in enhanced male vulnerability to death, disease and injury is the greater aggressiveness and readiness to take risks characteristic of males – and this, too, seems to be an effect of testosterone. Finally, testosterone depresses the immune system, and thereby increases vulnerability to disease.

If castrated males survive better than sexually intact ones, as they are indeed known to do, and if evolution does in fact select the fittest in the sense of personal survival, why has natural selection not selected males without testes? Put in plain terms such as these the answer is obvious. Males without testes would do somewhat better in terms of individual survival and resistance to all causes of death at all ages, but they would leave no descendants who could enjoy those advantages! From this we can draw the correct conclusion, insufficiently appreciated until astonishingly recently: selection selects ultimately for reproductive success, not necessarily or primarily for personal survival. If it does select for the latter – and, of course, it certainly does so to a large extent in practice – the only reason that it does is that personal survival, health, longevity or whatever are necessary factors in promoting an individual's ultimate reproductive success, rather than being factors selected in themselves irrespective of reproductive success.

dilute the 'fitness' of society as a whole. Here was 'survival of the fittest' perfecting, not merely individuals, but entire civilizations!

These views seem to be the inevitable consequence of errors about what natural selection actually selects and an outcome of the belief that evolution is primarily concerned with increments to individual health and welfare, rather than anything else. But if we take the correct view that true, Darwinian fitness is only another term for reproductive success, there is no way in which we could make these mistakes. In other words, Darwinian fitness implies a purely *quantitative* measure – differential reproductive success; it does not necessarily imply any other kind of necessary qualitative improvement, superiority or enhancement of an organism's individual attributes.[3]

Three assumptions about adaptations

Natural selection produces *adaptations*: that is, traits which serve to promote an organism's survival and reproductive success. As such, adaptations have a parallel in the traits selected in artificial selection, for example, long legs and speed in greyhounds. These characteristics of greyhounds are adaptations in the sense of being modifications of traits that can be found in all dogs. Every dog has legs, and all dogs can run, but in greyhounds the legs and other features have been adapted for speed, resulting in the characteristic, lean, long-legged look of the greyhound. However, we have already seen that natural factors could have selected for speed in a similar way and have indeed produced very similar adaptations in cheetahs.

Three assumptions are commonly made about adaptations, and it is important to understand these from the start, because failure to do so often leads to misunderstanding of evolutionary explanations and much unnecessary argument.

1   **Adaptive on average**   Because natural selection works on large numbers of organisms, the basis of selection is inherently statistical, rather than exact. This means that the effects of adaptations also need to be seen in a statistical, averaged-out context, and as applying to populations and typical cases, rather than to every individual and any particular case.

Any adaptation is not necessarily always and invariably adaptive in all circumstances. Wings in birds may be adaptive for flight, but they can be severe encumbrances on the ground or in water. Large tails promote an individual peacock's reproductive success, but peahens fly much better without them! An adaptive behaviour like freezing into stillness when a predator appears may save the life of an animal, but won't necessarily do so every time. On the contrary, there would have to be cases where an individual who froze but still got eaten might have escaped if it had tried to do so. However, the assumption is that freezing evolved as an adaptation to attack by predators because it worked more often than not, not because it necessarily worked every time.

2   **Adaptive all other things being equal**   There may be other factors that intrude to limit or negate the effect of an adaptation, and these need to be separated out from the effects of the adaptation itself. For example, it is clearly adaptive for parents to feed their offspring because such offspring are their reproductive success, and as we have already seen, reproductive success is the only currency accepted by natural selection. However, some birds who lay two eggs normally only feed the first to hatch, and ignore the second, who usually starves to death, or is killed (and sometimes eaten) by its elder sibling. How can that be adaptive? And why isn't an obviously adaptive behaviour – feeding the chick – directed towards both offspring?

The answer is that other things are not equal for the second chick because it is the second, rather than the first. Birds who lay two eggs like this often normally only fledge one chick per season. But that in itself makes it critical to have a chick to fledge. The second chick is a back-up who would be fed if the first failed to hatch, or to thrive when it did. Hatching order makes all the difference, and means that feeding the first chick to hatch is indeed adaptive. But feeding the second too is usually not adaptive, simply because the parents would normally not be able to find enough food to feed both chicks, and trying to do so would probably mean that neither fledged (Mock and Parker 1997).[4]

3 Adaptive in the conditions in which the adaptation originally evolved Obviously, human beings did not evolve originally in a modern, urban environment, and with the benefit of the things you would find there, such as technology, modern communications, plentiful food and sophisticated health-care. This means that our adaptations may have to be seen in an earlier evolved context, rather than in that of a modern society.

A good example might be our liking for sweet, salty or fatty foods. Such foods were scarce in our primal environment, and so natural selection arranged our preferences for them so that we would consume as much of them as we could when we got the opportunity. Dietary fibre, on the other hand, was impossible to avoid in primal conditions, and so no particular liking for it was necessary. Today the situation is quite different, and excessive and prolonged consumption of sweet, salty or fatty foods and insufficient consumption of dietary fibre can be severely maladaptive (Strassmann and Dunbar 1999). But that is simply because our tastes are adapted for the past, not for the present.

The EEA

This third point about adaptations is particularly pertinent to evolutionary psychology because some writers see it as distinctive of the field. They take the view that evolutionary psychology represents an advance over earlier evolutionary thinking as applied to human beings because it makes a central issue of the fact that we are not necessarily adapted to a modern, industrial way of life, but to an earlier, more traditional one. Some call this the *environment of evolutionary adaptedness*, or EEA for short (see box 1.2, 'The human environment of evolutionary adaptedness').

According to evolutionary psychologists, human beings have lived in small hunter-gatherer groups for over 99 per cent of the million-odd years our species has existed. Some think that 'This hunting and gathering way of life is the only stable, persistent adaptation humans have ever achieved,' and go on to claim that 'insufficient time has elapsed since the invention of agriculture 10,000 years ago for significant change to have occurred in human gene pools' (Symons 1979: 35). Other evolutionary psychologists castigate those who take current benefits of an adaptation into account when explaining it for not being 'adaptationists in the strict Darwinian sense' because only past conditions can explain present adaptations (Tooby and Cosmides 1997: 293).

Box 1.2

The human environment of evolutionary adaptedness

The term 'environment of evolutionary adaptedness', or EEA for short, was first introduced by the psychoanalyst, **John Bowlby** (1907–1990), and today has become a central tenet of evolutionary psychology.

Bowlby points out that no organism is so flexible that it is adapted to any and all environments. On the contrary, organisms are adapted to particular conditions that constitute their EEA. He adds that although it is usually safe to assume that the habitat occupied by a species today is the same, or very similar to, its EEA, this is not so in the case of human beings because today humans live in many more, very different, and often more quickly changing environments than they did in the past. This leads to the conclusion that the human EEA is represented, not by the present environments of human beings, but by the period of approximately 2 million years preceding the emergence of the diversified habitats seen today. He concludes that *'the only criterion by which to consider the natural adaptedness of any particular part of present-day man's behavioural equipment is the degree to which and the way in which it might contribute to population survival in man's primeval environment.'* (Bowlby 1982: 59, emphasis in the original).

Although there is understandable controversy about the details of the human EEA, most students of the subject would accept the following general characteristics as broadly likely:

- hunter-gatherer and/or scavenging subsistence;
- nomadic or semi-nomadic pattern of movement;
- low population density;
- relatively small, kin-based groups;
- stone-age technology at best;
- relatively high infant mortality and low life expectancy by modern standards;
- generally much greater vulnerability to the natural environment;
- fewer lifestyle options than in later societies.

In many respects the most sensible way to characterize the human EEA for the purposes of evolutionary psychology might be in negative terms: in other words, to realize that humans are not necessarily adapted for life in modern industrial societies, with high population densities, fixed places of residence, complex social groupings, bureaucracy, transportation, mass media, medicine, technology, plentiful food and minimal exposure to natural selection (at least as it would have operated in the EEA). This also meets the objection that there may never have been one EEA, or one continuous EEA, but rather multiple ones. Here the point would be that most modern human environments are simply not the same as the primal conditions in which our species first evolved.

However, as the evolutionary anthropologist William Irons has argued in a recent paper, the current reproductive consequences of an adaptation sometimes are a guide to what occurred in the past. Indeed, he points out that 'Saying that human beings were . . . hunter-gatherers for one or two million years creates a false picture of stasis during this period.' In his view, 'the statement that 10,000 years is not enough time for evolutionary change is hard to defend.' Irons adds that in the generational equivalent of just a tenth of that (30 generations, rather than 300–400), laboratory mice have been bred 'to obtain non-overlapping distributions of behavioral traits'. He also notes that there is strong evidence that certain human physiological adaptations, such as sickle-cell anaemia, have evolved in much more recent times (Irons 1998).

According to other critics of evolutionary psychology, you might just as well argue that Stone Age hunter-gatherers were maladapted to their way of life because for millions of years prior to that their ancestors were vegetarians. They add that a growing body of evidence suggests that evolved reproductive striving continues to translate into reproductive success in traditional, kin-based societies that have not undergone the demographic transition to smaller family sizes of the past century (Strassmann and Dunbar 1999). Indeed, if reproductive success is taken as the ultimate proof of successful adaptation, modern human populations have far outperformed our hunter-gatherer predecessors, despite being allegedly 'maladapted' for modern ways of life: 'Today we number approximately six billion. That would seem to be proof enough of our being adapted to current conditions' (Lopreato and Crippen 1999: 131).

Adaptations need not be relevant only to the EEA

Clearly, the present consequences for reproductive success of an adaptation do not necessarily tell us anything about how and why it originally evolved – but neither should it be assumed that they tell us nothing. Many psychological adaptations may still work in circumstances very similar to those in which they originally evolved simply because the major environmental factor shaping their evolution was the presence of other people who had evolved in a similar way. Despite dramatic changes in subsistence and population density, there may still remain much in the human, psychological environment that is essentially the same as it ever was. If so, modern conditions may be relevant to adaptive evolution, and present-day adaptive pay-offs could sometimes be a good guide to the origins of the adaptation concerned.

An example might be risk-taking. Numerous studies in many different contexts consistently and reliably indicate a marked difference between the sexes where taking risks is concerned. With one exception, women are much less likely to indulge in behaviour that risks life and limb by comparison to men. Indeed, a recent study showed that the predicted differences in risk-taking behaviour could still be found in kibbutzniks after three generations of socialization aimed at eliminating sex-role differences. Only in one respect were women ready to take greater risks than men, and that was in defence of their own children. With this one exception, men remained the prime risk-takers (Lampert and Yassour 1992).

Such findings readily fit evolutionary expectations because, as we shall see in more detail in a later chapter, a man's reproductive success normally varies much more than a woman's. Because a woman's ultimate reproductive success is determined by the number of pregnancies she can manage in one lifetime, and because her physical well-being is critical to successfully completing a pregnancy and raising her offspring, taking risks with her life or reproductive future is not normally rewarded by natural selection. However, a man has much more to gain from risky behaviour because his only obligatory contribution to a future offspring is a single sperm, and this even an injured or disabled man may well be able to provide. Furthermore, because men produce such sperms by the million each day, the only limit on a man's reproductive success is the number of women he can inseminate. If taking risks with life and limb can increase that number significantly for a man – for example by competing with other men for mates – then risk-taking will be selected in males in a way it is unlikely to be in females, who never need more than a single male per pregnancy as far as insemination is concerned (see below, pp. 152–5).

Despite the great differences between our modern and primal ways of life, there need be no essential difference where a readiness to take risks is concerned because all that is different is the circumstances that surround the risk, not the risk-taking itself. Driving fast, sky-diving, or betting large sums of money may not have been risky behaviours in which our primal ancestors could indulge, but there would probably have been just as many – if not more – risky alternatives that they encountered in their hunter-gatherer way of life. Given that risk-taking as such appears to be a naturally selected sex-specific difference, there is no reason to think that its expression today is in any way essentially different from what it was in the past: something that could (with the exception of defending children) benefit males more than females.

If you take evolutionary psychologists' view that human adaptations relate only and exclusively to the past, it implies that natural selection is not of much importance in the present. Nevertheless, even though modern technology and culture may protect human beings from some effects of natural selection, they clearly have not succeeded in making them totally immune to it – or in completely randomizing or equalizing reproductive success. Climate, disease and differential access to resources still take a systematic toll on the human population. According to the 1996 *World Health Report*, 17 million of 52 million human deaths during the previous year were the result of infectious disease. The Global Burden of Disease Study ranked respiratory infections and diarrhoeal diseases as respectively the first and second leading causes of death in 1990. It is estimated that half a billion people are infected with malaria, and half of all human beings are at risk of endemic disease of one kind or another. Twenty-nine new diseases, among them Ebola, Lyme disease and AIDS, have emerged in the last two decades (World Health Organization 1996).

Cultural developments, such as the invention of agriculture and the growth of urbanization, have greatly increased human vulnerability to many diseases, especially infectious ones. Measles epidemics will die out in places like isolated islands unless a fresh supply of victims arrives, and a convincing case has been made that the disease could not have persisted before the emergence of large population concentrations. The same is true of plague epidemics in France in the 1720s: 88 per cent of villages with fewer than one hundred people were spared, but all cities with more than ten thousand inhabitants were severely afflicted, while the fates of towns of intermediate size was proportional to their populations. Urban yellow fever is spread by a mosquito that breeds mainly in water stored in human habitations, and a sedentary life also increases vulnerability to schistosomiasis, malaria and other diseases that are transmitted through water or air (Strassmann and Dunbar 1999). Nor is this always limited to the poor and to those least protected by the advances of civilization. In the case of the 1950s polio epidemic, poorer people were protected by having been exposed to the virus in childhood and having thereby acquired a lifetime immunity which members of more affluent classes lacked. Because antibiotics select for resistance to themselves in the diseases they treat, natural selection interacts with human beings even at the forefront of technology and remorselessly reduces both the number of drugs available and their effectiveness (Armelagos 1997).

To the extent that evolution is ultimately a question of non-random reproductive success, there is again no reason to think that modern civilization has necessarily equalized or completely randomized natural selection. **R. A. Fisher** (1890–1962), one of the chief architects of modern Darwinism, concluded that human reproductive success is extremely uneven, and therefore subject to strong selection pressures. For example, Darwin's cousin, **Francis Galton** (1822–1911), drew attention to the unusually low fecundity of the English aristocracy and attributed it to the tendency for peers to marry heiresses as a means of adding to their estates. He suggested that in a society where wealth was inherited by sons, such heiresses were more likely to arise in small families with reduced fertility, and that marriages with them would have lower fecundity as a result. The 1912 Australian census found that 50 per cent of children were the offspring of one in nine of men and one in seven women. Three-fifths of all children born died unmarried, and 11 per cent of marriages were sterile (Cummins 1999). And according to *Social Trends 1996*, it is expected that just under 20 per cent of British women born in years before 1957 will be childless by the end of their reproductive lives (Office of National Statistics 1996).

Designer Darwinism

In many ways, you could see Darwin's discovery of evolution by natural selection as a refutation of the following famous argument by **William Paley** (1743–1805):

> Suppose that I had found a watch upon the ground, and it should be enquired how the watch happened to be in that place . . . the inference, we think, is inevitable: that the watch must have a maker, there must have existed, at some time and at some place or other, an artificer or artificers, who formed it for the purpose which we find it actually to answer; who comprehended its construction, and designed its use. (Paley 1986)

In this passage, Paley argued that because living organisms resemble things like watches in the intricacies of their working, they also pose the same question: who made them, and why? Paley's answer was obvious to him: God must have made them. As we saw earlier, Darwin proposed an alternative answer in natural selection. Now we need to explore the issue of adaptation somewhat further and specifically consider how it has been applied in evolutionary psychology.

Paley's approach is often called *the argument from design*. Natural selection doesn't deny that organisms are designed in some sense, but it does emphatically deny an agent – a creator – and any *intention* on the part of the evolutionary process. According to the theory of evolution by natural selection, any appearance of design in organisms is not the result of any plan in the mind of a conscious agent. On the contrary, evolution by natural selection requires no more than that randomly occurring mutations and variations should be preserved if they confer some benefit to the survival and reproductive success of the organism in question. The result may look like design, and might in some respects even be very close to what a human designer might propose, but it would not be design in the sense of something that was *intended* by anything or anyone. Indeed, you could say that the great strength of evolution by natural selection was that it dispensed with any need for considerations of intention in evolutionary explanation. Nevertheless, people can all too easily make the mistake of thinking that Darwinian evolution simply substitutes natural selection for God, and that everything that has evolved has been well designed by natural selection for its proper purpose, just as Paley thought that every living being had been created by God for some good reason.

For example, according to a recent account, evolutionary psychology 'is engineering in reverse ... The mind is a system of organs of computation, designed by natural selection to solve the kinds of problems our ancestors faced' (Pinker 1997: 38, 21). Writing the Introduction to *The Adapted Mind*, one of the first and most important collections of essays on modern evolutionary psychology, Cosmides, Tooby and Barkow claim that

> One can use theories of adaptive function to help one discover psychological mechanisms that were previously unknown. When one is trying to discover the structure of an information-processing system as complex as the human brain, knowing what its components were 'designed' to do is like being given an aerial map of a territory one is about to explore by foot. If one knows what adaptive functions the human mind was designed to accomplish, one can make many educated guesses about what design features it should have, and can then design experiments to test for them. (1992: 10)

However, according to another view, if you adopted the reverse-engineering approach to the human shoulder, you might conclude that it is designed well for swinging in trees. But if you reverse-engineered the human foot, you would find a rigid extremity designed for striding which was incapable of grasping anything, let alone swinging from it. On the strength of the foot you would probably conclude that human beings were wholly terrestrial and had never lived in trees. Laboratory tests would show that young humans can hang and swing by their arms (just as the design of the shoulder indicates), and that they even enjoy these activities. Nevertheless, hanging by the arms from trees has little to do with basic, evolved human activities, such as foraging, moving about or survival (Potts 1997).

As these examples show, the reverse-engineering approach raises many difficulties, even for quite simple physical adaptations like limbs, let alone much more complex ones, such as the human mind. The problems just mentioned in the case of human limbs relate to their evolutionary origins, and clearly, serious errors can result from not knowing what constraints evolutionary origins and individual development have placed on an adaptation. Given that we know even less about the evolution of the human mind than we do about human limbs, these considerations suggest caution and scepticism about reverse-engineering human psychology.

Writing 30 years ago, one of the foremost authorities on modern Darwinism, George Williams, remarked that

> Major difficulties . . . arise from the current absence of rigorous criteria for deciding whether a given character is adaptive, and, if so, to precisely what it is an adaptation. . . . adaptation is often recognized in purely fortuitous effects, and natural selection is invoked to resolve problems that do not exist. If natural selection is shown to be inadequate for the production of a given adaptation, it is a matter of basic importance to decide whether the adaptation is real. . . . adaptation is a special and onerous concept that should be used only where it is really necessary.

Williams concludes that 'This biological principle should be used only as a last resort' (Williams 1966: 4, 11). Nor is Williams alone: other prominent biologists have pointed out the weaknesses of adaptationism, notably Lewontin (1978, 1979a, 1979b) and Gould (S. J. Gould and Lewontin 1979).

Reverse-engineering is a variant of the argument from design

Whereas Paley assumed that the watch-like nature of living things obviously suggested a watchmaker, evolutionary psychologists assume that the characteristics of the mind obviously suggest that its maker – natural selection – made it to solve cognitive problems faced by our ancestors. In other words, reverse-engineering assumes that the presumed function of an adaptation gives you an insight into *why* something evolved, not just *how*. Clearly, this does the exact opposite of what George Williams recommends in the quotation above, because reverse-engineering begins with the assumption that the mind must be an adaptation for something, such as problem-solving. Rather than appealing to adaptation as a last resort in the way that he recommends, reverse-engineering makes it a first principle of evolutionary psychology.[5]

Design flaws in evolution

According to the evolutionary psychologists Leda Cosmides and John Tooby, in order to show that something is 'an adaptation to perform a particular function, one must show that it is particularly well designed for performing that function, and that it cannot be better explained as a by-product of some other adaptation or physical law' (Cosmides and Tooby 1987). The problem here is that judging how 'particularly well designed' something is introduces what might seem like a subjective value judgement, and certainly raises difficulties where adaptations are clearly flawed in their design or are complicated or compromised by other adaptations.

For example, the human eye appears to be the wrong way round as far as the layering of cells is concerned. The blood vessels and nerves are on top of the light receptors and this not only obscures the view, but creates a tendency for the retina to become detached. It also means that there has to be a hole in the retina through which the nerve fibres and blood vessels can exit. Ideally this would be in the front half of the eye, where no light falls. In fact, the hole is not far from the centre of vision and creates a significant blind-spot. An altogether better design would be the obvious one of having the wiring and plumbing behind the retina, which is what is found in molluscs like the squid and octopus.

The reason the eye is inverted in this respect is probably because the light-sensitive skin cells from which the vertebrate retina originally evolved were under the surface of the skin, rather than on top of it. Having started that way up, the eye remained so to this day. In short, the back-to-front design is probably a legacy of the eye's evolutionary origin; it is not necessarily an adaptive feature in itself.

Sometimes maladaptive outcomes and suboptimal design are the result of developmental constraints on an organism. Here an example is nipples in men, which can even produce milk in some circumstances. Yet men have never evolved to share breast-feeding with women, despite the obvious advantages. On the contrary, men bear the cost of breast tissue in the form of a vulnerability to breast cancer, without gaining any real benefit from it. A rationally designed man would either have functional breasts and thereby gain the benefit, or develop with no breast tissue at all, and thereby avoid the cost. Why then, has evolution produced nipples in men?

The answer probably is that mammals like human beings begin with a female body plan in the embryo, and males then deviate from it. Nipples are started before differentiation of the male is complete, and so they are left in place, but never finished, so to speak. In other words, nipples in men are not necessarily adaptations in themselves, but may simply be by-products of a critical adaptation – mammary glands – in women. Retaining them in adult men may be no more optimal than the design of the eye. Again, the sperm ducts in men are vastly longer than need be, looping around the ureter rather than running direct from testes to penis. This is because during development the testes migrate to the scrotum from the position in which the female ovary remains, trailing the sperm ducts after them.

A further constraint is that an adaptation may confer a benefit at one stage of development, but a cost at another. An example is the finding that non-insulin dependent diabetes and the stroke and coronary heart disease with which it is often associated correlate strongly with low birth weight. However, other components of insulin resistance syndrome may be persisting effects of adaptations which enabled the fetus to continue growth in the face of limited nutrient supply and to protect key organs and tissues, especially the brain. Such responses to deficits in early development are likely to be favoured by natural selection even though they may lead to disease and premature death in later life (Barker 1998, 1999).

Indeed, senescence – something which is absolutely fundamental to all organisms that have a determinate life cycle – hardly seems 'adaptive' because its ultimate effect is to kill the organism, rather than to contribute to its survival or reproductive success. But like non-insulin dependent diabetes, senescence appears to be a case of paying the cost of genes that benefit the organism during development and reproduction. Effectively, this is a 'live now – pay later' situation: genes that promote survival and reproductive success early in development are strongly selected, but natural selection acts much more weakly to select out those that reduce it late in development when contributions to reproductive success are slight or non-existent (Williams 1966; Hamilton 1996: 83–128).

Another factor that can complicate and confuse adaptations is the way that a single organ or feature of an organism can come to serve more than one adaptive function. Both food and drink and air have to share the same pathway down the human neck. This means that you risk choking every time you eat or drink, and results in a small, but significant number of deaths from food particles getting stuck in the air-way. A further example is the way that the digestive tract has been co-opted for reproductive functions in many organisms. Because reproduction demands handling fluids like semen or expelling solids like eggs from the body, openings and tracts already present for digestion and excretion have tended to be used for reproductive purposes too. In human beings, the female digestive and reproductive tracts only converge at the point where they leave the body, but in men serious complications can arise because both systems use much of the same plumbing. Organs like the penis and urethra come to serve two adaptive functions, and these don't always co-exist happily because what goes wrong with one system can – and often does – affect the other.

The lesson taught by all of these examples is that just because something has evolved doesn't necessarily mean that it is 'particularly well designed' for performing its function. On the contrary, these cases suggest that many important adaptations in the human body are not particularly well designed for their adaptive purpose and are certainly far from optimal in the way they work.

Suboptimal design is often found in human artefacts

Suboptimal or perverse design in evolved adaptations should not surprise us because we find it even in human artefacts, where you would think that rational, intentional design was more likely to ensure an optimal outcome. Nevertheless, the fact that a product might be well designed and better than another is no guarantee that it will be a marketing success. The fact that the Betamax system of video recording or the Macintosh personal computer operating system were in many ways technically superior to the alternatives available at the time did not ensure that these systems were in fact adopted in the marketplace. On the contrary, both were supplanted by inferior systems which nevertheless managed to sell in much greater numbers – because they were cheaper to buy, for example, or more compatible with other systems. If this can happen in the evolution of products consciously optimized in many respects, how much more likely is it in the case of natural selection, where there is no such design philosophy – or indeed any designer whatsoever. Clearly, what we can't even always ensure in our creations we should not assume in nature's!

The Swiss army knife model of the mind

Cosmides and Tooby are fond of using a Swiss army knife to illustrate
their concept of the adapted mind. Just as such a knife has many different blades, each shaped for its specific purpose, so the mind, they
claim, is composed of many different modules, each evolved for a different adaptive purpose (Horgan 1995; Barkow et al. 1992). A common reaction on seeing such a knife is to wonder, not just at how
many strange blades and attachments it has, but what they could be
for: trying to reverse-engineer it, in other words.

To the extent that a Swiss army knife comprises many different
blades, it makes a passable analogy with the many different components which we now suspect underlie something like IQ. In part, the
Swiss army knife metaphor has been put forward as a corrective to the
idea that the mind was a general purpose learning device that could be
taught more or less anything because cognitive skills were general,
rather than specific.

The problem with using a Swiss army knife as a metaphor for the
'adapted mind' is similar to the one discussed just now that arises
when adaptations are defined in terms of how 'well designed' they
appear to be to fulfil their function. It suggests that, just as each blade
in such a knife is optimally engineered from scratch for just one application, so each 'module' of the mind has been specifically designed by
adaptive evolution for its proper purpose. In his account of evolutionary psychology, Wright observes that, faced with having to explain
instances of remembering and forgetting, the evolutionary psychologist 'can relax and come up with different explanations for each one'
(Wright 1994: 320). Mental modules, it seems, like Swiss army knife
blades, can be made to order. The question is: to whose order – evolution's or evolutionary psychologists'?

Darwin saw adaptations more as swords beaten into ploughshares

Although many evolutionary psychologists make much of their self-
proclaimed Darwinism, it is important to point out that Darwin's own
view of how evolution went about meeting adaptive needs was very
different from that suggested by a Swiss army knife:

> If a man were to make a machine for some special purpose but were to
> use old wheels, springs and pulleys, only slightly altered, the whole

machine, with all its parts, might be said to be specially contrived for its present purpose. Thus throughout nature almost every part of every living being has probably served, in a slightly modified condition, for diverse purposes, and has acted in the living machinery of many ancient and distinct specific forms. (Darwin 1886: 283)

In this quotation Darwin compares natural selection to someone using pieces of old machinery to make something improvised from existing parts rather than to producing a pristine artefact made from raw materials like the blades of a Swiss army knife. Inevitably, natural selection has to work by modifying an existing, working design, and can only innovate on the basis of what is there already. Taking Darwin's view of the matter, beating a sword into a ploughshare would be a better analogy than the blades of a Swiss army knife.

Although the belief that the brain is a general purpose learning device has been discredited, there is much evidence for plasticity in the brain's internal organization and development. For example, research by V. S. Ramachandran and others on phantom limbs (that is, limbs that have been amputated but still generate sensations such as pain) implies that new pathways that are precisely organized and functionally effective can emerge in the adult human brain in less than three weeks (Ramachandran 1994).

These findings have possible relevance to language, which evolutionary psychologists claim is both a unique human adaptation, and one based on distinct mental modules (Pinker 1994). Gesturing with the hands emerges in young children before the development of language, and is even reported in phantom limbs in the case of a woman born without arms (Ramachandran and Blakeslee 1998)! Linking such movements with speech is found in all parts of the world and in association with all languages. One possible explanation is that these are simply social conventions, learnt by imitation in childhood. However, experiments show that people who have been blind since birth use exactly the same kinds of gestures that sighted people do, and in exactly the same way. Another possibility is that people use gestures to add to what they are saying as a kind of visual aid. But when people speak to listeners who are blind they gesture just as much, even though they know that the person to whom they are speaking can't see what they are doing with their hands (Iverson and Goldin-Meadow 1998). Nevertheless, experiments in which people are asked to describe a story with or without the use of their hands reveal that subjects remember the details better if they are allowed to gesture while they speak (Cohen 1998).

This suggests that the primary function of gesturing might not be to communicate with others so much as to facilitate the speaker's use of language (a possibility also suggested by the common observation that when people are having difficulty with what they are trying to say they tend to gesture much more). Brain-imaging certainly suggests considerable overlap between language, motor control and other centres in the brain. Other recent studies suggest that words may be encoded in different parts of the brain, depending on their meaning and associations: words referring to movement, for example, could be coded in the motor cortex, while hearing-related words may be stored in the auditory parts of the cortex (Motluk 1998). If language evolved fairly recently out of parts of the brain that originally did other things, such findings might be easily explained. Evolution might indeed be using older, more basic cerebral functions for language, just as Darwin believed that it would. To this extent, a language 'module' would certainly be more like a sword beaten into a ploughshare than the purpose-built blade of a Swiss army knife.

Ramachandran concludes from his studies of phantom limbs that

> there must be a great deal of back and forth interaction between vision and touch, so that the strictly modular, hierarchical model of the brain that is currently in vogue needs to be replaced with a more dynamic, interactive model. . . . This result flatly contradicts the view held by the AI [artificial intelligence] community that the brain is composed of a number of autonomous 'modules' that sequentially perform various 'computations' on the sensory input. . . . our results are much more consistent with the dynamic, interactive view of the brain. . . . we must give up a strictly hierarchical, modular view of the brain . . . and replace it with a more dynamic, interactive model. (Ramachandran and Rogers-Ramachandran 1996)

The triune brain

According to a theory put forward by Paul D. MacLean, the three fundamental parts of the brain each reflect a different stage in brain evolution, so that evolutionary constraints may affect its architecture and function, just as they do the features of the human body discussed earlier (MacLean 1990).

1 **The brain stem, or reptilian brain** You could compare the central nervous system to a tree, and the nerves that run throughout the body to its roots. These come together in the trunk, which would cor-

respond to the spinal chord. The top of the trunk would be the brain stem or what MacLean calls the 'reptilian brain' (figure 1.1). This controls basic functions such as breathing, circulation and digestion. According to MacLean, the largely automatic functions of the brain stem evolved in reptiles some 300 million years ago, and have remained the basis of the brain in all subsequent animals that evolved from them. The responses of the reptilian brain are instinctual, and concerned with typical reptilian behaviours, such as territoriality, self-defence, asserting dominance, aggression and mating.

2   The limbic system, or palaeo-mammalian brain   The lower limbs of the tree that emerge from the top of the trunk correspond to what MacLean calls the 'palaeo-mammalian brain' by contrast to the reptilian one. This is more often called the *limbic system* (not because it has anything to do with limbs, but because some writers saw it forming the rim or margin – *limbus* in Latin – to the rest of the brain: figure 1.1). The limbic system comprises a number of main parts, each serving different functions. Some are closely associated with the sense of smell and have proved to be involved in oral and genital functions so

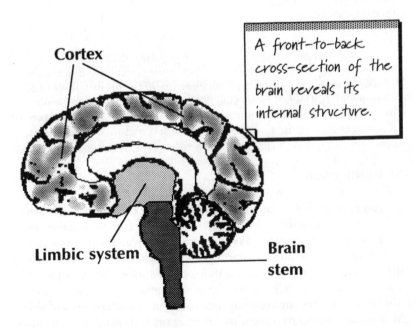

Figure 1.1   The cortex, limbic system and brain stem

that these parts of the brain have also been called the 'visceral brain' or *rhinencephalon* – literally, the 'smell-brain'.

The limbic brain is 'mammalian' to the extent of being concerned with temperature control (mammals, of course, are warm-blooded), parental care (another mammalian speciality), vocal communication, play and long-term memory (all found in mammals more than in reptiles). Numerous findings, such as the clinical study of epilepsy and direct stimulation of the brains of conscious patients during surgery, provide good evidence that the limbic system is involved in the experience and expression of emotion. Many authorities see the limbic system as the main cerebral representative of the internal state of the organism, expressed in the form of emotions and motivation. For these reasons the limbic system is sometimes called the 'emotional brain' (LeDoux 1996).

A critical part of the emotional brain is the *amygdala*. This is an almond-sized component of the limbic system that triggers the fight-or-flight reflex that primes the body for whichever response the higher brain centres decide is appropriate. The amygdala is the link between sensory systems and fear responses. Fear conditioning occurs in all animals, and in all those that have an amygdala, the amygdala appears to be the key. The list includes reptiles, birds and a host of mammals, including humans. Indeed, the amygdala has been called 'the heart and soul of the fear system' (LeDoux 1996). In human beings, direct electrical stimulation of the amygdala produces sensations of anxiety and apprehension (Gloor 1986). Brain-imaging research shows that when people are shown disturbing pictures the amygdala lights up immediately, and the same response is seen to faces registering fear – but not to those showing happiness (Morris et al. 1996). In cases of damage to the amygdala, emotionally loaded memories are impaired or distorted, suggesting that it plays a role in the storage and processing of emotional responses (Allman and Brothers 1994).

3   **The neocortex or neo-mammalian brain**   The crown of a tree, and especially its foliage, might be likened to the final part of the brain, the neocortex, the highly convoluted, sponge-like covering of the brain. This 'new cortex' is so-called to distinguish it from the limbic cortex, which appears to be older in certain respects, at least from the evolutionary point of view, and certainly has not undergone the same dramatic expansion as the neocortex in recent evolution. The deep folds of the neocortex account for the fact that it has a surface area of about 2,500 square centimetres, despite being crammed inside a skull that is only 20 centimetres across. If you opened the cortex and flattened it

out, it would correspond to a square 50 centimetres to a side – about the size of an open tabloid newspaper. Overall, it accounts for about two-thirds to three-quarters of all nerve cells in the human brain (figure 1.1).

The neocortex is connected to the senses and appears to be primarily concerned with reacting to the outside world. Much of it is given over to processing sensory inputs, especially from the eyes, ears and the surface of the body. This is the part of the brain that has to decide whether to fight or take flight after arousal by the limbic system. Mammals whose neocortices have been removed continue to live, but will not react very much to outside stimulation and appear to be incapable of initiating anything but the most basic behaviour. In human beings the neocortex is concerned with problem-solving, learning and detailed, conscious memory. Major parts of it are devoted to speech and verbal comprehension, so that on occasions it has been called the 'word brain' by contrast to the limbic system, which has been described as 'illiterate' (MacLean 1949). The neocortex is sometimes portrayed as the 'cognitive' or 'executive' brain because of its prime role in decision-making, intention and reasoning (Keverne et al. 1996a).

Evolutionary psychologists reject MacLean's theory

MacLean's 'triune brain' theory has not been accepted by all authorities, but, whatever reservations they might have about its details, you might have expected evolutionary psychologists to be prepared to consider it – at least as a rough approximation. After all, it is one of the few attempts that have been made to understand the structure of the human brain in terms of its evolution, and has many facts and findings to support it. You would have thought that evolutionary psychologists more than anyone else would be ready to at least consider the possibility that evolutionary constraints may have complicated the brain and produced elements of suboptimal design in the way in which they have so many other features of human anatomy.

But according to one account of evolutionary psychology, MacLean's theory fails to see that the forces of evolution do not just heap layers on an unchanged foundation but modify existing structures to present adaptive needs – a process which includes the older parts of the brain, as well as the new. Looked at from this point of view, the human cortex does not ride piggyback on an ancient limbic system or serve as the terminus for a processing stream beginning there. On the contrary, it works in tandem with it, integrated by many two-way connections.

The amygdala is a case in point, receiving not just simple signals from lower stations of the brain, but abstract, complex information from the brain's highest centres. The amygdala in turn sends signals to virtually every other part of the brain, including the decision-making circuitry of the frontal lobes. MacLean's evolutionary model of the brain is dismissed as a 'Romantic doctrine of the emotions . . . translated into an incorrect theory' (Pinker 1997: 370–2). It is certainly not what the reverse-engineered-Swiss-army-knife approach to the brain would lead you to expect.

Nevertheless, there is nothing necessarily Romantic or incorrect about MacLean's claim that our intellectual functions are carried out in the newest and most highly developed part of the brain, but that our emotional behaviour continues to be dominated by a simpler and more primitive system, which provides a clue to understanding the difference between what we 'feel' and what we 'know' (MacLean 1949).

To return to the amygdala as an example, the neuroscientist Joseph LeDoux has pointed out that neurological projections from the amygdala to the neocortex are much stronger than neocortical projections back to the amygdala. The implication is that the ability of the amygdala to control the cortex is greater than the ability of the cortex to control the amygdala. This may explain why it can be so hard to will away anxiety: emotions, once set into play, can be very difficult to turn off. Hormones and other long-acting substances released in the body during emotions can return to the brain and lock it into a particular state. Once in that state, it can be very difficult for the cortex to find a way of working its way down to the amygdala and shutting it off. Indeed, LeDoux suggests that psychotherapy may be such a long and difficult process because the neocortex is using imperfect channels of communication to try to control the amygdala. The amygdala can control the neocortex very easily, because all it has to do is arouse lots of areas in a very non-specific way. But for the cortex to then turn all of that off is a very difficult job (LeDoux 1997). Summarizing current brain research, LeDoux concludes:

> The remarkable fact is that at the level of behaviour, defense against danger is achieved in many different ways in different species, yet the amygdala's role is constant . . . When it comes to detecting and responding to danger, the brain just hasn't changed much. In some ways we are emotional lizards. I am quite confident in telling you that studies of fear reactions in rats tell us a great deal about how fear mechanisms work in our brains as well. (LeDoux 1996: 174)

In *The Origin of Species* evolutionary psychology got just a single sentence – and that was more of a hope than a statement of fact: 'Psychology', wrote Darwin in 1859, 'will be based on a new foundation, that of the necessary acquirement of each mental power and capacity by gradation.' If LeDoux is right about the amygdala, Darwin's expectation would be wholly justified in the case of basic emotions such as fear. If we are in some ways close to reptiles in our fear reactions, it is because natural selection has indeed beaten the sword of our animal ancestors' amygdalas into the ploughshare of an emotional brain that we still have today. What it has not been able to do is to manufacture a purpose-made Swiss army knife blade specifically for the purposes of having distinctively human fear reactions. On the contrary, a genuinely Darwinian evolutionary psychology would suggest that in our emotions perhaps more than anywhere else we would have retained much of our evolutionary past, with fewer gradations separating us as feeling organisms from our ancestors than some evolutionary psychologists might suppose.

To put it another way, you could say that LeDoux's point is that the amygdala-neocortex connection is a bit like the eye. From the point of view of connectivity to the cortex at least, it is the wrong way round. But, having started out that way long before the human neocortex evolved, we are stuck with something that evolutionary psychology evidently has difficulty accepting: primitive emotional responses built into the brain irrespective of optimal design for cognition.[6]

The benefits of human brain evolution

Seeing something as adaptive has often been criticized as little more than evolutionary story-telling, because it is not difficult to think up adaptive explanations, and often there seems no reason to prefer one adaptive interpretation over another (S. J. Gould and Lewontin 1979). Nevertheless, adaptationist theorizing can be kept within realistic limits if – and only if – questions are asked and satisfactorily answered about both the costs and the benefits of adaptations, and about the evidence on which such answers are based. Nowhere are such issues more critical or important for evolutionary psychology than in relation to the organ on which our evolved psychology relies – the brain.

Human brain expansion has been one of the fastest and most astonishing developments in evolution. Expressed as a ratio of actual brain size to that of an average ape or monkey of similar size, or *encephalization quotient*, chimpanzees have a quotient of 2.0, early humans 3.1, and modern ones 5.8 (Lewin 1993). In two to three million years, the volume of the human brain increased threefold from approximately that found in modern apes (about 450 cc) to its present value (about 1350 cc), while the cortex increased to account for 70 to 80 per cent of the total. According to some authorities, this increase was not continuous, but may have been interrupted by a long static period between about 1.8 million and 150,000 years ago (Ruff et al. 1997). The trend was exponential: in other words, it increased like compound interest, rather than by simple addition (Henneberg 1987). By comparison, average human height increased by only about a quarter, and weight by approximately 70 per cent in four million years (Mathers and Henneberg 1996).

Many attempts have been made to find the cause of brain evolution. Examples are: hunting, tool use, warfare, language, social life, sexual conquest, consciousness, politics and so on. These theories assume that the brain is to human achievement in these respects what the wing of a bird is to its ability to fly: an organ exquisitely adapted to a particular useful function. All of these theories take it for granted that the evolutionary benefits of whatever they propose explain why the brain evolved to facilitate it. They assume that those with just a little more grey matter devoted to tool-making, talking, consciousness or whatever, would have left slightly more descendants who inherited that critical ability than others with less brain in the right place. Their descendants in turn would have had slightly more descendants if they had possessed even more of the little grey cells where it most mattered, and so on. The trouble with such explanations is that they are always ultimately a question of interpreting the results of evolution, and often one interpretation looks as good as another.

You can get round the problems of specific adaptations for brain development by appealing to a general selective trend, for example for increased intelligence. A difficulty here is the finding that humans and other closely related members of the order of primates, such as apes and monkeys, do not grow their brains faster than other mammals, but grow their bodies slower. From an early embryonic stage, primates have smaller bodies than you would expect for their age. The apparent increase in relative brain size in primates is more accurately described as a decrease in relative body size. This poses a serious challenge to the traditional view of primate evolution as characterized by selection for increased intelligence. If primates were selected for increased intelligence, why should this produce a change in body growth but not brain growth (Deacon 1997)?

One of the most plausible and well-argued theories to have been advanced recently is Robin Dunbar's theory linking brain growth, group size and language. According to him, animals cannot maintain the cohesion and integrity of groups larger than a size fixed by the information-processing capacity of their brain. He argues that social networks function as coalitions whose main purpose is to buffer their members against harassment by the other members of the group. The larger the group, the more harassment and stress the individual faces and the more important these coalitions are. A coalition's effectiveness (in the sense of its members' willingness to come to each other's aid) seems to be directly related to the amount of time its members spend grooming each other. Hence, the larger the group, the more time individuals devote to grooming with the members of their coalitional clique (Dunbar 1993).

Dunbar goes on to propose that in human beings grooming has been supplanted by gossip, and that language evolved to allow us to gossip. Plotting the size of the part of the human brain involved with speech and consciousness – the neocortex – against time spent in grooming/gossip, he concludes that the primary human social network numbers about 150, and claims that this is the typical size of effective social units found in armies, business organizations and societies in general. Nevertheless, we are still left with the puzzling question of what drove the increase in group size. Dunbar candidly admits that he doesn't really know, but suggests as possible answers social and environmental factors to do with vulnerability to predators, and the sizes of groups needed to colonize new areas of the world (Dunbar 1996).

Brain expansion has ceased, and we don't have the largest brains

Most of the big-brains-evolved-to-enable-us-to-do-this-that-or-the-other theories are put in doubt by the fact that the now long extinct Neanderthals had larger brains than modern humans – and certainly didn't have significantly smaller ones (R. D. Martin 1983). According to Dunbar's theory, this would indicate group sizes as large or even larger than that of modern humans, and if these are in turn linked to colonization or an ability to resist predators, you wonder why today the world isn't full of Neanderthals.

Again, there is good evidence that brain growth in living humans has not increased in recent times. Indeed, the data suggest that brain size may actually have declined by a factor of about 10 per cent in the last 30,000 years (Henneberg and Steyn 1993). Yet human beings have done much more with their brains since brain growth appears to have stopped and gone into reverse, and many human groups have grown markedly with cultural advances such as agriculture and urbanization. You would think that if selection selected for large brain size in order to allow human beings to apply their brains in larger social groupings, a burst in new brain applications represented by technological, cultural and social advances would have gone with a further increase in brain volume – especially if brain and group size were correlated in the way suggested by Dunbar.

But brain size simply hasn't increased in this way during recent history. On the contrary,

> there may be no very tight relationship between relative brain size and specific behavioral capacities. The latter may be far more dependent on the internal wiring of the brain rather than its overall size. While it is undoubtedly true that large brains are generally superior to small brains, no convincing case has been made for the proposal that any particular feature of behaviour (e.g., feeding ecology, complexity of social organization) has exerted a specific selection pressure for favouring an increase in brain size . . . when the effects of confounding variables such as body size and socio-economic status are excluded, no correlation is found between IQ and brain size among modern humans. Until some behavioral advantage of increased brain size per se has been demonstrated, there is no basis for arguing that specific selection pressures have favoured the development of a very large brain in humans. (R. D. Martin 1996: 155)

As long ago as 1966 George Williams candidly admitted that

> Despite the arguments that have been advanced, I cannot readily accept the idea that advanced mental capabilities have ever been directly favored by selection. There is no reason for believing that a genius has ever been likely to leave more children than a man of somewhat below average intelligence. It has been suggested that a tribe that produces an occasional genius for its leadership is more likely to prevail in competition with tribes that lack this intellectual resource. This may well be true in the sense that a group with highly intelligent leaders is likely to gain political supremacy over less gifted groups, but political domination need not result in genetic domination, as is indicated by the failure of many a ruling class to maintain its members. (Williams 1966: 14–15)

The standard response to such criticisms is to point out that where brain development is concerned size isn't everything, and that it is the relative expansion of areas of the human brain – such as the prefrontal cortex – that really counts. In humans the prefrontal cortex amounts to some 30 per cent of the cerebral hemispheres, and is known to be the site of many distinctively human mental capacities, such as social awareness, conscience and self-restraint.

However, in the case of the *echidna*, or spiny ant-eater *(Tachyglossus aculeatus)*, an allegedly 'primitive', marsupial mammal, the prefrontal region takes up a remarkable 50 per cent of the cerebral cortex as a whole, proportionately more than in any other animal (Augee and Gooden 1993). According to one authority, if human beings had brains with a prefrontal cortex the size of the echidna's, we would have to carry them around in wheelbarrows (Winson 1985)! Writing as long ago as 1902, an authority on brain evolution confessed that the reason the echidna has this large prefrontal neocortex 'is quite incomprehensible. The factors which the study of other mammalian brains has shown to be the determinants of the extent of the cortex fail completely to explain how it is that a small animal of the lowest status in the mammalian series comes to possess this large cortical apparatus' (Griffiths 1968: 101). Today the situation is no different, and the echidna continues to confound adaptationist theories of brain evolution.

However obvious the benefits of human brain evolution may be to most people, scientifically credible explanations are currently unknown, and no single theory has given either a completely convincing answer or one that is universally accepted. An honest answer would be that, although some impressionistic and approximate reasons may be known, no rigorous account of human brain evolution has yet been given, despite a century of unremitting effort. The truth is that, contrary to the assumptions of reverse-engineering evolutionary psychologists, we don't really know why the human brain evolved, what purpose it evolved to serve, precisely who or what benefited from it, how they or it benefited, or why. Given that the brain is the key organ as far as evolutionary psychology is concerned, failure to establish credible and generally accepted answers to these questions leaves the whole undertaking completely without a foundation and makes the reliance of evolutionary psychology on dubious adaptationist argumentation even greater.

The costs of human brain evolution

One of the things that makes adaptationist story-telling most dubious of all is its tendency to concentrate on the presumed benefits of an alleged adaptation without considering the inevitable costs that it will also impose. If we now turn to the question of the costs of the brain as an adaptation, we once again find that the picture is far from simple, and its meaning by no means as clear as the more simple-minded adaptationist explanations would suggest.

In terms of its energy consumption, the brain consumes up to ten times more than the average of the whole human body. Unlike other tissues, the brain can only burn pure glucose, while having little capacity to store significant reserves. Although only 2 per cent of body weight, the brain consumes 20 per cent of the available oxygen and glucose, and even more in childhood. At birth the brain represents 10 per cent of total weight but consumes up to 65 per cent of the body's energy, while only 8 per cent of an infant's total metabolic rate is devoted to muscle tissue (Holliday 1978). In the first year and a half of life a human infant needs almost 10 per cent more energy per day to run its brain than a chimpanzee of the same size. At six years of age the brain's consumption of total oxygen intake peaks at about 50 per cent. If you replaced the brain with a light bulb, it would be rated at just under 15 watts (the wattage of a refrigerator light). The ever-beating heart, by comparison, would radiate at 10 watts, and the skin would barely glow at one-and-a-half. Energy consumption always produces heat as a by-product, and the human head has been engineered by evolution to radiate away as much of it as possible through a complex system of veins and an ability to sweat profusely (Falk 1992).

So significant is the energy cost of the brain that some believe that economies have had to be made elsewhere in the human body to accommodate it. The digestive tract also uses a lot of energy, but its total mass is only 60 per cent of what you would expect to find in an ape or monkey of similar size to a human being. The increase in mass of the human brain appears to have been balanced by an almost identical reduction in the length of the intestines. This in its turn suggests that, whatever may have driven human brain size enlargement, it was accompanied by an increasing reliance on a high quality, meaty diet that could be digested efficiently by a shorter gut, in its turn aided by food-processing and cooking skills made possible by the expanded brain (Aiello and Wheeler 1995).

Finally, the large size of the human brain imposes significant costs in the form of obstetric complications. The longest axis of the foetal head only just fits the widest axis of the human mother's birth canal. In order to allow the minimum cross-section to pass through the maximum diameter of the outlet, the foetal head must rotate from facing sideways to facing towards the back of the mother as the baby squirms through the narrow opening. Because the human foetus emerges from the birth canal facing in the opposite direction from its mother, it is difficult for the mother, whatever her position, to reach down as ape and monkey mothers often do to clear a breathing passage for the infant or remove the umbilical cord from around its neck. If a human mother tries to assist in the delivery by guiding the infant from the birth canal, she risks damaging the baby. However, expansion of the diameter of the mother's birth canal also imposes costs in terms of the efficiency of walking, so that evolution has had to strike a balance between the obstetric constraints imposed by human brain enlargement and those dictated by the adoption of an upright posture. The result is that the fit between the human pelvic opening and the typical newborn baby's head is a tight one. Largely thanks to this, human birth is painful, difficult and dangerous – and yet another example of distinctly suboptimal adaptive design.

Thanks to the constraints of having to give birth to a large-brained baby through a narrow pelvic canal, three-quarters of human brain growth has to take place after birth, rather than before it. This in its turn results in human newborns being notably retarded in their development by comparison with other primates. Whereas most monkeys are sufficiently developed to actually assist their own birth once their hands are free, human newborns are totally passive, not just during birth, but for some considerable time afterwards. This long period of helplessness in turn imposes huge costs on the mother, who must compensate by nurturing the baby much more intensively and for much longer than any other primate (Rosenberg and Trevathan 1996).

The costs of human brain development fall on the mother

The importance of considering cost as well as benefit in evolutionary explanation is illustrated by the *maternal energy hypothesis*. Once again, this raises complications glossed over by most adaptationist accounts, and highlights the very different way that the costs of brain development fall on individuals. While adaptationist accounts usually assume that everyone benefits from a large brain, they notably fail to point out that some individuals pay much more of the cost than others, and completely fail to advance any credible adaptive explanation of why this should be so.

Because most of the growth in size of the brain has taken place by the time of weaning in mammals, recent research has found that the size attained by the brain is dependent on the input made by the mother during gestation and lactation. This suggests that it is the mother's energy turnover that primarily constrains the final brain size achieved by her offspring. According to this way of looking at it, all mammals have the largest brains that are compatible with the resources available to their mothers during gestation and lactation (Martin 1996). Indeed, it has even been suggested that the recently discovered 3–5 per cent shrinkage in the size of the mother's brain at the end of pregnancy may be because human mothers not only contribute the greatest amount of free resources they can to building their babies' brains, but even raid their own brains in doing so (Horrobin 1998). (See box 6.3, 'Why breast is best', pp. 215–16 below.)

In the case of human brain development, one of the critical questions is: why should mothers pay the exorbitant costs of human brain development, rather than anyone else? Any rigorous theory of human brain evolution ought to be able to answer this question, but it is seldom asked and even more rarely answered – least of all by reverse-engineering evolutionary psychology.[7]

The evolutionary psychology of evolutionary psychology

Whatever the truth about its evolution, it would be naive to think that the human brain was in any way specifically adapted to understand evolution in general, or evolutionary psychology in particular. On the contrary, the likelihood is that natural selection would have built into the human mind attitudes and capabilities primarily concerned with individual survival and reproductive success in primal hunter-gatherer societies. One of the most important of these would probably be a feeling of your own significance and of the necessity of your own survival. The problem here is that, looked at objectively, any individual human being in the past would only be in the order of a millionth part of the human race, and so, as far as evolution is concerned, probably next to totally insignificant. (And of course, today, with billions of people on the planet, the problem is a thousand times worse!)

The result is that individual human beings suffer from a psychological myopia where their own existence and importance in the grand evolutionary scheme of things is concerned. They see themselves and their immediate environment clearly, but their minds cannot grasp the vast expanses of other humans and evolutionary time that surround them. But this is exactly what you have to grasp in some fashion if evolutionary insights are to be credible. Again, the mindless cruelty of natural selection offends moral sentiments which evolved to foster human co-operation in primal societies. But the fact that natural selection did not design us to treat our friends and relatives the way it effectively treated us in evolution is no reason why we should not face the fact that ultimately nature is neither moral nor immoral, but mindlessly amoral.

These cognitive and emotional difficulties show themselves negatively as resistance to and rejection of evolutionary insights, which seem implausible to a mind that simply can't grasp the numbers or dimensions concerned. They also show themselves positively as a hankering after things we can understand and would prefer to find: sudden, dramatic events or catastrophes, rather than slow, remorseless evolution over inconceivably long periods of time; the playing out of a structured drama with heroes and villains, winners and losers, rather than a mindless culling by infinitesimal differences in the reproductive success of vast numbers of individuals; above all, the wish that someone could be credited or blamed for the whole thing and that, above and beyond the evolution of life on Earth, there was some cosmic principle, spirit or being who had devised the whole thing the way a human mind might have done. In short, our cognitive abilities and emotional sensibilities evolved to equip us for life in primal societies, not to understand the great, but cruel and alien forces that created us. For tiny moral-minded, self-interested creatures like us, this makes evolution difficult at best, and confronts us not simply with intellectual problems, but with emotional and moral difficulties as well. We may not know what our minds are adapted for in general, but we do know one thing that they are not adapted for in particular: a full, complete and unbiased comprehension of our own evolution.

Suggestions for further reading

Darwin, C. (1968)   *The Origin of Species* (first published 1859).
Deacon, T. (1997)   *The Symbolic Species: The Co-evolution of Language and the Human Brain.*
LeDoux, J. (1996)   *The Emotional Brain: The Mysterious Underpinnings of Emotional Life.*
MacLean, P. D. (1990)   *The Triune Brain in Evolution.*
Pinker, S. (1997)   *How the Mind Works.*
Williams, G. C. (1996)   *Plan and Purpose in Nature.*

2

Genetics and Epigenetics

Darwin's theory of evolution by natural selection required heredity to preserve and pass on useful adaptations to the descendants of organisms. Yet, as we shall now see, Darwin himself was completely wrong about how heredity worked. Nevertheless, his error is an instructive one because it arose from what seems at first sight an obvious fact: that heredity is the means by which organisms are reproduced. However, what appears obvious and what is scientifically true are often two quite different things, and nowhere is this more so than in the case of heredity. My aim in this chapter is to explore Darwin's error and show how modern insights have transformed our view of heredity thanks to the discovery of the gene and the genetic code that translates genes into organisms.

This is a critical issue for evolutionary psychology because psychology is an attribute of organisms, not of genes. Yet, as we shall see, genes are the ultimate units of heredity, and so it is important to understand how and why heredity works in the way it does. We shall see that Darwin was particularly wrong about heredity where psychology was concerned, and today no issue is more bedevilled by misunderstandings and confusions than is that of the relation between heredity and human psychology. Although this is a big subject, and will take several chapters to introduce in anything like the proper detail, this chapter will concern itself with the basic issue of how heredity does – and, just as important, does not – work. As we shall see, it leads to a new and challenging view of how and why organisms evolved – human beings not excepted.

Inheritance of acquired characteristics

Charles Darwin's theory of *pangenesis* asserted that the characteristics of the whole organism are reproduced in its offspring. 'The chief assumption', said Darwin,

> is that all the units of the body, besides having the universally admitted power of growing by self-division, throw off minute gemmules which are dispersed throughout the system. . . . we further assume that the gemmules grow, multiply and aggregate themselves into buds and sexual elements. Hence, it is not the reproductive organs or buds which generate new organisms, but the units of which each individual is composed. These assumptions constitute the provisional hypothesis which I have called pangenesis. (Darwin 1988: 350, 370)

To use a modern analogy, you might say that pangenesis sees reproduction rather like a photocopying machine, and the whole body of the organism as the original which is copied by it. This view proposes that information flows from the organism to its reproductive cells and from them to the next generation. It implies that acquired characteristics, such as development of the body or learning in the mind, might also be heritable.

Today the belief that acquired characteristics can be inherited is often called *Lamarckism* after **Jean-Baptiste Lamarck** (1744–1829). However, such a belief was widespread and, as we have just seen, shared by Darwin in the form of his doctrine of pangenesis. Darwin may in fact have acquired it from his grandfather, **Erasmus Darwin** (1731–1802), rather than from Lamarck, but the fact remains that until well into the twentieth century it was almost universally believed that, in one way or another, acquired characteristics could be inherited. Although Darwin may have formulated the details in his own particular way, the general supposition was widely taken for granted.

Darwin was particularly prone to appeal to the inheritance of acquired characteristics where psychology was concerned, remarking that 'even in the first edition of the "Origin of Species", I distinctly stated that great weight must be attributed to the inherited effects of use and disuse, with respect both to the body and the mind.' In *The Descent of Man* he claimed that 'some intelligent actions – as when birds on oceanic islands first learn to avoid man – after being performed during many generations, become converted into instincts and are inherited.'

He also believed that 'the vocal organs would have been strengthened and perfected through the principle of the inherited effects of use' (Darwin 1871).

Even when Darwin did mention natural selection in a psychological context, it appears only as an alternative to Lamarckian evolution: 'some instincts', claimed Darwin, 'have been developed simply through long-continued and inherited habit, other highly complex ones have been developed through the preservation of various pre-existing instincts – that is, through natural selection.' But notwithstanding this recognition of natural selection, he candidly admitted to seeing no real alternative to Lamarckism where habitual actions were concerned: 'That some physical change is produced in the nerve cells or nerves which are habitually used can hardly be doubted, for otherwise it is impossible to understand how the tendency to certain acquired movements is inherited.'

Darwin seemed to credit the idea particularly in psychology, explicitly stating regarding instincts that 'it was necessary to show that at least some of them might have been first acquired through the will in order to satisfy a desire, or to relieve a disagreeable sensation' (Darwin 1998). His observations of one of his own children even led him to 'suspect that the vague and very real fears of children, which are quite independent of experience, are inherited effects of real dangers and abject superstitions during ancient savage times' (Darwin 1877). Indeed, Darwin was of the opinion that 'the constant inculcation in a belief in God on the minds of children' might have produced 'so strong and perhaps an inherited effect on their brains not yet fully developed, that it would be as difficult for them to throw off their belief in God, as for a monkey to throw off its instinctive fear and hatred of a snake' (Darwin 1958: 93).

Given Darwin's belief in the inheritance of acquired characteristics, and given that psychological factors like instincts or reflexes are demonstrably inherited, it did not seem absurd to him to say that they must first have been acquired before they could be inherited and to assume that, before they were inherited as instincts or reflexes, they were intentional acts. Darwin explicitly states this when he says that 'it seems probable that some actions, which were at first performed consciously, have become through habit and association converted into reflex actions, and are now firmly fixed and inherited.' Only when an originally voluntary action had become converted into an inherited reflex through frequent repetition did Darwin see the mechanism of natural selection taking a hand in its evolution by way of preserving variations of it that were beneficial (Darwin 1998).

But as Darwin himself also saw, pangenesis can't result in every feature being inherited:

> it appears at first sight a fatal objection to our hypothesis that a part or organ may be removed during several successive generations, and if the operation be not followed by disease, the lost part reappears in the offspring. Dogs and horses formerly had their tails docked during many generations without inherited effect. . . . Circumcision has been practised by Jews from a remote period, and in most cases the effects of the operation are not visible in the offspring. . . . If inheritance depends on the presence of disseminated gemmules derived from all the units of the body, why does not the amputation or mutilation of a part . . . invariably affect the offspring? The answer in accordance with our hypothesis probably is that gemmules multiply and are transmitted during a long series of generations. . . . Therefore the long-continued inheritance of a part which has been removed during many generations is no real anomaly, for gemmules formerly derived from the part are multiplied and transmitted from generation to generation. (Darwin 1988: 340)

Darwin used a similar argument to explain why acquired mental abilities, injuries and other transient characteristics of parents are not necessarily inherited by their offspring. Effectively he argued that gemmules had a resistance to short-term changes and a tendency to reproduce only long-term effects typical of the species. To this extent pangenesis regarded inheritance essentially as a means of reproducing not simply the individual organism but the species as a whole.

Further problems with pangenesis were revealed by experiments carried out by Darwin's cousin, Francis Galton. Seeking to find out if gemmules really did exist, Galton carried out blood transfusions between rabbits of different kinds and then waited to see if the offspring were in any way affected, as the presence of gemmules from the blood of another rabbit might lead you to expect. No such effect was found.

Three reasons why inheritance of acquired characteristics won't work

1   There is no way to scan the organism   If heredity worked liked a photocopier of the organism, it would have to have something like Darwin's gemmules: that is, some means of carrying information from the organism to be reproduced to the sex cells which would reproduce it. In photocopiers, the document is scanned with light to achieve this, but no biological equivalent exists which can scan the organism, explaining why Galton's experiments failed.

2   There is no 'original' of the organism that can be reproduced   If heredity worked this way it would need an original 'document' or copy to reproduce: in other words, a particular, definitive version of the organism that it could copy. If it chose the newborn or immature form, it would not be reproducing the whole, complete organism but an immature form that would lack essential characteristics of the mature one (such as functioning sexual organs, or a fully developed brain). If it were to choose the adult, finished form, it would inevitably include acquired characteristics like the effects of injuries and ageing on the body, and experience and learning on the mind.

3   In order to know what to copy in the organism, there would have to be a process of selection   In order to exclude characteristics that were acquired but not wanted in reproduction, such as effects of ageing or injury, heredity would need some means of selecting which characteristics to copy. It would need to know which characteristics to avoid, and this would require some method of selection or some kind of catalogue of the organism, listing its typical, normal characteristics, but excluding abnormally acquired ones. As a result, you would need a second source of information, independent of the organism, in order to reproduce the organism – which contradicts the whole idea of heredity reproducing the organism as such. It would be like expecting a photocopier only to reproduce correctly spelt words in a document. But clearly, in order to be able to do this, the photocopier would need to have its own spell checker, and that would mean a second source of information, independent of the document to be copied.

Nevertheless, the inheritance of acquired characteristics has proved a tenacious idea, perhaps because it seems so obvious to an organism like a human being that its reproductive system should be designed to copy itself (Jablonka and Lamb 1995). Again, the idea has retained positive associations in some quarters despite its disastrous application in the Soviet Union and the murder, misery and mass starvation to which it ultimately led (see box 2.1 on Trofim Denisovich Lysenko).

Blending inheritance and mutation

Although the offspring may be thought of as a copy of the parent, it is clearly never an identical one in a sexually reproducing species because there the offspring has two parents, and never exactly repro-

Box 2.1

Trofim Denisovich Lysenko (1898–1976)

The Soviet plant-breeder, Lysenko, had little scientific education, and was pro-moted thanks to a post-revolutionary programme of 'positive discrimination' in favour of peasants. Set the task of acclimatizing beans in Azerbaijan, Lysenko got promising results, thanks to the mild winter of 1925–6. In 1927, a journalist on *Pravda* publicized Lysenko as 'the barefoot professor' whose discoveries would save the peasants of Azerbaijan from starvation.

Despite a total lack of scientific evidence, Lysenko went on to orchestrate a noisy press campaign in favour of his belief that plants could be 'educated' to grow in adverse climates. According to him, plants were indivisible organisms, without separate hereditary or environmental influences. He attributed what amounted to free will to plants, who could not only select food, but enter into 'love marriages'. In association with the Marxist ideologist I. I. Prezent, Lysenko went on to denounce genetics as a 'capitalist' and 'clerical' conspiracy, and to deny the existence of the gene. He said that 'Lamarckian propositions, which recognize the active role of the conditions of the external environment in the formation of the living body and the inheritance of acquired characteristics . . . are indeed not faulty, but on the contrary perfectly correct and entirely scientific.'

According to Lysenko, there is no struggle for survival among members of the same species, but mutual co-operation for the common good. He also claimed that plant hormones do not exist, and to have transformed wheat into rye, barley, oats and cornflowers; even the successful and permanent transforma-tion of small white fowl into large black ones by blood transfusions was said to have been achieved! This may be explained by his belief that 'if you want a particular result you obtain it,' and by his statement that 'I need only people who will obtain what I require.'

Critics and associates who knew too much about Lysenko for his comfort were brutally dealt with. In 1934, N. M. Tulaikov, the only surviving witness of Lysenko's appropriation of another scientist's work, was denounced in *Pravda*, and then shot. Another victim was N. I. Vavilov, who had had responsibility for genetics under Lenin. A botanist of international reputation, Vavilov was one of the few non-Communists to become a member of the Central Executive Committee of the Soviet state. Under his leadership, a network of research institutes and experimental stations was built up, eventually employing more than 20,000 people, and doing much valuable genetic research. Vavilov had begun by endorsing Lysenko. However, following a vicious campaign of char-acter assassination, lies and political intimidation, Vavilov's powers were cur-tailed after 1936, and in 1940 he was arrested as a spy, sentenced to death, and died in prison three years later.

Lysenko's stranglehold tightened further in 1948, when thousands of scien-tists were dismissed in a purge of those who had opposed him, and the teaching of Mendelian genetics became a crime. Lysenko received three Stalin Prizes, six Orders of Lenin, and the Order of the Red Banner. He was proclaimed a Hero of Socialist Labour, became a deputy and vice-president of the Supreme Soviet and of the Central Committee of the Communist Party. Monuments and statues were erected in his honour, and busts were on sale in shops. Khrushchev was a personal friend, and continued to patronize him as dictator of Soviet genetics after the fall of Stalin. Only in the 1960s was his work exposed as wholesale fraud sustained by violence, lies and intimidation.

duces either one of them. As a result, it was obvious that some kind of blending or combination of characters occurred in heredity – what is often termed *blending inheritance.*

This created another problem for Darwin because, as we have already seen, his theory needed mutations. By *mutation* we mean some heritable variation which appears in an individual by chance. Obviously, such chance variations were necessary for Darwin's theory because they provided the raw material of genetic variation on which natural selection could then go to work. Without heritable mutations, evolution had no starting point, and without selection and conservation of some of those mutations evolutionary change would not occur in the way Darwin had suggested (see above, pp. 5–6).

The problem was that, according to apparently well-founded views of the mechanism of inheritance current at the time, any mutation occurring in any one individual would be diluted by half every time it was passed on. Consider the following hypothetical, but crucial example. Suppose that a mutation occurs in an individual organism that enhances its reproductive success – the number of offspring it leaves, in other words – by 100 per cent. If, as is likely in the vast majority of cases, the mutant in question reproduced sexually, only half the mutation would be passed on to its offspring because the other half of their inheritance would come from the other parent. In the second generation, the grandchildren of the original mutant, it will already be down to 25 per cent, and in the third to 12.5 per cent, in the fourth to 6.25 per cent, and so on. In only eight generations the percentage contribution to increased reproductive success of a mutation which originally conferred a very significant 100 per cent advantage will be down to less than 1 per cent, and beyond that its contribution will be negligible. What chance, asked contemporary critics of Darwin's theory, would a mutation have of becoming fixed in the species as a whole?

Mendel

The irony of all this is that the foundations of the true science of genetics had been discovered and published as early as 1865 by **Gregor Mendel** (1822–1884), but Darwin – and just about everyone else who ought to have known about it at the time – unfortunately remained ignorant of his work. In meticulous breeding experiments with peas, Mendel found that if he crossed a plant with purple flowers with one that produced white ones, all the offspring would be purple. But if he interbred these offspring, the white flowers reappeared in the ratio of one white pea plant to every three purple. These, and many similar findings, made Mendel realize that traits like flower colour were being inherited complete, rather than by degrees. They were not being blended, because white or purple colour was passed on as an indivisible unit – as if there were 'atoms of heredity' just as there are atoms of matter. Today we know that this is because the traits in question are produced by individual *genes* that normally are indeed passed on as single units, explaining why purple or white colour is inherited on an all-or-nothing basis and without diminution or blending over time.

Mendel was able to explain the proportions in which genes were inherited by supposing that each individual pea plant had received a single (or, in the technical jargon of genetics, *haploid*) set of genes from each parent. We now know that Mendel's peas were representative of most organisms that reproduce sexually, and that normally an offspring receives a full complement of genes from each parent so that it usually ends up with a double set (*diploid*). Every new organism passes one haploid set on to each of its offspring in its turn (but exchanges between the sets of genes mean that identical sets are not normally passed on from generation to generation). Mendel showed that in a sexually reproducing plant like the pea it was not a question of any gene being half inherited by all the offspring of the parent, but rather a question of *all of that particular gene being inherited by half the offspring*.

This solved the problem of the apparent dilution of beneficial mutations because such a mutation would not be diluted, but handed on complete. Admittedly, it might only be handed on to half the original mutant's offspring, but in those offspring where it was expressed it would retain its entire effect. So to return to our original example, we can see that although only half the offspring might inherit a gene which enhanced their reproductive success by 100 per cent, those offspring would gradually become more numerous in each generation, thanks to the fact that the gene's effect was not being diluted and the numbers of its bearers constantly increased.

Mendel realized that if every individual has two complete sets of genes, it means that each gene received from one parent must have a corresponding, paired gene inherited from the other, nowadays called an *allele*. He also realized that the inheritance of an allele and its expression are not the same thing. If purple and white pea plants interbreed and produce only purple offspring, Mendel saw that this must be because the purple gene is both inherited and expressed while the white one is inherited but silent. However, if the white gene were to be passed on to an offspring in whom it was paired with the same white allele from the other parent, it would have to be expressed because there would be no purple alternative to take precedence over it. Today we would call alleles that have such precedence in expression over others *dominant*, and alleles that are silenced by being paired with dominant partners *recessive*.

Mendel showed that a pea plant with two alleles of the dominant gene for purple colour which was crossed with another with two copies of the corresponding recessive allele for white colour would produce a new generation of peas each with one dominant and one recessive allele simply because offspring inherit a single, complete set of genes from each parent. This new generation of peas would resemble the purple parent rather than the white one because the dominant allele for purple colour would be expressed while the recessive one for white would remain silent. However, the fact that offspring inherit half their genes from each parent also meant that the recessive allele for white colour would be present in the new generation and could be passed on to its offspring in turn. If the peas each carrying one white and one purple allele were crossed with each other, they would give rise to a new generation of whom about half would be just like the parents: they would inherit one dominant and one recessive allele and so would express the dominant, purple colour. On average, a quarter of the new generation would have two of the dominant genes, and so would also produce purple flowers. But the other quarter would probably inherit the recessive, white allele from both parents, and so would produce white flowers. The same pattern of inheritance of dominant and recessive genes is seen in human beings (figure 2.1).

As so often happens in science, Mendel's discovery was partly luck because he just happened to choose traits in peas that are dominant or recessive on an all-or-nothing basis, producing effects that were unmistakable. However, dominance is not always complete, and can produce the illusion of blending inheritance. Again, many genes may be

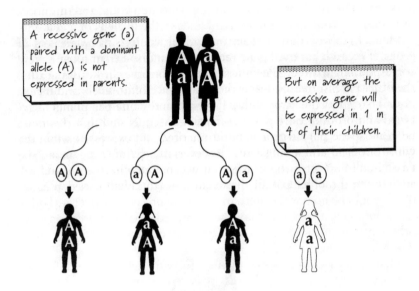

Figure 2.1 Mendelian inheritance

involved in characteristics such as size, colour or behaviour, and so strict Mendelian inheritance may be obscured by the complex interactions between them. Nevertheless, the important thing is that Mendel made the fundamental distinction between inheritance of a gene and its expression, and this turns out to be crucial.

Mendel's discovery that what you see is not necessarily what you get in genetics not only explained why traits could skip generations and reappear later, but also why recessive traits could often injure their carriers. If a gene for a harmful trait were to be dominant rather than recessive, it would be expressed every time it was inherited, and so might soon be lost, thanks to its ill effects on so many of its carriers. But injurious alleles that are recessive are not expressed so often and consequently can be spread by carriers, thanks to being coupled with harmless or beneficial dominant alleles.

Sex chromosomes are exceptions

Genes are packaged in *chromosomes*, so-called because they were discovered by dyeing them and thereby making them visible under a microscope. The term chromosome means 'coloured body' and this is just how they showed up – as coloured bands in the nucleus of a cell. Human beings have a total of 46 chromosomes, comprising two sets of 23 – one from each parent. So a gene on a chromosome from one parent will be paired with an allele on the corresponding chromosome from the other parent. In each set there is a single sex chromosome, labelled X or Y by vague analogy with its appearance. Female mammals have two X chromosomes, but males have a single X and a Y. *Gametes* (sperms and eggs) carry a haploid set of 22 *autosomes* (or non-sex chromosomes) and a single sex chromosome. Because a woman has two Xs, all her eggs carry one X, but because men have an X and a Y sex chromosome, half of all sperm carry a Y and half carry an X sex

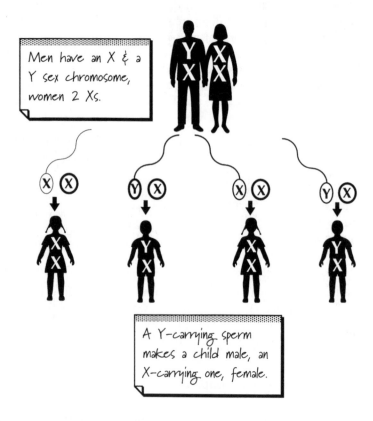

Figure 2.2   The inheritance of sex chromosomes

chromosome. This in turn means that an egg fertilized by a Y-carrying sperm will be male and one fertilized by an X-carrying one will be female. (Figure 2.2, see also box 2.2, 'Queen Victoria's haemophilia'.)[1]

The discovery of DNA

A further advance in our understanding of genetics was made by **August Weismann** (1834–1914). Weismann pointed out that in many organisms there is a distinction between what you might call the *germ-line* – the cells that give rise to the reproductive cells and thereby to the next generation – and the *somatic*, or body cells. For example, the precursors of a woman's egg cells are formed during embryonic development, and all the genetic information that they contain is copied long before she is born. As far as she is concerned, her last genetic will and testament was signed, sealed and deposited in her ovaries several months before her birth. In some organisms, only 13 cell divisions occur between the constitution of the germ-line cells of one generation and the next. This hardly allows for much modification of the genetic message through inheritance of acquired characteristics, even if it were possible.

However, it was not until 1953 that **Francis Crick** (1916–) and **James Watson** (1928–) finally showed what genes actually were. For some time before, it had been known that chromosomes seemed to be largely constituted of *deoxyribonucleic acid*, or *DNA* for short (along with the very similar RNA: ribonucleic acid). Crick and Watson proposed a model which suggested that DNA comprised two sugar-phosphate helical spirals linked together by four chemical bases, abbreviated as A (adenine), C (cytosine), G (guanine) and T (thymine). Crick and Watson explained the ratios in which these bases always seemed to appear by suggesting that an A on one strand was always paired with a T on the other, and a G on one always bonded with a C on the other. If the two helical strands were unzipped and collected new complementary bases and sugar-phosphate chains corresponding to them, complete duplication could occur, and this was found to be the mechanism by means of which genetic information was copied and transmitted from cell to cell and generation to generation (see figure 2.3).

DNA isn't the biochemical equivalent of a photocopier

When the first photocopiers were introduced they were adopted by architects and designers in spite of their very large size and considerable cost

Box 2.2

Queen Victoria's haemophilia

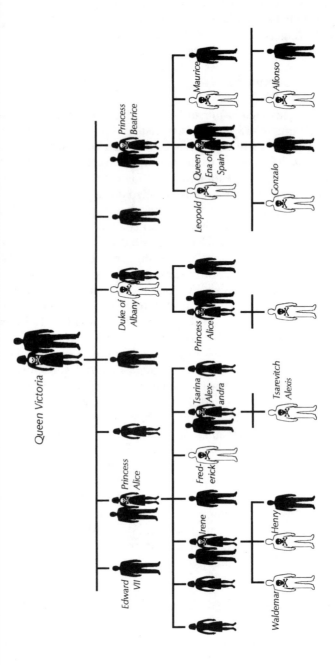

Queen Victoria carried a recessive gene for the blood-clotting disorder, haemophilia, on one of her two X chromosomes. She and all her female descendants were safe from the disease because it was paired with a dominant gene on the other X chromosome. Men have only one X chromosome because the other, paired sex chromosome is a Y. The result was that males who were unlucky enough to inherit the gene for haemophilia from Queen Victoria on their one and only X chromosome suffered from the disease (highlighted). Queen Victoria's family tree shows that some of the sufferers lived long enough to pass their haemophilia on to their offspring. It also shows how sex chromosome inheritance works: although the Duke of Albany was a sufferer, he could only pass the haemophilia gene on to a daughter, Princess Alice, because a son would not inherit his X chromosome. Alice in her turn passed it on to a son in the form of his one and only X chromosome.

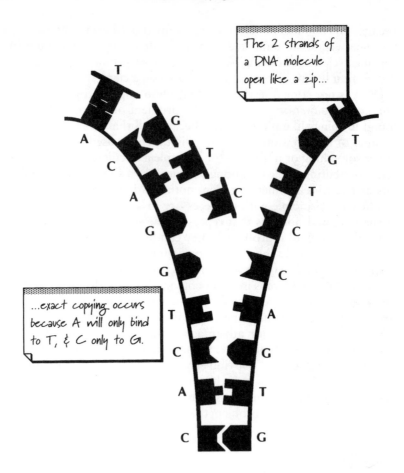

Figure 2.3 The genetic code

because they offered an alternative to the manual copying of drawings. Rather than spending hours reproducing a drawing by hand, it could now be photocopied in a few minutes. However, there was a problem. Copies were usually needed not just as records but as the starting point for new drawings that modified the original one. This would often be photocopied in its turn, further modified, then photocopied again, and so on. This meant that many drawings went through repeated cycles of photocopying in which each copy was made from a previous photocopy.

Because no copy was perfect and each copy started from a previous one, the imperfections accumulated to the point that after a certain number of copying cycles, the drawing became more or less completely illegible. At this point it had to be completely redrawn on a clean sheet of paper.

DNA is not copied in the way that photocopiers copy documents. *Digital reproduction* gets round the problem of loss of information found in things like photocopiers because all that has to be copied is an item of information that in the digital codes used in computers is either something or nothing – for example a circuit that is either on or off, representing a one or a nought. Since it is a simple and unambiguous matter to tell something from nothing, digital records can be reproduced in principle with no necessary loss of information. As long as the ones and noughts that represent the something or nothing are faithfully read and reproduced, they can be copied as often as necessary because exactly the same information is read and reproduced in each and every cycle of reproduction. There is no inherent loss or degradation the way there is in photocopying. Indeed, this is the way that plans and drawings are copied by designers and architects nowadays. Instead of using pen and paper, drawings are made on computers and stored digitally. A major advantage is that they can then be reproduced and modified limitlessly, without any inherent loss of information or accumulation of copying errors. Much the same happens with DNA: bases strung out along the molecule are copied in a similar, all-or-nothing way, ensuring an astonishing level of accuracy and avoiding the cumulative error problem that bedevils the photocopier method.

The genetic code

Proteins are the principal active constituents of living matter. Many of the most important are *enzymes*: substances that accelerate or control reactions involving other chemicals. The genetic code is written in triplets of DNA bases, each corresponding to a particular constituent of a protein, or to stop and start 'punctuation marks' in the code. Genes are decoded one triplet of bases at a time by *ribosomes*, subunits of the cell responsible for the assembly of proteins. In terms of the genetic code, a gene can be described as a sequence of base-pairs on a strand of DNA that code for any one particular protein, and are typically found to be thousands or millions of base-pairs long – and not necessarily all in one piece. Overall, the total complement of DNA in a human being, what is termed the *genome*, is believed to be about three billion base-pairs long. Laid end to end these would be about five feet in length, although far too fine a thread to be seen with anything but the most powerful microscope. If imagined as a rope about two inches in diameter, the total complement of DNA in a human cell would be approximately 32,000 miles in length – enough to circle the Earth at the equator one and a quarter times.

Since all known organisms appear to encode their genetic material in DNA (or the very similar RNA), and similar genes for similar things are found in organisms as diverse as yeasts, human beings and plants, it seems very likely that all organisms are descended from originals which used a DNA-like genetic code. Evolution can be seen as occurring by means of chance changes in this code – mutations, in other words – which have gradually accumulated in countless organisms over immense periods of time. But the fact that DNA-like substances are highly vulnerable to chemical attack and certainly can't survive in an oxygen atmosphere like that which now exists on earth means that ever since the oxygen atmosphere developed – and probably long before – DNA had to be packaged, or enveloped in some kind of protective covering. To account for this, nothing more than natural selection need be supposed: genetic information which could survive and leave more copies of itself because it included genes for containment and protection would probably be the only genetic information to be selected once competition among DNA began.

Organisms are the evolutionary packaging of their genes

Nevertheless, it would be wrong to think that every bit of DNA was a gene and that the entire genome of an organism was devoted to genetic information that was expressed in building the organism. In fact, the amount of DNA in an organism is not necessarily related to that organism's size or complexity. If we take the total size of an organism's genome as a measure of the information stored in its DNA, we find no such relation: toads and mice have much the same amount of DNA as human beings, chickens have about half as much, corn almost twice as much, newts more than five times as much, and lungfish 40 times more! Even within a single type of organism, such as flowering plants, genome sizes range from a tiny fraction of the human one to 37 times larger. At the very least, you might expect to find the biggest difference between multi-celled and single-celled organisms. Yet the greatest range is found within single-celled ones, where the variation from yeast to amoeba is 80,000-fold and within green algae is 3,000-fold (Maynard Smith and Szathmáry 1995: 179).

In part this can be explained by the fact that not all DNA appears to be accounted for by functional genes – that is, by genes that are expressed as proteins and so directly contribute to the organism. So-called *pseudogenes, junk genes* or *selfish DNA* exist that are not translated into protein, even though they are faithfully copied along with the rest of the genome. In general, the larger the total quantity of DNA, the greater is the proportion that appears to be redundant in this respect, with more than 99 per cent of all DNA being like this in the most extreme cases.

DNA existing simply to reproduce itself is graphically illustrated by so-called 'jumping genes' (alias *transposable elements*). Because genes are strings of DNA, they are dealt with sequentially, like people standing in a queue. Jumping genes are like cheats who rejoin the queue after being served in order to get a second helping. Having got themselves copied once, such genes jump to a part of the genome that has yet to be copied, and so get themselves copied again. Other genes can change the sex of an offspring or distort the sex ratio in a way favourable to themselves if they are preferentially transmitted by one sex rather than the other.

If DNA in general and genes in particular existed simply to reproduce the organism as a whole in the way that Darwin imagined his gemmules did, any DNA that did not perform this vital function would seem to be free-riding because it did not pay its way, so to speak, by building the organism. But if you look at things the other way round, and see the organism as being generated by its genes, rather than genes being generated by the organism, there is no reason why junk genes should not exist, nor why DNA should not be selfish and copy itself, rather than the organism.

Indeed, we might go further and conclude that essentially this is why organisms as such exist: as the temporary containers, or packaging, of the genes which they contain. Mendel's discovery – and especially that of Crick and Watson and the whole science of molecular biology that has followed from it – leaves little doubt that the essence of evolution by natural selection is the containment and transmission of genetic information encoded in an organism's genes. Without such genes an organism could not develop, and without developing as the vehicle for such genes an organism could have no evolutionary future (Dawkins 1978).

Development and preformation

Genes not only encode and transmit genetic information, they also direct the development of organisms. In the second half of this chapter I want to focus on the fundamental issue rather than give a survey of everything that is known, and just as in the first half, I shall begin by discussing a historical error. As we shall see, this is of more than academic interest because it still affects how many people think about the developmental role of genes today and is at the root of the most common misunderstandings, particularly where psychology is concerned. A correct understanding of what genes can – and perhaps even more importantly, *cannot* – do is essential if we are to avoid the common error of thinking that genes control behaviour the way that strings control puppets, or digital programming controls industrial robots. On the contrary, we shall see that it is precisely because genes can't act in this way that they have to build bodies and brains that can act as independent agents on their behalf.

The belief that everything about an organism is preordained and laid down at the moment of conception is often called *preformation*. People are born as small babies, apparently complete in all their limbs and organs. Babies grow larger in the womb, so it follows that they must begin smaller. This suggested to so-called *Ovists* that at the moment of conception there is present in the egg a tiny person, or *homunculus*, just like the one that will be born, but of microscopic size. *Spermists*, on the other hand, believed each sperm 'contains a little male or female animal of the same species hidden under a delicate skin' (Jacob 1976: 61). Some even went so far as to link preformation with biblical creationism, seeing each generation nested within the previous one like a series of Russian dolls:

> Most of these men teach that there is in fact included in the egg a germ or perfect little human machine. . . . And not a few of them say that all human bodies were created fully formed and folded up in the ovary of Eve and that these bodies are gradually distended by alimentary humour until they grow to the form and size of animals. (S. J. Gould 1977: 29)

Others claimed that 'even original sin may stand on this principle as on a firm foundation, since all mankind have been laid up originally in the loins of their first parents' (Pinto-Correia 1997: 28).

In this way the doctrine of preformation insisted that development from egg to adult was predetermined and simply a question of the incremental growth of the homunculus, which was complete in every detail save size. The problem is that many people today still think of genes in preformationist terms, especially where behaviour is concerned. Such erroneous thinking probably fuels much of the heat that is generated by genetics in people's minds today, and certainly explains much of the phobic reaction to genetics seen in the media, where what you might call 'DNA preformationism' appears to be the rule. You sometimes see illustrations that try to express this idea by portraying people as puppets whose strings are pulled by genes or a hand labelled 'DNA'. Alternatively, the situation is sometimes represented as one in which genes 'program' human beings in the way that someone might program a computer to do something. Either way, you get the impression that what people do has already been decided by their genes and that they are just playing a part already written for them in the genetic code. But as we shall now see, neither physical development nor behaviour is or can be preformed by genes.

Development is not preformed

Embryonic development is not simply a matter of growing larger, or even of continuous addition. Sometimes structures are begun and left unfinished – the best example being the nipples of male mammals (see above, pp. 19–20). Again, not all cells that are added to an embryo or foetus are retained. Many are programmed to die in the process of development, such as those that lie between the digits of the embryonic hand and foot. Failure results in webbed extremities in the case of limbs, and a similar defect causes cleft palate in the case of the head. At birth babies are born with many more neurones than they will retain as adults, the surplus dying along the way. In some locations in the nervous system, up to 70 per cent of neurones may suffer this fate. To this extent, brain development is more like sculpture than building: rather than being built up brick by brick, the finished product is carved out of a mass of which much is discarded.

Even well after birth, growth is not always cumulative. The thymus gland, for example, is a critical part of the immune system, but shrinks after puberty to be a shadow of its former self. Even at its most active in childhood, the thymus produces vast numbers of cells that die within it, apparently unwanted. An embryo is not at all like an adult, and at certain stages shows features such as gill slits and a tail which no adult human being would ever have. At even earlier stages of development there is not even a remote resemblance to the adult body form. Organisms like human beings do not begin as tiny, complete models of themselves and then just grow larger. They do not grow by simple accumulation or enlargement at a constant, linear rate. In a word, they are not *preformed*.

Epigenesis

In order to avoid preformationist thinking about genes and development it would be helpful if we could find a concept that would represent the true view. Fortunately one already exists. **Aristotle** (384–322 BC) used the example of making a net to illustrate the process of *epigenesis* understood as generating the organism from the raw materials that make it up. Today *epigenetics* is the name given to the study of the way in which genes bring about their effects on growth and development (King and Stansfield 1997). Nets are made by knotting string. The nature, number and spacing of the knots determine the final form of the net. We now know that Aristotle's analogy is an even better one than he could have realized, because ultimately genes are codes for proteins, and proteins are essentially molecular strings whose pattern of folding is critical to the way they work. So we could regard the folded proteins as the knots, and genes as the directions for making the knots.

Looked at from this point of view, genes are like the programs that control looms or knitting machines (whose output of woven material is essentially a tightly woven and very complex net). Although these programs determine the pattern, texture and overall characteristics of the cloth, they do not do so by being a blueprint or plan for it. All that these programs do is to specify the type of stitches to be woven, the number and sequence in which they are to be made, and the threads to be used. The finished cloth emerges from the process of weaving or knitting as a result of the application of the program just as a net emerges from the process of knotting string. A tartan pattern in a woven cloth, for example, is generated in a way that is quite different from a tartan pattern which is printed on to a material. In the latter case a preformed tartan pattern must be prepared that is imprinted on the cloth, whereas in a woven tartan the pattern emerges from the weaving process by the way coloured threads are combined together in making the fabric.

Genes are not blueprints in any strict sense

Thanks to thinking in terms of preformation rather than epigenesis, many people believe that an organism's DNA does indeed preform it to the extent that genes contain a complete plan or model of it, albeit in coded form. But DNA is no more able to preform an organism than is a homunculus.

Box 2.3

Epigenesis of the immune system

Surprising as it may seem to those who take the view that DNA is a complete genetic blueprint for the organism, many genes that play a critical role in keeping us alive are not present when we are conceived, or even when we are born. And contrary to those who see genes as rigidly fixed and limited by the evolutionary past, the fact is that the human genome can generate a practically infinite number of different gene products when it needs them. Indeed, were it not so, no human being would survive infancy, let alone reach adulthood.

Large, long-lived creatures like human beings need defences against the threat posed by many much smaller, more numerous and more quickly reproducing organisms that would like to exploit them. There are believed to be anything up to a million species of bacteria, and at least 5,000 viruses, many with generation spans as short as 20 minutes. Protection against this threat is the function of the immune system. Its purpose is to detect and destroy diseases, parasites and infections of all kinds – what we might collectively call *antigens*. These are countered by *antibodies*, specially manufactured proteins that bind to antigens and thereby label and disable them. The problem for the genes of the immune system is that they have to generate antibodies to fight antigens which might not have existed at the time the individual was conceived and which can evolve rapidly within an individual's lifetime.

But what preformation can't achieve, epigenesis can. What happens is this: antibodies are composed essentially of two principal parts – a constant region common to all, and two variable ones, producing a characteristic 'Y' shape. On each of one pair of chromosomes in a fertilized egg there are about 300 gene segments that code for the variable region of an antibody. Some considerable distance away on the same chromosome there are some further short segments that contain more code for the variable region. Somewhat further still, the constant region is coded, along with a terminal part. As cells of the immune system mature, the DNA coding for the variable regions is randomly combined and mutated with that for the constant region and the terminus. As a result, new genes are produced which were not present in the original genome. A nearby regulatory sequence turns on the newly created gene, which is then expressed, producing a unique antibody. There are five regions in the second set of variable segments, which, with the 300 in the first set, can produce up to 1,500 different genes. However, this number is vastly increased by the fact that joining of the randomly chosen segments is itself highly variable, so that ultimately as many as 100 billion different antibodies can be formed in as many different immune system cells (Berg and Singer 1992).

Today it is believed that humans have in the order of 100,000 functional genes. If each antibody needed its own gene, and if 100 billion is the right kind of figure for the number of different antibodies that could in principle be made, then clearly human beings would have to have a million times more genes than they do. In other words, if every antibody that we could produce was blueprinted by human genes, people would need not just 46, but 46 million chromosomes in each one of their cells! But in reality only 300 or so DNA segments are required, all of them located on a single chromosome. This is an example of epigenesis, not of preformation.

In architectural plans, every detail, dimension and attribute of the finished building is exactly specified and to that extent preformed. Architects often make scale models of the building that can in principle be complete to any degree of detail. Indeed, you could see the finished building as the ultimate, full-size, fully detailed model. But genes are not blueprints in this sense. For a start, a fully detailed working drawing or blueprint is a specification of every part of the finished product. Genes do not specify every detail of the organism in this sense because they always rely on pre-existing cell machinery to read and translate them. Even viruses, which are little more than DNA in a protein container, rely on the gene-reading and protein-producing capacities of the cells they infect to make more copies of themselves. Today DNA can't do it on its own (even though its first precursors may have been able to do so to some limited extent, as RNA still can).[2]

Indeed, it is generally true that genes need not – and indeed cannot – contain all the information that would be necessary if they really were completely detailed blueprints for organisms. The human genome could not possibly store enough data to detail every connection between brain cells, for example, simply because there are so many billions of them. Although there are thought to be in the order of 100,000 functional human genes (10^5), there are believed to be at least a billion times more connections between nerve cells (10^{14}–10^{15}). This is nothing like enough to code them all in DNA, even if every one of the three billion bases available in the entire genome were used. Identical twins – so-called because they share identical genes – often have patterns of blood vessels that are visibly different, proving that a detailed, specific map of them cannot exist in their common genome.[3] (Box 2.3, 'Epigenesis of the immune system', gives an even more striking example.)

The role of the single gene

The fact that there are tens of thousands of genes in the human genome and that each gene codes for one protein suggests that no single gene can count for very much. It would seem that any significant trait would have to rely on many genes acting together, and that consequently the contribution of single genes would be relatively trivial. However, taken too far, such a view transfers to development the fallacious argument that Darwin's critics used against his theory where the inheritance of favourable mutations was concerned. As we saw earlier in this chapter, critics ignorant of the true nature of inheritance argued that mutations would be diluted by half in each generation, and so quickly reduce to insignificance. Today similar fallacious reasoning is applied to genes where development is concerned when it is claimed that no single gene can have much influence on its own, but is blended with and diluted by many others in its development outcome.

On the contrary, single genes can and do have far-reaching, critical effects. For example, height in human beings has always been regarded as a complex outcome of the interaction of many different genes with environmental factors, such as food supply. But according to the latest findings, 70 per cent of the variation in height in adults can be attributed to a single gene known as *PHOG*, found on both the X and Y sex chromosomes (Knight 1998).[4] Again, a number of seriously debilitating or fatal diseases are now known to be caused by single genes. One of the most striking is *Lesch-Nyhan syndrome*. The gene that causes this disorder has been traced to a place in the genome that normally codes for a single enzyme involved with basic cell chemistry. Affected individuals perform bizarre self-mutilating behaviour, typically biting off their lips and fingertips. *Huntingdon's disease* first shows itself as poorly co-ordinated movement but eventually results in dementia and death. Once again, a single gene has been isolated as the cause, but in this case it is not a loss but a gain that is the cause. The gene responsible often contains tens, hundreds or thousands of repeats of a single triplet of the genetic code that seems to determine the age of onset: the more repeats, the earlier it claims its victims. So in these cases not just a single gene but a single 'word' in the genetic code seems to cause the problem. A similar case is *fragile X syndrome*. This is a relatively common disorder causing mental retardation. Unaffected individuals have up to 60 one-word repeats, carriers who pass it on to their children without being affected themselves have 60 to two hundred, while victims have hundreds or thousands of them.

Box 2.4

Colouring Siamese cats

Many Siamese cats are notably darker at the extremities of the body – the tail, paws, ears and face. Why is this so? Is there a gene for colouring the corners of the cat? And if so, how does the gene 'know' where those corners are, and how to colour them? Is there a biological equivalent of painting-by-numbers where mapped regions of the cat are allocated specific colours according to a predetermined plan?

Photo © Photodisc

The answer is that the cats in question have a gene, not for colouring their corners as such, but for a particular enzyme that is both responsible for their colouring and sensitive to heat. Where the body is hotter – that is, in the middle – the enzyme results in less colouring. But where the body is cooler – the extremities – its colouring effect is strongest, and so the cat ends up with darker tail, paws, ears and face. The 'gene for colouring the corners of the cat' is in reality one for a heat-sensitive enzyme involved in colouring chemistry. This is not painting-by-numbers, but colouring by temperature.

If you artificially change the temperature of parts of a growing Siamese cat's body, for example by keeping its feet in socks, those particular extremities of the body will be warmer, and so will be coloured less. This shows that the final effect of the gene is also dependent on environmental factors, in this case temperature. Nor is this exceptional. On the contrary, because genes do not exactly preform every final aspect of the characteristic to which they contribute, it is often true that the way a gene is expressed can be drastically affected by other factors, such as the products of other genes, other organisms, or the external environment. The point is that if genes did indeed completely and perfectly preform the organism in the same way in which working drawings preform a finished product, such environmental effects would not appear. The colouring of Siamese cats illustrates the fundamental truth that development is not preformed, but *epigenetic*.

Sex is determined by a single gene

One of the best examples of the far-reaching effect that single genes can have on normal development is the *Sry* gene (for Sex-determining Region of the Y chromosome), which determines sex in mammals. As we have already seen, development in mammals begins with a female body plan, probably explaining the epigenetic effect of nipples in males. Male development deviates from this if the *Sry* gene is present on the Y chromosome. It functions as an epigenetic switch, which turns on many other genes downstream of it in the developmental cascade. Essentially, it converts what would have been ovaries into testes, and then the hormones which the testes produce masculinize the foetus. *Sry* is a prime example of the way in which genes control development, because there is no way in which it could map, plan or list all the manifold features of masculinity in a mammal. However, it can and does change the pathway of embryonic development from a female to male one. (For another example, see box 2.4, 'Colouring Siamese cats').

Genetic and environmental determinism

When most people think of something being determined by a single gene they usually assume that environmental factors are completely ruled out of account. However, the case of sex determination in crocodiles and turtles shows that this is by no means necessarily true. Sex is something absolutely fundamental, is usually determined early in development, and can't normally be changed later. It should be the epitome of 'genetic determinism', but in the case of some reptiles at least appears to epitomize environmental determinism of a very radical kind!

A single gene that is similar to the *Sry* gene in mammals determines the sex of crocodiles, alligators and turtles, but does so in a very surprising way. What is surprising about it is that, like the gene for colouring a Siamese cat, the sex-determining gene in these reptiles is temperature sensitive. Eggs incubated above a critical temperature all develop as males in crocodilians and the snapping turtle, while those incubated below it all develop as females. In other turtles the reverse is true: the higher temperature produces females, the lower one males.

The case of temperature-sensitive sex determination gives the lie to the vague generalizations that you often hear about genes and the environment always being equally important. Clearly, where sex is set by environmental temperature, the environment is more equal than where it is predetermined by inheritance of a sex-defining gene of the kind we find in mammals. It simply isn't true that genetics and environment as they are usually understood are always mixed in equal measures to produce any outcome. Pretending that they are only deepens confusion about the true facts of development and obscures the often differing ways in which genes and environment interact in any particular circumstance.

What environmental sex determination exemplifies is not a characteristic mix of genetic and environmental determinism, but epigenesis as opposed to preformation. Preformation rules out any environmental influence on development. If the organism begins as a tiny, complete and perfect prototype of itself, and merely grows larger to reach maturity, nothing can change its essential nature. Environmental factors in the form of more or less resources for its development may perhaps contribute to its final size, but overall nature triumphs over nurture. Preformationism would have you believe that sex must always be determined in advance, as it appears to be in mammals like human beings.

What happens in reptiles with temperature-sensitive sex determination, however, is that a usually reliable environmental cue is used by epigenesis to decide sex. Normally, a higher incubation temperature produces larger offspring in reptiles. Larger final body size often promotes the reproductive success of one sex more than the other. In the crocodilians and the snapping turtle, larger size benefits males, who fight for females. A gene that effectively said 'Make males in warm nests' would promote itself if it produced males who would be more successful in passing such a gene on to their descendants. In most turtles, however, larger body size normally benefits the reproductive success of females more than that of males, because it allows them to carry more eggs. In these species a gene that set sex the opposite way, with higher incubation temperature producing females, would also promote its own reproductive success if larger body size did indeed benefit females' egg-laying abilities. In both cases the gene defining sex would be taking advantage of an environmental cue to determine the most desirable outcome for itself.

The problem with programming behaviour

If genes can't and don't preform every detail of the final appearance of an organism because they are not blueprints or plans, it is even less likely that they could preform the organism's behaviour. Yet people all too easily think that if genes are involved in behaviour, they act mechanically, like programs that specify every last point and detail with total precision.

The idea of genes controlling behaviour suggests the image of the robot spot-welders nowadays used in car factories. As body shells advance down the production line in the factory, automated spot-welding machines swing into action and make a series of welds, repeating the process when the next body comes along. Robot welders like this are computer controlled, and execute a precise and unchanging sequence of actions. They respond to their programming very much as a puppet responds to the person pulling the strings. But this image of puppet-on-a-string control by genes is as wrong as the view that the physical form of an organism is preformed and mapped by its genes.

To see how wrong this is, take some real robots as a starting point, and consider the following problem: three robots have the task of collecting an evenly spread array of pucks into one pile. Each robot can move independently and has a scoop at the front with enough room for up to three pucks. How can the robots be programmed to complete the task?

One way would be to program every move of each robot in much the same way that spot-welders are programmed. Each puck-pushing robot would need an on-board computer and a memory to choreograph its movement. The memory would contain the list of actions that the robot would have to follow and the computer would have to read the list and convert it into patterns of movement. Like the spot-welder, the robot would be working as a preformed system because all its programming would be internal, fixed and installed before it began.

Although this sounds simple in principle, in practice it would turn out to be a very complex task. This is because a rigid, preformed program of the kind that is perfect for spot-welders would certainly fail for free-moving robots. Spot-welders are fixed, repeat an unchanging and closed cycle of actions, and work on car bodies that are presented to them at exact locations on a production line that moves in a manner perfectly synchronized with them. Free-ranging robots with disposed objects on which they must work face a quite different prospect. Errors of various kinds would be bound to creep in. Wheels might slip, pucks might stick, and even minute inaccuracies of direction or timing would build up cumulatively so that eventually they would become major divergences from the plan. Inevitably, linear programming for such a task would have to include error-correction procedures and complex subroutines to allow for a step in the program to be repeated or compensated for if it failed initially. The on-board computers and memory would grow, and the robots would require sophisticated senses to measure their performance against the listed plan, to take account of what the other robots were doing, and to correct or vary their own movements where necessary. Many thousands of lines of programming would probably be required for even so simple a task as concentrating the pucks, and sophisticated artificial intelligence would probably be needed to complete the task at all.

Applying this insight to genes that control behaviour leads to the same conclusion we came to when considering genes that build bodies: there simply isn't enough room in the genome of an organism to program its behaviour in the way that spot-welders are programmed, and even if there were, such programming probably wouldn't work in the real world! How then, could genes do it?

Free-ranging robots with only one programming rule can complete the task

A second, quite different approach has recently been proved to work in solving the robot puck-concentration problem. Rather than attempting to program the robots for every move they make, it has been found that they can do the job thanks to a very much simpler set-up. Each robot is free-moving and has a pressure switch mounted behind the scoop that is triggered if the scoop is pushing three or more pucks. Each robot is programmed with only one rule that says, 'When the pressure switch is triggered, stop, back off and move away in a random direction.' Observation of robots operating on this basis shows that the same thing always happens. First, pucks are pushed into piles of three. Then larger piles emerge from which one or two pucks are randomly removed or to which they are added. Eventually only one

Box 2.5

Puck-pushing robots

Three robots must push 81 evenly spaced pucks into a single pile. Each robot can move in any direction, stop and start. Each has a scoop with a pressure switch that stops the robot if it is pushing at least three pucks, hits another robot or the fixed boundary. The robot is programmed to back off and start again in a random direction each time it stops.

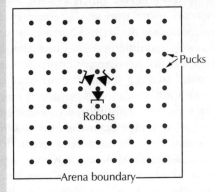

At first, pucks are collected into many piles of three:

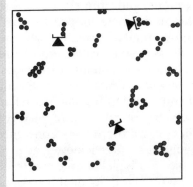

Then fewer, larger piles are formed. Finally, a single, complete pile is formed (Beckers et al. 1994).

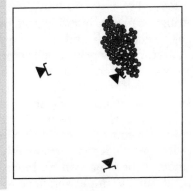

pile is left, containing all the pucks (Beckers et al. 1994). (See box 2.5, 'Puck-pushing robots'.)

In this example, the first, linear programming solution corresponds to preformation because every move by the robots is listed and foreseen in the design of the system, including error correction and compensation subroutines that may, or may not, be executed. The second, random-search method corresponds to epigenesis because, rather than having a complete, preformed plan of every move and action, the robots simply repetitively apply one simple rule, based on an environmental signal given by the pressure switch.

Today there is considerable evidence that a close equivalent of the puck-pushing robot approach is seen in many cases of animal behaviour. A striking case is the way in which ants collect their dead. Observations show that ants tend to put corpses of dead nestmates together in cemeteries which occur in certain places far from the nest and which grow in size with time. If a large number of ant corpses are scattered outside a nest, the ants from the nest pick them up, carry them about for a while, and drop them. At first, the corpses are put into small clusters, but as time goes on the number of clusters decreases and their size grows until eventually all the corpses are in one or two large clusters (Beckers et al. 1994). Another example is the way in which termites build their mounds. These begin as patterns of mud-balls dropped by individual termites at random, and the accumulations of mud-balls gradually grow to become the pillars and walls of the nest. Darwin himself gives the example of the way in which bees build honeycombs. In these cases the insects concerned act very much like the puck-pushing robots and achieve a goal without the need for any program that specifically defines the end result, which emerges naturally from the sum of their individual behaviour. 'All this beautiful work can be shown', says Darwin, 'to follow from a few very simple instincts' (Darwin 1968: 248).

Putting the matter in more modern terminology, you could say that although genes can't and don't normally program behaviour in the linear, preformed way in which computer codes control the behaviour of spot-welders, genes can and do build *epigenetic rules* into organisms. Such epigenetic rules are naturally selected tendencies for an organism to react in one way rather than another (Lumsden and Wilson 1981), and are applied recursively, just like the single rule that we have just seen controlling the behaviour of the puck-pushing robots or the analogous rules that presumably control the construction of termite mounds or honeycombs. Indeed, as we shall see in a later chapter, if the rule is simple and general enough, it can certainly control much that passes for normal and abnormal behaviour in human beings (see below, pp. 125–8).

Epigenetic agents

A common complaint is that genes can't be the ultimate authority for any aspect of behaviour because genes are biochemical recipes, not sets of instructions for actions. Of course, this is true, as I have pointed out repeatedly. However, genes can and do build bodies and brains, which in their turn can act independently for and on behalf of the genes that built them.

Designers of mobile probes intended to explore the surface of other planets realized early on that such vehicles would have to be able to control themselves to a large extent, simply because it was impractical to think that they could be operated remotely from the Earth. This is because signals would take time to travel to and from the vehicle, which might be on Mars, for instance. If a vehicle attempted to cross Martian terrain under remote control from Earth, it would have to move very slowly in order to allow for the best part of an hour that two-way transmission would take before it could be stopped, so as to avoid an obstacle, for example. Under these conditions it would obviously be much better if the vehicle could make its own decisions about whether to go over or around, or back off from an obstacle it encountered.

Genes act in a comparable way. Like a space agency that builds a probe and sends it to explore a distant planet, genes can build an organism, but once it is committed to its mission, it has to be left largely to its own devices. Like a planetary probe's mission controllers, genes can't constantly intervene in an organism's activity to dictate the best behaviour for every situation. On the contrary, all that they can normally do is to provide epigenetic rules likely to enhance ultimate reproductive success, like 'avoid fire or deep water', and leave it to the organism to decide for itself what to do if it encounters fire or flood. Freedom to act on its own behalf, in other words, is as much of a necessity for an organism built by genes as it is for a planetary probe. In both cases, the nature of the system positively demands such independence because of the constraints under which it operates.

To the extent that autonomous planetary probes are carrying out research on behalf of their designers, you could see them as *agents*: that is, expert systems which carry out a task on behalf of clients. The clients, however, do not need to be able to carry out the service for themselves. On the contrary, the whole point of employing agents is that they can do things for you that you can't do for yourself. Nevertheless, it is the client who is the ultimate beneficiary of the services provided by the agent.

When you want to go abroad, the fact that it is a travel agent who actually makes the bookings for you does not alter the fact that it is you who actually makes the journey. Similarly with genes. Although genes build bodies and brains to act and make decisions on their behalf, it is only an organism's genes that will arrive – or not arrive, if the decisions are wrong – in future generations. All organisms die, but genes are potentially immortal. Organisms are the vehicles that genes use for travel in both time and space. Those vehicles are their agents, and have all kinds of expertise, knowledge and capabilities that genes don't have and don't need. You don't need online connection with the airlines' booking system as long as your travel agent has it and can use it on your behalf. You don't have to bother your head with detailed knowledge about the travel business if your agent can advise you of what you need to know. And you certainly don't need to know how to build airliners, fly planes or operate air traffic control systems to arrive safely at your destination. Similarly, genes don't need to be able to act, decide, think or remember as long as they can commission epigenetic agents who can do all these things for them. But just as you have the ultimate responsibility for commissioning your travel agent and making your own journeys, so genes retain ultimate authority over their agents. Those epigenetic agents that deliver them safe, sound and digitally copied to the future will go on getting commissioned; those that don't, won't. Evolution by natural selection is as simple as that.

Those who balk at the idea of genes building behaviour as well as bodies are probably doing so in some part because they have failed to understand not just epigenesis, but the concept of epigenetic agents. Their problem is that they jump directly from the gene to behaviour without thinking of the agent that must lie in between. The concept of the epigenetic agent explains how and why genes can be the units of inheritance and yet the agents that they generate can have capabilities that far exceed their own. The fact that you retain ultimate authority over your travel agent doesn't mean that you won't listen carefully if you are given advice or that you should try to do the agent's job, for example by using the booking system yourself. The whole point of employing agents is that they can do the job better than you can. Consequently, you have to allow them to get on with it and exercise the appropriate freedom, initiative and judgement in doing so.

Genes are in the same position. They have to allow their agents the appropriate freedom they need to do whatever it is they have to do on their behalf. Consequently, organisms will have all kinds of independent competencies, expertise and abilities that their genes in themselves lack. They will be expert systems in their own right and will have to have the freedom and discretion to act as such. Genes don't deny individual freedom: they positively guarantee it because their agents could not function without it. And without their agents genes would go nowhere save to extinction.

Suggestions for further reading

Berg, P. and M. Singer (1992)   *Dealing with Genes: The Language of Heredity.*
Coen, E. (1999)   *The Art of Genes: How Organisms Make Themselves.*
Dawkins, R. (1989)   *The Selfish Gene.*
Maynard Smith, J. and E. Szathmáry (1999)   *The Origins of Life.*
Plomin, R., J. C. DeFries and G. E. McClearn (1997)   *Behavioral Genetics.*
Wolpert, L. (1991)   *The Triumph of the Embryo.*

3

The Evolution and Psychology of Co-operation

Human beings' capacity for co-operation with others is one of our most distinctive characteristics, and one that is often regarded as setting us apart from the rest of nature. Selfishness, aggression and competitiveness have always been easy to explain in terms of evolution by natural selection – and indeed are synonymous with it in the minds of many. However, it was not until the later part of the twentieth century that Darwinian theory was able to begin to put the evolution of co-operation, self-sacrifice and altruism on a rigorous genetic and mathematical basis. The result is that today evolution by natural selection can explain co-operative behaviour as readily as it can self-seeking behaviour, and no longer deserves to be blamed for appearing to condone anti-social tendencies. On the contrary, the greatest triumph of modern evolutionary theory has been to explain altruism as an epitome of natural selection at the level of the individual gene.

In this chapter we shall consider the question of how and why co-operation can evolve, and what some of its psychological consequences might be. As we shall see, it is a subject that has been revolutionized by the genetic insights explained in the previous chapter, and it is one to which evolutionary psychology has made a distinctive and important contribution.

Super-organisms and group selection

According to Herbert Spencer, there were three grades of Evolution (with a capital 'E', see above, pp. 1–2): Inorganic, Organic and Super-organic. Super-organic evolution pertained to 'all those processes and products which imply the co-ordinated actions of many individuals'. Of these, 'the most familiar and in some respects the most instructive, are furnished by the social insects.' Spencer pointed out that 'Just as the germ of a wasp evolves into a complete individual; so does the adult queen-wasp, the germ of a wasp-society, evolve into a multitude of individuals with definitely-adjusted arrangements and activities' (Spencer 1885: 1–5). Applying the principle to human beings, the German Social Darwinist **Ernst Haeckel** (1834–1919), held that the Germanic race had 'discovered the factor of organization', which made it superior in the scale of evolution to other peoples who still 'live under the regime of individualism' (Kemp 1998).

This Spencerian, super-organic tradition of thinking about social evolution continued into twentieth-century Darwinism associated with the concept of *group selection*. Group selection holds that, for the purposes of natural selection, the individual who belongs to a group or species is not necessarily the relevant unit. Instead, selection should be seen as acting on the entire group or species. Furthermore, selection demonstrably does act on groups at all levels. This can best be seen by recalling the point just made about organisms and super-organisms. Individual organisms are indeed groups of cells, and to the extent that selection acts on an individual organism, you could say that it acts on a group. Again, it is easy to imagine situations in which changes in the natural environment might affect large groups of organisms, or even entire species or classes of animals. For example, some people think that changes in the Earth's oxygen level have occurred in the past. To the extent that the oxygen concentration in the atmosphere would affect all oxygen-consuming organisms, you could see it as a selective force that acted on very large groups indeed, and to that extent, was an instance of group selection. Indeed, some adaptations – such as sex – make no sense in terms of the individual because at least two members of a sexual population are required: one male and one female.

Group selection will seldom if ever affect all members equally

Nevertheless, there are some important qualifications that need to be borne in mind when considering group selection. The first is that group selection will never affect every individual in a group or species identically because every member will differ somewhat in its genetics, location or other circumstances, so selection for behavioural traits that benefit groups will not benefit all members equally or in the same way.

Again, because every benefit will normally carry some kind of cost, the costs of behavioural adaptations that would benefit entire groups or species will not necessarily fall equitably on all. Where cost is greater and/or benefit is less, there will be less incentive for the organism to co-operate with the interest of the group or species.

Group selection was implicit in much biological and evolutionary thinking until the early 1960s. Then the British biologist V. C. Wynne-Edwards published a book explicitly arguing that group selection was both predictable and observable in animal behaviour. According to Wynne-Edwards, species were constantly threatened by breeding and by eating themselves out of existence. To remedy this, he proposed that adaptations would evolve which limited population growth and the consumption of resources in the overall interests of the species even if this meant sacrifices by individuals for the greater good of the majority (Wynne-Edwards 1986).

However, careful experiments and field studies by many workers soon discredited this idea. For example, clutch sizes in birds are not adjusted to benefit the species but to maximize an individual parent's reproductive success. A good example of the effect is the fact that many bird species who normally raise only one chick in each breeding season often nevertheless lay two eggs. The waste of the species' resources in laying two eggs is considerable, because it means that one in two hatchlings usually starves to death, ignored by its parents and/or pecked to death by its first-hatched and better-fed sibling. In one species of eagle, for example, 200 nests with clutches of two eggs were found, but in only one case did both chicks survive to fledge. If the species as a whole decided the clutch size, you would think that one egg would be the norm because 99.5 per cent of all second eggs appear to be wasted.

But from the point of view of the parents, laying two eggs does pay, despite the considerable cost of the extra, wasted egg. This is because being able to raise only one chick per season makes it very important to the parents' reproductive success to have one chick to raise. From this point of view, the second egg can be seen as a back-up if for any reason the first one fails to produce a viable chick. Again, laying two eggs can pay if resources are unusually good. In this case, it may in fact be possible to raise both chicks, and the parents would thereby double their reproductive success in that season. The inescapable conclusion is that the potential gain to the individual parent's reproductive success of laying two eggs outweighs the cost to themselves, explaining why clutch size is not necessarily adjusted to benefit the species as a whole (Magrath 1989). (For another example, see box 3.1, 'Getting away with murder'.)

Box 3.1

Getting away with murder

Langur monkeys live in groups with several females and their young, controlled by a single, dominant male. When a male manages to supplant another in such a group, he systematically murders infants up to six months of age. He also kills infants born in the next six months. Initially, this was interpreted as population control in the interests of the species. Males were prudently culling the new-born so as to prevent groups from growing too large, and thereby destroying the scarce resources on which they relied. Unfortunately, the facts don't fit this complacent picture:

- Population size is determined by the number of females, because these are the individuals who will have the offspring. Where animal populations are scientifically culled to control numbers, it is nubile females that are killed, not infants of both sexes.
- Males often control groups for several years, but they only kill infants during the first six months. Yet periods of takeover do not correlate with population fluctuations.

However, the facts can be elegantly explained in terms of the reproductive interest of the dominant male:

- Lactating female langurs are infertile, and infants are weaned at seven to eight months. Killing infants still being suckled brings their mothers into estrus (sexual receptivity) within a few days and so makes them much more immediately available to carry the offspring of the new male.
- The gestation period in langurs is six months. This means that offspring born up to six months after a takeover are likely to be those of the previous male. However, offspring born after that date are likely to have been fathered by the new male, explaining why his campaign of infanticide only lasts for six months.

According to the species-advantage view, langur mothers should acquiesce to the murder of their offspring in the interests of the social whole. However, in the context of selection for individual reproductive success, langur mothers should resist because it is their offspring who are being murdered, even if they are not those of the new male. Adult females band together to protect their offspring from attack, and lactating mothers attempt to avoid the centre of the group where the male is usually found. Langur infants tend to avoid adult males, even their fathers, and this contrasts with behaviour in other species where such infanticide does not occur. Finally, a case has been described in which a female came into oestrus while the old male was still resident, and mated frequently with him. In the next three months, she showed signs of being pregnant, and then a new male took over the group. Within a week, this female appeared to have come into oestrus but gave birth only five months later to an offspring who was not attacked by the new male, presumably because he thought that it was his. In this case, a show of pseudo-oestrus by a female may have misled a new male into thinking that the offspring was his when in fact it was that of his predecessor.

As Robert Trivers points out,

in group- or species-advantage thinking, one individual's self-interest is typically elevated to that of the entire group. In this example, the adult male's self-interest has been elevated to that of the species. . . . The individual with the power to get away with murder becomes the benefactor, a patron of the weak and foolish. Elevating the self-interest of the powerful to that of the species tends to make the behavior of the powerful appear justified. This must be one of the reasons for the popularity of species-advantage reasoning. (Trivers 1981: 6–7)

Individualism in groups

Consider an insect sitting on a leaf, or a grazing animal on grassland. As figure 3.1 suggests, a lone individual is vulnerable to attack by a predator from 360 degrees. However, if that individual stands next to a neighbour, its vulnerability is halved because any predator will hit the neighbour first if it comes from the neighbour's side. If four individuals group, the angular vulnerability of each is again halved to 90 degrees. With six or more, some individuals have effectively 0 degrees vulnerability, because they can be entirely surrounded by others. In groups that exceed a critical size, such as that at the bottom of figure 3.1, the number of those with such zero vulnerability exceeds those on the periphery, and in their case vulnerability is down to 20 degrees. The practical effects of this can be seen in the way that herding animals bunch up if predators or dogs come into view. Fish shoals show the same effect in three dimensions – and with dazzling dynamism as individuals displaced to the outside attempt to enter the shoal again, producing a turbulent, rolling aggregation that seems to have a mind of its own. Clearly, grouping behaviour does not require any necessary top-down social constraint to be effective. It can and does emerge naturally from the self-interest of members to use others as a shield or hiding place (W. D. Hamilton 1971).

Grouping can also occur in the time dimension. Newborn wildebeest are extremely vulnerable to predators such as lions and hyenas

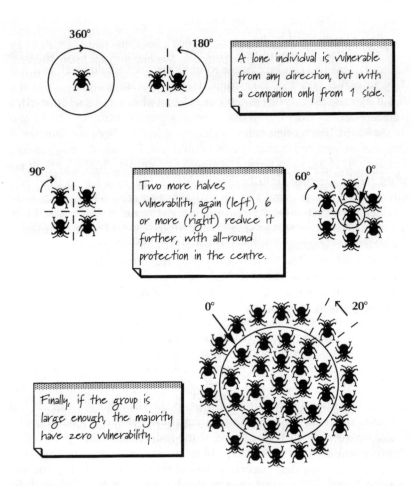

Figure 3.1 Social geometry

on the African plains where they are born. Although there may be little that any individual female wildebeest can do to protect her newborn calf from predators, she can make a dramatic difference to its chances of survival if she times its birth to coincide with that of the calves of other females. As a result, the vast majority of wildebeest calves are born in a short period of just a few days. During this time, predators feast on the spoils, but so vast is the number born, and so short is the period during which calves are vulnerable, that the predators can only take a small fraction of the total newborn population, reducing an individual's chances of being a victim to the lowest possible figure.

What is true of grouping is also true of restraint on aggressive behaviour. This too can be explained in terms of individual self-interest. Any animal that comes into conflict with another member of its species may meet an opponent who in fighting ability is equal to itself, is inferior, or superior. It will not normally pay an animal to be in conflict with an antagonist who is clearly superior, because injuries or exhaustion incurred in that conflict could – and almost certainly would – reduce its chances in later, less unequal contests. Again, individuals who are of superior fighting ability will seldom find it in their self-interest to keep proving the fact to subordinates if the latter avoid conflict with them for the reason just given and if there always remains a chance, however small, that injury or depletion incurred in such contests might prejudice the superior animal's prospects in more critical conflicts. Only protagonists who are of roughly equal standing are likely to fight to the point where one or the other has to retire, admit defeat, or suffer serious injury or death:

> the most spectacular social interactions of sheep are the dominance fights of rams. They are by no means common, but they may occur at any time of the year when strange rams meet. If the strangers differ conspicuously in horn size, the smaller one at once acts like a subordinate, and a normal dominant–subordinate interaction results between them. If strangers of equal horn size chance upon each other, they have no means to judge each other's fighting potential except by fighting. . . . Seen in this light, the reluctance of a dangerously armed dominant to engage with a subordinate is less a consequence of altruism than of self-preservation. (Geist 1971: 189, 234–5)

In other words, simple self-interest can be seen to reduce the incidence of conflict within a group or species quite markedly once both the costs and the benefits of aggressive behaviour are taken into account. Since the costs will often outweigh any likely benefit, conflict will often be avoided, not for the benefit of the group or species as such, but for the benefit of the individual concerned.

The problem of altruism

To see the evolutionary problem of social behaviour at its clearest, we must consider the issue of *altruism* defined as *any contribution to the reproductive success of a recipient at a cost to the reproductive success of an actor.* The crucial question is, can altruism as defined here be selected by group selection? This is effectively what Wynne-Edwards's theory demands, because clearly, self-imposed restraint in reproduction or the consumption of resources is indeed such a benefit to others' reproductive success at the organism's expense.

To see the problem here, first assume that an altruistic species exists in which all individuals promote the reproductive success of the others at a cost to themselves, just as our definition of altruism requires. Now imagine that a selfish mutant appears. By definition, the altruistic majority must promote the selfish mutant's reproductive success at a cost to their own reproductive success. However, because the selfish mutant does not by definition promote the reproductive success of the altruists in return, its own reproductive success is likely to be greater than theirs – it will be the archetypical free-rider, profiting from their altruism but giving nothing in return. Before long, altruists will be driven to extinction, and only the selfish will remain.

Much the same occurs if we try to imagine how an altruistic mutant could appear in an otherwise wholly selfish population. Such a mutant would, by our previous definition of altruism, have to promote the reproductive success of the selfish at a cost to itself, and would seemingly never become established, let alone dominant in the species. Here the selfish majority would be the free-riders, exploiting any altruistic mutants to the latters' complete extinction.

Group selection is not the same thing as selection for group benefit

The error that people often make is to think that, just because selection can affect entire groups, it can also select traits that benefit the group at a cost to the individuals who carry that trait. The free-rider theorem corrects this and points out that selection will also act on individuals within groups in such a way as to frustrate the group benefit: *individuals will be selected to gain a benefit to their reproductive success without paying its attendant cost, or to avoid paying an additional cost from which they gain no more benefit than anyone else.*

Hamilton's inequality

Although we seem to have proved that altruism as defined in terms of reproductive success cannot possibly evolve by natural selection, the fact remains that altruistic acts as we have defined them are surprisingly common throughout nature. Furthermore, it is possible to imagine one way in which such naturally selected self-sacrifice could evolve.

Suppose that a species of insect lays eggs in a nest, where the eggs and larvae that develop from them are tended by the mother. Now suppose that a mutation occurs in such a mother, so that some of her daughters are sterile. All that would be required to achieve this would be a detrimental change in a gene critical for reproduction, such as an enzyme affecting fertility in some way (and we have already seen that detrimental mutations are highly probable: see above, pp. 5–6). Suppose further that normally females leave their mother's nest to make nests of their own when they produce eggs. The sterile daughters will fail to produce eggs, and as a result may stay on in their mother's nest. However, the stay-at-home daughters will have inherited all the nest-tending behaviours they would have needed for their own nests, and so the result might be that, instead of raising their own offspring, they help their mother to raise more of hers.

At first sight, you might think that such a mutation as the one we are imagining would be likely to be selected out. After all, it produces sterility, and that can hardly promote the reproductive success of an organism! But the English biologist **William Hamilton** (1936–2000) realized that circumstances existed where it might do so. For example, imagine also that, at the same time that the gene for occasional sterility appears, so there is a marked shortage of nest sites. The result might be that the gene for producing some sterile females who stayed at home and helped their mothers have more of their sisters found its reproductive success enhanced by comparison with an allele that had no such effect on fertility. It could easily happen in these circumstances that a sterile female who stayed at home and helped her mother produce more sisters would have greater reproductive success that way than would a fertile female who left home but produced no offspring because of the lack of nest sites.

Hamilton saw that the reproductive success of sterile individuals could be indirect: instead of passing on their genes to their own offspring, identical genes might be passed on by their mother to the sisters they helped their mother raise. If such sisters were raised more successfully and/or in greater numbers than the offspring of fertile females without helpers, females with the gene for occasional sterility in their daughters might find their reproductive success increased. In other words, the gene for occasional sterility would have been selected because it conferred greater reproductive success on its possessors than they would have had had they not possessed it! (See box 3.2, 'Eusociality and haplo-diploidy'.)

Box 3.2

Eusociality and haplo-diploidy

The *hymenoptera* – bees, wasps and ants – are *haplo-diploid*. Females are diploid in the usual way, and receive one set of genes from each parent, making two sets in all (see above, pp. 45–7). However, males develop from unfertilized eggs, and so are haploid, because an egg, like a sperm, carries only one set of chromosomes. As a result, male hymenopterans are the product of a biological one-parent family: they have a mother, but no father.

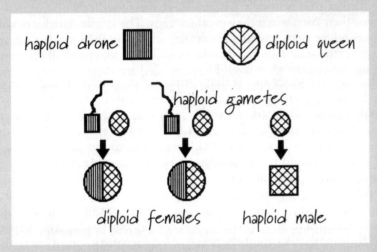

This strange arrangement has some intriguing consequences. For one thing, it means that a male cannot have any male offspring, because these develop from unfertilized eggs, and have no need of a father. All a male's offspring must be daughters. Again, a male's sperm cells carry exactly the same set of genes that all his other cells do, and his daughters each receive exactly the same set of genes from him, meaning that through him their shared relatedness amounts to one half of their total complement of genes. However, the set of genes that hymenopteran females get from their mother amounts to only a half of the total because their mother is diploid, and so has two complete sets. This means that, on average, sisters will share half of a half of their mother's genes, or a quarter. Consequently, the total relatedness to one another of hymenopteran females who share the same parents is half via their common father and a quarter via their mother, making three-quarters, or 0.75 in all. In other words, females with the same parents are more closely related to their mother's offspring – their sisters – than they would be to any offspring which they might have themselves. This explains why it could pay a gene in a sterile female worker to help her mother have more offspring: that way, the gene is copied at a 75% level of probability, whereas if the worker reproduced herself, the gene would only be present in her offspring with 50% probability.

Such considerations also go far towards explaining why so many hymenopteran species are *eusocial*: that is, why their communities feature sterile castes of workers, soldiers and nurses, along with reproductive queens and drones. However, it would be wrong to think that haplo-diploidy is the only – or necessary – basis for eusociality because it is also found in the conventionally diploid termites and even in a mammal: the naked mole rat. What is essential for eusociality is high levels of relatedness between community members, and this is achieved in the non-hymenopteran cases by close inbreeding, rather than by haplo-diploidy (W. D. Hamilton 1964).

The importance of this is that sterile castes of insects had always posed a serious problem to evolution by natural selection, as Darwin himself candidly admitted. Darwin also correctly intuited that the solution lay in relatedness, but lacking any real understanding of heredity, Darwin himself could never explain exactly how natural selection could create sterile castes. However, Hamilton triumphantly solved the problem by the realization that selection could act indirectly on a gene shared by close relatives. Put in its simplest terms, Hamilton proved that traits like sterility or self-sacrifice could be selected where $Br > C$, and B was the benefit to the copy of the gene for altruism in the beneficiary of an altruistic act, C was the cost to an identical copy of the gene for altruism in the altruist, and r was the degree of relatedness. (See box 3.3, 'Calculating relatedness'.)

For example, suppose that situations occur where a parent could sacrifice its life to save offspring from fire, flood or predators at a cost to its own life. In a normal, sexually reproducing, diploid species it would not pay a parent to do this to save a single offspring (on average and all other things being equal) because the gene for self-sacrifice in the parent would be lost with 100 per cent probability while it would be saved in the offspring only with 50 per cent probability. Nevertheless, saving two offspring would not cost the gene anything (100 per cent lost, 100 per cent saved), but saving three would confer a real benefit: 100 per cent lost in the parent, but 150 per cent saved in the three offspring (on average, all other things being equal and in the circumstances in which the trait first evolved: see figure 3.2).

Box 3.3

Calculating relatedness

The *coefficient of genetic relatedness*, or **r** for short, expresses *the statistical likelihood that two individuals share identical genes by common descent.*

Sexually reproducing organisms are usually diploid (that is, have two complete sets of genes) and usually produce haploid sex cells (one set of genes) which come together to create a new, diploid offspring. However, the haploid set of genes that each parent passes to its offspring is not usually simply one of its own two sets. Normally, genes are exchanged between the parent's diploid sets to create a new, haploid one, which is a mixture of both original sets.

If a diploid organism like a human being gets half its genes from each parent, its relatedness to each parent must be 0.5, or one-half. Relatedness between half-siblings – that is, a brother or sister who share only one parent – is 0.25, or one-quarter. This is because half of each half-sibling's genes come from half of the genes of the shared parent, so that relatedness of half-siblings through the shared parent is a half of a half, or 0.25. Because full siblings are related through both parents, their relatedness through both mother and father has to be added together so that their overall relatedness is twice 0.25, or 0.5.

Normally, stepping back a generation in a sexually reproducing, diploid organism halves relatedness between offspring of the same parents. Grandparents and grandchildren share r = 0.25, or a quarter of their genes, because each grandparent passed half their genes to their children, who in turn passed half of them on to the grandchildren. If those grandchildren have children of their own, their relatedness to their parent's grandparents – their great-grandparents – is clearly one-eighth, or 0.125, and so on. Relatedness with the mother's or father's collateral relatives can be worked out the same way. Cousins (children of siblings) are related by one-eighth of their genes (r = 0.125) because they share a quarter of their parents' genes, who themselves share half their genes as siblings, and a half times a quarter is one-eighth, or 0.125.

Although the vast majority of genes are contained in the nucleus of a cell, there are some that remain outside it. For example, *mitochondria*, which are important subunits of a cell involved in energy metabolism, have some of their own genes. These mitochondrial genes are normally inherited only from the mother in most sexually-reproducing organisms because the male sex cell contributes only nuclear genes to the fertilized egg. Sex chromosome genes are again different. This is because in mammals like human beings females have two X chromosomes, whereas males have only one, the other being a Y (see above, pp. 47–9). This means that Y chromosome genes never find themselves in a female body, and so are not inherited in the way that autosomes (non-sex chromosomes) are. Clearly, relatedness between a man's Y chromosome and his mother is zero, because he got his Y chromosome from his father. For the same reason, relatedness between a man's Y and his father is 1.0. Relatedness between a man's X chromosome genes and his mother's X chromosome genes is 0.5, because his mother carried two copies of the X chromosome, and the one he inherited is a random mixture of genes from both, so he has a 50% chance of inheriting any particular X chromosome gene of his mother's.

Immediately, this made parental sacrifice as easily explicable as any other kind of behaviour in which one organism incurs a cost to the benefit of another. Because relatedness to offspring is so obvious and because its evolutionary utility is so unmistakable, sacrifices by parents for their offspring were never seen as paradoxical. But Hamilton proved that his principle could explain all such sacrifice, and that the altruism of sterile workers who kill themselves defending their kin is no more difficult to explain than that of parents who risk their lives to save their offspring. Indeed, Hamilton's inequality explains why the billions of cells in a human being consign themselves to certain evolutionary death and allow the germ line alone the privilege of potential immortality (see above, p. 49). Cells in a multi-cellular organism like a human being are normally related by 100 per cent, so any net benefit to a sex cell by the sacrifice of the majority of non-sex cells can pay – and clearly does. In other words, brain, liver or muscle cells sacrifice their evolutionary future to sperm or egg cells in human beings because they are clones of those cells.

Taking such a 'gene's eye' view of things may seem strange, but there are good reasons for arguing that it is a more realistic and objective way of looking at things than is our conventional, and rather self-centred, attitude to ourselves. We have already seen that our genes do not exist to reproduce us so much as we exist to reproduce them, and if on occasions this means making sacrifices – perhaps even the ultimate one – then, from the individual gene's point of view, that is how it must be. Natural selection ultimately selects, not for human improvement, health, comfort, a balance of nature, advances in complexity, or whatever, but for one thing and one thing only: the reproductive success of genes for which organisms are nothing more than their biodegradable packaging. Only this view of things can make sense of suicidal altruism from the point of view of natural selection (see above, pp. 54–5) (W. D. Hamilton 1963, 1964).

Figure 3.2 How relatedness encourages altruism

Kin altruism

Numerous studies of animal behaviour strongly support the contention that what we might term *kin altruism* is indeed strongly correlated with close genetic relatedness. Alarm calling, for instance, has been found to be more marked when kin are the beneficiaries, and suicidal self-sacrifice by soldier ants and termites occurs in the context of very high degrees of interrelatedness among the individuals concerned.

So common is co-operation with kin among human beings that we have a special term for it – or, at least, for when we disapprove of it. We call it *nepotism*, and mean by that term favouritism towards relatives, usually at the expense of non-relatives. Several scientific studies indicate a positive effect of kin on human health and survival. For example, a study of who-helped-whom during the air raids on the Israeli city of Haifa during the Gulf War showed that relatives were more likely to share shelters and to call each other to see if help was needed than were non-relatives. However, less costly forms of aid (such as advice about how to prepare for the raids) was more likely to be shared among friends than among kin (Shavit et al. 1994). These findings support a study which showed that modern Americans rely on friends for companionship, but are more likely to borrow money from kin (Fischer 1992). During the first winter after their arrival at Plymouth Rock in 1620 more than half the Pilgrim Fathers died, but individuals with more kin survived better than those with fewer (McCullogh and York Barton 1991). On Dominica in the Caribbean, children lacking kin support are at risk of high levels of stress hormones (such as cortisol) and have a higher incidence of illness (Flinn and England 1995). Indeed, even the symbolic kin support offered by a pet has been found to improve survival in nursing homes (Strassmann and Dunbar 1999). Nor are kin effects limited to health and survival alone; studies of marriage in the Third World show that marrying a first cousin has greater average reproductive success than marrying a non-relative thanks to a greater number of pregnancies (which more than compensate for slightly increased child morbidity) (Bittles et al. 1991).

Altruism can also mean avoiding doing harm

Hamilton's principle should also apply in reverse in the sense that, not merely might positive acts of altruism on behalf of relatives be selected in the way he proved they would be, but acts of selfishness which do harm to relatives might be selected against for similar reasons. For example, if I had a gene that made me preferentially sacrifice three of my offspring to save my own life (the exact converse of the example above and in figure 3.2), 100 per cent of my genes for selfishness would be preserved, but 150 per cent of those genes present in my children would have perished. Because more copies of the genes for selfishness would have been destroyed than were saved, we can conclude that natural selection for the reproductive success of individual genes would select against such selfish acts that are injurious to kin in precisely the same way that it selects for acts of altruism that benefit kin.

Putting the matter another way, we might say that natural selection could favour self-restraint where acts injurious to kin were concerned. If you make the important distinction between blood relatives and relatives by marriage, statistical evidence of homicide does appear to bear out the prediction that genetic relatives tend preferentially to avoid killing one another. For example, in 1972, 75 per cent of all murders of relatives in the city of Detroit were by non-blood related relatives. In the same sample, co-residents unrelated by blood were 11 times more likely to be murdered than genetic relatives living in the same household. If the frequency of interaction were the important factor in deciding who murdered whom, genetic relatives would be no different from any other category of persons who might cohabit. This would mean that two individuals who carried out a murder together ought to be just as likely to be related to one another as would victims be likely to be related to their killers. However, figures for collaborative murders in Miami showed that 30 per cent were relatives, as compared with 2 per cent of murder victims being blood relatives of their murderers. Nor are such figures exceptional in any way. On the contrary, the degree of relatedness between collaborative killers is far higher than that between victim and killer in every society for which a relevant sample of cases is available, including tribal horticulturalists, medieval Englishmen, Mayan villagers and urban Americans (Daly and Wilson 1988).

These findings become particularly striking if we compare them with data regarding relatives who have no genetic tie, but a purely social one, such as step-parents. An interview study of middle-class step-parents in Cleveland, Ohio, who were not experiencing any particular kind of stress in relation to their stepchildren found that only 53 per cent of stepfathers and 25 per cent of stepmothers claimed any 'parental feeling' towards their stepchildren, and fewer still professed to feel 'love' for them. That such subjective reports are not misleading is suggested by the finding that an American child living with one or more substitute parents in 1976 was approximately 100 times more likely to be fatally abused than was a child living with its natural parents. Nor are such figures a peculiarity of the United States: similar findings

are reported for Canada and England. Indeed, a recent study concluded that 'Stepparenthood per se remains the single most powerful
risk factor for child abuse that has yet been identified' (Daly and Wilson
1988).

Inclusive fitness

We can now see that, far from being paradoxical, altruism which reduces an organism's personal reproductive success is to be expected
and derives from exactly the same determinants as those which dictate
that organisms should on occasions be ready to sacrifice their own
bodily health and welfare for their offspring. Even though such acts of
altruism may reduce *personal* reproductive success, they may increase
the *shared* reproductive success which copies of the gene or genes for
altruism may have in beneficiaries of the altruistic act. The term *inclusive fitness* was coined by Hamilton for this measure of the effects of a
gene on identical copies in related organisms, and is defined as *an
actor's own reproductive success plus or minus the effects of its actions on the reproductive success of related organisms, discounted by
the degree of relatedness between the parties*. In practice, inclusive
fitness is difficult to work out without complex mathematics, and an
altogether easier alternative is the 'gene's eye view' which sees organisms as packages of interacting genes, whose reproductive success is
correlated and affected by those interactions (Grafen 1982).
    What the concept of inclusive fitness reveals most clearly is that,
whether in the same body or in a near relative, natural selection determines that the benefit to the reproductive success of individual genes
should on occasions exceed the cost of sacrifices to personal health or
reproductive success of particular organisms who carry them. In a
manner that reveals the true character of natural selection with particular clarity, it seems that both the reproductive success and the personal survival of some organisms should on some particularly revealing
occasions be compromised in the interests of selection at its most fundamental: that of differential reproductive success of individual genes.[1]

Prisoner's dilemma

If you take both cost and benefit to the actor and recipient of a social
interaction of the act into account, there are four possible outcomes as
far as the actor is concerned:

- if the actor gets a benefit, and the recipient of the act pays a cost, the action is *selfish* (an example would be stealing something);
- if the actor pays a cost and the recipient gets the benefit, the action is *altruistic* (an example would be giving someone a gift);
- if the actor gets a benefit and the recipient also gets a benefit, the action is *co-operative* (an example would be sharing something);
- finally, if both actor and recipient incur costs, the action is *spiteful* (an example would be destroying something you couldn't have so that no one else could have it either, see table 3.1).

A real-life example might be going out for a meal with a partner. The benefit would be eating, the cost, paying for the meal. Each of you would face a choice, either to pay, or not to pay. Let's call paying the bill *co-operating*, and not paying it *defecting*. If you both co-operate, you both pay and you both eat: this is the co-operative outcome. But now suppose that you co-operate and pay, but your partner does not for some reason: the outcome is obviously an altruistic action on your part if it means that you pay for your partner's lunch. However, your partner gets a free lunch, which is a benefit without any cost, so this corresponds to the selfish outcome as far as your partner is concerned. Finally, we could imagine a situation in which neither of you were prepared to pay anything and so neither got any lunch: the spiteful outcome.

This situation, in which two actors face the dilemma of either co-operating with each other to their mutual benefit, or defecting in their private self-interest, is often called a *prisoner's dilemma*. The reason is that law enforcement agencies often use such a situation when interrogating suspects involved in the same crime. The usual practice is to isolate the suspects and interview them separately in the hope that one will incriminate the other if there is an inducement to do so, such as the promise of more lenient treatment, or a shorter sentence for the one doing the incriminating.

Table 3.1 Four fundamental forms of social action from the point of view of the actor

Actor	Recipient	Action
gets benefit	pays cost	**selfish**
pays cost	gets benefit	**altruistic**
gets benefit	gets benefit	**co-operative**
pays cost	pays cost	**spiteful**

If we now think about the relative value of these outcomes to you or your partner, we can see that a free lunch is always best: you get a benefit without a cost. We could call this T, perhaps for the *temptation* to free-ride at the other's expense. This is better than a lunch with a shared cost, because, although you still get your lunch, you have to pay for it. We could call this outcome R for *reciprocity*. This is in turn better than no lunch at all, which although imposing no cost, also carries no benefit whatsoever. We could represent this by P, for the *punishment* of mutual defection. Finally, the worst outcome is having to pay for someone else's lunch – a cost without a benefit to you. This is the *sucker's* pay-off, S. In the formal symbols usually used to express the prisoner's dilemma mathematically: $T>R>P>S$. To put the matter another way, you might say that, in a classical prisoner's dilemma, reciprocity pays both players, but exploiting the other pays better; and whereas mutual non-co-operation costs both players, co-operating when the other doesn't costs you more.

Additionally, the pay-off for mutual co-operation must be greater than the average pay-off of co-operation and defection: $R>(T+S)/2$. Otherwise (if $R<(T+S)/2$), there is no incentive to co-operate, and prisoner's dilemma becomes a game of chance (or can easily be resolved by allowing the players to take turns at defecting). If, and only if, both these conditions are satisfied, the game is a classical prisoner's dilemma. Table 3.2 sets out the *pay-off matrix* for such a classical prisoner's dilemma.

At first sight, prisoner's dilemma doesn't seem very interesting because it is obvious what to do. If you have the choice to co-operate with or defect against a partner with whom you can't communicate and who you know has been offered the same inducements, it is obvi-

Table 3.2 The prisoner's dilemma pay-off matrix

		Partner's choice	
		Co-operate	Defect
Actor's choice	Co-operate	Co-operate (pay) = R	Co-operate (pay) = S
		Co-operate (pay) = R	*Defect (don't pay) = T*
	Defect	Defect (don't pay) = T	Defect (don't pay) = P
		Co-operate (pay) = S	*Defect (don't pay) = P*

ous that you should defect. This protects you from the worst pay-off (S) if your partner defects, and promises you the best (T) if your partner co-operates. Clearly, in such a *one-shot prisoner's dilemma*, there is no point in co-operating. Nor does a series of such encounters look any more promising. This is because the last in the series is just like a one-shot: you should defect in case the other player does the same. However, since we assume that the other player knows this as well as you do, you can take it for granted that you will both defect on the last move. This means that you should also defect on the second-to-last move, just in case the other player does, given that you know that the other will do so on the last. But that in turn means that you should defect on the third-to-last move, and so on.

Prisoner's dilemmas are everywhere, and can be strikingly real

People often say that prisoner's dilemma is just a formal, mathematical game, with no application to real life. A major problem in biological applications is that to be objectively quantified, pay-offs would have to be translated into some measure of reproductive success, and that is notoriously difficult.

Nevertheless, a recent experiment with viruses showed that prisoner's dilemma can be applied to the simplest form of life. The virus in question is one that infects bacteria (a so-called *bacteriophage*, or bacterium-eater). It comes in two versions: co-operator and defector. The co-operator is so called because it produces by-products that help other viral particles to form: in other words, it promotes their reproductive success. The defector produces few of these, but benefits from those produced by co-operators. Many bacteriophages can infect one cell. The reproductive success of a co-operator in a cell infected by other co-operators was set at 1, and obviously corresponds to the pay-off for mutual reciprocity: R. The reproductive success of a defector in a similar cell was found to be 1.9, which corresponds to T: the defector's pay-off. The reproductive success of defectors in a defector-infected cell was found to be 0.83, and that of co-operators in such a cell was 0.65. In other words, T (1.9) > R (1.0) > T (0.83) > S (0.65) – just as a classical prisoner's dilemma pay-off matrix demands. As the experimenters showed, this insight explained why, even though both defectors and co-operators would have greater reproductive success if all were to co-operate, defectors still appeared to the mutual detriment of all once infections had reached a level that could sustain them. Although viruses are in a sense the ultimate free-riders because they are parasitical on other living organisms whose cellular machinery they use to make more copies of themselves, there is a poetic justice in realizing that free-riders can and do evolve to exploit the free-riders in their turn (Turner and Chao 1999)!

Another common response is to reject prisoner's dilemma on the grounds that even if it might apply to simple biological organisms like viruses, it doesn't correspond to the much more complicated social interactions of organisms like human beings. Nevertheless, if you think about it, every sexual relationship – not to mention marriage – is a prisoner's dilemma (at least if you define fidelity as co-operating, and infidelity as defecting). Furthermore, far from being limited to simpler organisms, prisoner's dilemma has been widely applied to human be-haviour of all kinds in psychology, sociology, strategic studies, eco-nomics, law and social philosophy. (See box 3.4, 'The school run prisoner's dilemma', for an example of its application to an everyday situation.)

Iterated prisoner's dilemma

The real-life situation depicted in the box also illustrates another di-mension of prisoner's dilemma interactions: what happens when they are *iterated*, or repeated over a period of time. In the early 1980s, Robert Axelrod invited participants to submit computer programs to play iterated prisoner's dilemma. The computer programs entered for Axelrod's tournaments each had to make a choice with knowledge of the previous choices of its opponent (although obviously not of the current choice). Programs were played against each other in a round-robin tournament (meaning that each entry was played against every other entry including itself), and scores totalled. Points in each round were allocated as follows: 5 for T, successful defection; 3 for R, mu-tual co-operation; 1 for P, mutual defection; and 0 for S, unsuccessful co-operation. Each game had 200 rounds, but scores were discounted in a way that effectively made each game of infinite or of indefinite length (overcoming the unravelling effect mentioned earlier) (Axelrod 1984).

Two tournaments were played. The winner was the shortest, sim-plest program submitted. Called *TIT FOR TAT*, its strategy was to co-operate on the first move and thereafter do exactly what its opponent had done on the previous move. TIT FOR TAT won despite the fact that it was known beforehand to be a good strategy, and a number of the other programs submitted were attempted improvements on it. But

Box 3.4

The school run prisoner's dilemma

A mother made an agreement with another woman to co-operate in taking their children to school. The agreement was that one mother would take the children to school at the beginning of the day and the other would collect them at the end. Obviously, both had a real incentive to co-operate in this way because it meant halving the time spent taking and collecting her child to and from school, petrol consumed, and so on.

At first, all went well, but then, towards the end of the first term, the second mother's car began to let her down and the first did significantly more journeys than she did. The holidays came and went, and the next term things got going on an equitable footing again. However, as the end of the term approached, the second mother's car once again began to be afflicted with mechanical problems. Finally, when exactly the same thing occurred at the end of the third term, the first woman made a polite excuse and established another – and more successful – arrangement with another mother for the next school year.

Although a real-life situation, this was also a classic prisoner's dilemma, with an implicit pay-off matrix illustrated here. T, the pay-off for successful defection is represented by one mother having her child transported to school and back entirely by the other woman; while S represents the corresponding cost to the other woman of taking both her and the other's child to school each

| | Second woman | |
	Co-operate	*Defect*
Co-operate	**Co-operate** **(take both children one way)** **= R** *Co-operate* *(take both children one way)* *= R*	**Co-operate** **(take both children both ways)** **= S** *Defect* *(don't take children either way)* *= T*
First woman **Defect**	**Defect** **(don't take children either way)** **= T** *Co-operate* *(take both children both ways)* *= S*	**Defect** **(take own child both ways)** **= P** *Defect* *(take own child both ways)* *= P*

way. P represents the cost to each woman of taking just her own child to school without any help from the other, and is less than S, since it does not include the very real cost of collecting, waiting for, and delivering the other woman's child. R, mutual co-operation, represents exactly half S, unilateral co-operation, since it means taking both children only half of the time, but is clearly less costly than P, taking only one's own child both ways all the time. In other words, T, no cost at all, is a greater benefit than R, half the cost of taking both children; this is in its turn a greater benefit than P, the cost of taking one's own child both ways; and the latter, finally, is less costly than S, taking both children both ways each day. In short, $T>R>P>S$, a classical prisoner's dilemma.

whatever the discipline of the rival inventors or the greater complexity of their programs, they could not better it. Axelrod comments that 'expert strategists from political science, sociology, economics, psychology and mathematics made the systematic errors of being too competitive for their own good, not being forgiving enough, and being too pessimistic about the responsiveness of the other side' (Axelrod 1984: 40).

In a variant of the basic round-robin tournament, an 'evolutionary' or 'ecological' variant was played, made possible, like the main tournament, only by the speed of modern computers. In this tournament, programs were 'selected out' as they fell to the bottom of the score sheet, and their representation was weighted according to their past success. Once again, TIT FOR TAT emerged as the winner, and went on winning by a steadily growing margin.

The secret of the success of TIT FOR TAT lay in four factors.

- *Niceness*   TIT FOR TAT did well by never being the first to defect, and thereby eliciting co-operation wherever it was forthcoming.
- *Robustness*   Because TIT FOR TAT retaliates immediately after every defection of the other player, it can't be exploited, and so no strategy playing against it could ever get more than one defection ahead.
- *Forgivingness*   TIT FOR TAT was ready to return to co-operation as soon as it found its protagonist doing so, and this encouraged co-operation with it to the mutual benefit of both players.
- *Clarity*   Because TIT FOR TAT was such a simple, transparent rule, other players could readily understand it and respond appropriately. Complex programs, by contrast, encourage defection in the other player because of their unpredictability (Axelrod 1984).

Is TIT FOR TAT an evolutionary stable strategy?

According to John Maynard Smith, who coined the term, an *evolutionary stable strategy* (or ESS) 'is a strategy such that, if all members of a population adopt it, no alternative, "mutant", strategy can invade the population' (Maynard Smith 1988: 194). The concept of ESS is important, because it shows that we don't have to think of individuals as always being co-operators or defectors. It is perfectly possible to see strategies like TIT FOR TAT or ALL D (always defect) as subject to natural selection in themselves, and as existing to a large extent independently of the organisms who might adopt them. So an individual might follow the ALL D strategy some of the time, but TIT FOR TAT or ALL C (always co-operate) at others. To see how these strategies compare on the basis of their evolutionary stability, consider the following simulation.

In figures 3.3 and 3.4, TIT FOR TAT encounters ALL D and ALL C in a territorial tournament in which strategies occupy spaces on a computer screen and play prisoner's dilemma with neighbours, winning points that determine their reproductive success. The surprising thing is that although ALL C cannot resist invasion by ALL D, and certainly cannot invade populations of ALL D itself, TIT FOR TAT can both invade ALL D populations and promote the reproductive success of ALL C.

To see how and why, consider the situation in figure 3.3 (top). Here ALL D is indicated by a minus sign on the left, ALL C by a plus on the right, and the centre player is TIT FOR TAT. After 15 generations during which each player plays every other with which it is in contact (figure 3.3, bottom), ALL C is in the lead, largely because of protection from the exploitative ALL D players by a wedge of TIT FOR TAT. By generation 35 (figure 3.4, top), all the available space has been filled, and ALL C continues to do well, thanks to the fact that the ALL D population is now entirely surrounded by TIT FOR TAT. ALL D finally becomes extinct at generation 125 (figure 3.4, bottom) because it has no ALL C players it can exploit, can't make headway against TIT FOR TAT, and does poorly in interaction with itself (gaining P). However, ALL C, the weakest possible strategy, continues to thrive in interaction with itself and with TIT FOR TAT (gaining R each time). As these figures show, TIT FOR TAT both benefits ALL C and punishes ALL D, promoting its own reproductive success and that of any strategy able to co-operate with it to an equal extent. Gradually, TIT FOR TAT invades populations of ALL D and encourages the co-operation of ALL C with itself. In Maynard Smith's terminology and in this particular simulation, TIT FOR TAT is an evolutionary stable strategy.

However, it is important to point out that TIT FOR TAT is not always evolutionarily stable. In part, this is a consequence of the fact that, as Axelrod himself pointed out, there can be no best strategy independent of the strategy of the other player (Axelrod 1984). Clearly, if you are playing ALL C, it is better to follow an ALL D strategy than TIT FOR TAT. If you interpret being an ESS to mean being a strategy that *always* succeeds in invading any population, then, as a number of writers have proved, TIT FOR TAT is not an ESS. On the contrary,

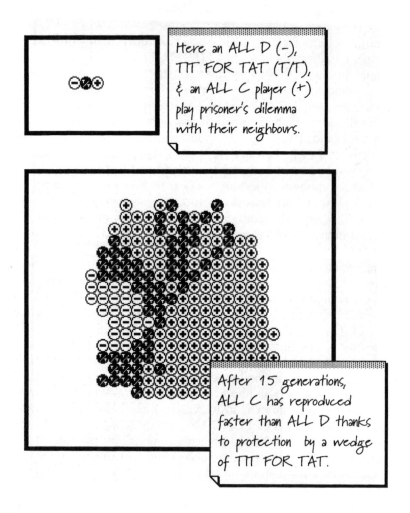

Figure 3.3   ALL D, TIT FOR TAT and ALL C in a territorial tournament

you can show that no reactive strategy with a memory restricted to the opponent's preceding move is evolutionarily stable when there is no discounting of future moves. Nevertheless, the proof of this suggests that TIT FOR TAT-like strategies may be the best response to representative collections of other strategies derived from it. In particular, and as my example above suggests, TIT FOR TAT-like strategies may be the only ones that can benefit from the positive features of a wide range of both co-operative and defector strategies (Lorberbaum 1992).

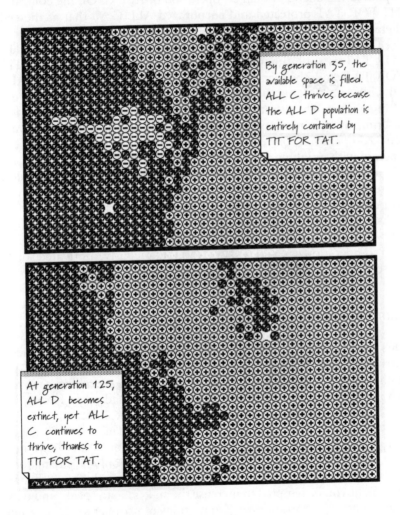

Figure 3.4   Co-operation triumphs

Axelrod's achievement is perhaps best understood as having established how TIT FOR TAT-style reciprocity can evolve by natural selection (Binmore 1998: 319). Contrary to those who thought that evolution by natural selection inevitably means selfishness, aggression and spite, we can now see what is perhaps the most astonishing development of all: naturally selected co-operation gradually invading a population of selfish exploiters. Perhaps even more surprising still for those who equate evolution with slogans like 'weakest to the wall', TIT FOR TAT never exploited the unconditional co-operation of ALL C. On the contrary, TIT FOR TAT protected and encouraged ALL C, so that at the end there were more ALL C players than there were TIT FOR TAT ones.

Reverting to the earlier discussion, you could see the success of TIT FOR TAT as a solution to the free-rider problem. This is because TIT FOR TAT could be seen as countering the spread of free-riders (ALL D) while encouraging the emergence of altruists (ALL C) without exploiting them. The secret of the success of TIT FOR TAT is that it is a discriminating kind of co-operation, one whose basic rule is *co-operate with co-operation, but defect against defection.* Its readiness to co-operate with anything that will co-operate with it means that it rapidly reaps the rewards of mutual co-operation, and does not exploit those more indiscriminately co-operative than itself. But its readiness to punish defection with defection protects it from exploitation by selfish players who capitalize on the co-operation of others. The fundamental lesson of modern evolutionary insights into co-operation is that co-operation can and will evolve spontaneously, motivated solely by self-interest. (See box 3.5, 'Live-and-let-live in World War I'.)

Familiarity and reputation

One obvious limitation of prisoner's dilemma simulations of social interaction is that co-operation and defection must occur on an all-or-nothing basis. Sometimes, real-life relationships are like this, as in the school-run example, where each woman either had to do her run or not (box 3.4). However, there are many more real-life situations in which players can modulate their co-operation, and increase it by stages. For example, the first time you encounter something like the restaurant prisoner's dilemma with someone you might only be paying for a drink. Only if you found your partner to be trustworthy in small matters might you be tempted to increase the stakes, so to speak, and trust them in more important ones. Simulations of prisoner's dilemma-like interactions in which players can vary the degree of co-operation or

Box 3.5

Live-and-let-live in World War I

Historical accounts from World War I show that an astonishing live-and-let-live co-operation between the opposing armies emerged. It relied in large part on the fact that trench warfare produced a situation where small, evenly matched units faced one another for considerable periods of time. Peaceable restraint, which originally began on both sides during mealtimes or bad weather, became extended to the point where open fraternization became possible, and where on occasions soldiers on one side would actually apologize to the other for unintended breaks in the informal truce. A British officer who discovered it in a French sector recounted that it was maintained by means of the French firing only if fired on, but always returning two shots for every one fired at them. Sniper or artillery fire, ostensibly intended to inflict damage on the other side, was in fact used as a means of maintaining the peace. Snipers would demonstrate their skill by repeatedly shooting at the same place on a wall to bore a neat hole, while artillery would show off its accuracy by hitting non-military targets. These apparently ritualized expressions of the conflict served to maintain the overall pattern of co-operation because they showed that, if necessary, the other side could be provoked into telling retaliation.

Live-and-let-live was an iterated prisoner's dilemma in which co-operation meant not attacking, and defection attacking, the enemy. Clearly, attacking the enemy when they were not attacking you (T) was always the best pay-off, because it maximized the chances of military success and minimized the danger of being killed in the process; while being the victim of such an unprovoked attack was the worst pay-off (S). However, mutual restraint (R) was preferable to continuing conflict (P) because of the danger involved in the latter. Taken together, we have the classical set of inequalities required for a prisoner's dilemma: T>R>P>S. Finally, since both sides would prefer continuing mutual re-

		The enemy	
		Co-operate	*Defect*
Own side	**Co-operate**	**Co-operate (don't attack) = R** *Co-operate (don't attack) = R*	**Co-operate (don't attack) = S** *Defect (attack) = T*
	Defect	**Defect (attack) = T** *Co-operate (don't attack) = S*	**Defect (attack) = P** *Defect (attack) = P*

straint with no casualties to random alternation of attack and restraint with the inevitable casualties on both sides, R was indeed greater than the average of T and S: R>(T+S)/2.

The system was eventually broken by the institution of unexpected raids, often carried out by troops not familiar with the local conventions. These did much to undermine the implicit truces which had come to dominate long tracts of the front line. These sudden and vicious defections roused the enemy to retaliate in kind and undermined the trust and mutual confidence that had earlier built up so that eventually live-and-let-live was replaced by kill-or-be-killed (Axelrod 1984).

defection confirm the findings set out above. Here, the equivalent of TIT FOR TAT is Raise-the-Stake, a strategy which begins with a small degree of co-operation, and increases it in increments if the other player reciprocates, but decreases it if the other does not. Competing against a number of other strategies such as Give-As-Good-As-You-Get, which matches what its partner last invested, and Short-Changer, which does the same, but invests less, Raise-the-Stake emerged as a robust strategy in much the same way that TIT FOR TAT had done in Axelrod's tournaments. Like TIT FOR TAT, Raise-the-Stake is resistant to exploitation by other strategies, while making the most of co-operative opportunities (Roberts and Sherratt 1998, but see also Killingback and Doebeli 1999).

Co-operation can evolve even if recipients have no opportunity to reciprocate

Another limitation of the prisoner's dilemma model is that it assumes that interaction can be reciprocal: both parties can both co-operate or defect. But in real life things may not be so simple, and co-operation might be completely one-sided. Indeed, co-operation frequently is one-sided, because people often help others whom they will never meet again or who have no opportunity to reciprocate.

Recently Nowak and Sigmund published a mathematical model in which players are unlikely to interact more than once. The donor co-operates at cost c to itself, and the recipient benefits by b such that $b>c$ (that is, benefit exceeds cost). However, individuals can monitor the behaviour of others, and assign 'image scores' to them on the basis of whether they co-operate or not (observed co-operation gets one point, defection loses one point). Now, when asked to co-operate with a partner, the partner's image score encourages co-operation if it is high, but discourages it if it is low, or negative. Your own image score, of course, is determined by others: if you are judged co-operative, you get a positive image score, but will get a negative one if not. Nevertheless, suppose that you encounter low-scoring partners, and punish them by defecting. You avoid paying the cost c, but others may rate you a defector yourself, and your own image score may go down. Yet if you ignore others' image scores, and co-operate indiscriminately, you run the risk of becoming a sucker who is exploited by defectors. You could call this the Good Samaritan's Dilemma: do you pass by on the other side, avoiding the cost of co-operation, or do you help out, gaining a positive image score from onlookers?

Nowak and Sigmund simulated the effect of natural selection on a population of strategies with various levels of discrimination and limited knowledge of image scores. These ranged from unconditional co-operators (the equivalent of ALL C in prisoner's dilemma) to equally unconditional defectors (ALL D). In each generation there was a random pattern of interactions, and the prevalence of a strategy was determined by its score. As in iterated prisoner's dilemma, unconditional co-operation encouraged defectors, whose prevalence was often cyclic, depending on the size of the population they could exploit. Repeated simulations suggested that the winning strategy was an equivalent of TIT FOR TAT: one that discriminated the most, but was also co-operative. Specifically, Nowak and Sigmund showed that if the probability of knowing the image score of the recipient exceeds the cost-to-benefit ratio of the altruistic act, the resulting strategy is a stable one. The authors conclude that the relevance of this to human social behaviour is that information about another person does not require a direct interaction, but can be obtained indirectly either by observing the person or by talking to others. They speculate that the evolution of human language as a means of obtaining such information must certainly have helped in the emergence of co-operation based on indirect reciprocity (Nowak and Sigmund 1998).

More recently still, Sigmund and Nowak's model was modified to include so called *phenotypic defectors*: individuals unable to co-operate under any circumstances. Whenever there are such defectors in a population, there is a persistent advantage for discriminating co-operators over non-discriminating ones because the former avoid the costs incurred in helping defectors. But this advantage disappears as soon as all defectors are eliminated from the population, producing the fluctuations and long-term cycles in the number of discriminating co-operators seen in Sigmund and Nowak's original model. In the presence of phenotypic defectors, however, a large population of discriminating co-operators is maintained. Given that the equivalents of phenotypic defectors are found in all human populations in the form of the young, old, sick and disabled, you could argue that this modification of the basic model is a major step forward in realism (Lotem et al. 1999). Indeed, you could also see it as yet another vindication of the fundamental validity of TIT FOR TAT-style co-operation.

The evolved psychology of reciprocity

In a pioneering paper, **Robert L. Trivers** (1942–) considered the whole issue of the evolution of co-operation and its psychological consequences (Trivers 1971). Trivers points out that helping in times of danger, sharing food, helping the sick, wounded, young or old, sharing implements, and sharing knowledge would all have been common instances where reciprocity would be likely to evolve in primal human populations. This is because help given in each case might be worth much more to the recipient than its cost to the helper, and help given at one time by the helper would create an obligation on the recipient to return it at a later one, when the original helper might need it. Trivers argues that in our evolutionary past our species would have met the conditions for the evolution of reciprocal altruism: long lifespan, low dispersal rate, life in small, mutually dependent, stable social groups, and a long period of parental care.

Trivers makes a particular point of considering deceit, cheating and other forms of free-riding in reciprocal relationships and their implications for human mental adaptations. He distinguishes between *gross cheating*, in which the recipient doesn't reciprocate at all, and *subtle cheating*, in which there is reciprocation, but not quite enough of it. He adds that because human co-operation may last a lifetime and be expressed in hundreds or thousands of exchanges of many different kinds and quantities, computing the totals, detecting inequities and deciding whether they are due to chance or subtle cheating is extremely difficult. Even then, he points out, an individual is in a difficult position because, even if they are the victim of subtle cheating, receiving some reciprocation may be better than the none that might result if the cheating were confronted and the relationship severed as a result. He comments that the subtlety of the discrimination necessary to detect this form of cheating and the awkward situation that ensues makes some subtle cheating adaptive. This in turn sets up a dynamic tension in the system to counter and control it. Trivers argues that the existence of discrimination against non-reciprocating individuals can't be explained by kin selection, because there the advantage to kin is what matters, not whether it will ever be reciprocated. He claims that 'the strongest argument for the operation of reciprocal-altruistic selection in humans is the psychological system controlling some forms of human altruism', and lists the following factors (Trivers 1981).

A complex regulating system   Given that some degree of cheating is adaptive, natural selection will favour a complex psychological system in individuals regulating both their own altruistic and cheating tendencies and their responses to these tendencies in others. As more subtle forms of cheating are selected, so too there will be selection of more acute abilities to detect it. The system that evolves allows individuals to get the benefit from co-operation, to protect themselves from cheats, and to practise the forms of co-operation or cheating that the situation makes appropriate. Individuals will differ not in whether they are co-operators or cheats, but in the degree to which they cheat or co-operate. For example, children in experimental situations do not divide simply into altruists and cheats, but are distributed normally. Almost all the children cheated in the study in question, but they differed in how much, and under what circumstances they cheated (Krebs 1970).

Friendship and the emotions of liking and disliking   Selection will favour those who are themselves co-operative, irrespective of relatedness. Liking others will motivate co-operation with them, whereas disliking will discourage it. Mutual co-operation will cement friendship, while cheating will destroy it. For example, all groups in all experimental situations tested showed more altruistic behaviour towards friends than towards neutral individuals. Attractiveness of a friend is the feature that correlates most highly with altruism towards them, and several studies show that the relationship between liking and altruism is a two-way street: people are more altruistic towards those they like, and tend to like those who are most altruistic (Sawyer 1966; Krebs 1970).

Moralistic aggression   Indignation and expressions of moral approval or disapproval will evolve to control and educate individuals in the standards expected. Because much cheating may be subtle, but may still take a heavy toll over a very long period, selection would probably favour a strong show of aggression when the cheating was finally uncovered. Trivers suggests that moralistic aggression and indignation in humans was selected

- to counteract continued altruism in the absence of reciprocity by those receiving it;
- to educate non-reciprocating individuals by frightening them with immediate harm or the withdrawal of future aid;
- to select directly against non-reciprocating individuals by injuring, killing or exiling them.

Gratitude and sympathy   If the cost/benefit ratio is important in determining the value of co-operation, the emotions of gratitude and sympathy could be seen as having evolved to motivate reciprocity, and to be sensitive to the net cost or benefit in each particular case. Gratitude could be seen as a wish to repay a benefactor in emotional currency, and sympathy a pledge expressed in similar terms. Sociological findings suggest that the greater the need of the recipient of altruism and the scarcer the resources of the altruist, the greater will be the tendency of the recipient to reciprocate (Gouldner 1960). A study of American undergraduates showed that they thought they would feel more gratitude when the altruistic act was more valuable and cost the benefactor a great deal (Tesser et al. 1968). Experiment shows that more altruism is induced by a gift of 80 per cent of 1 dollar than by 20 per cent of 4 dollars even though both amounts are the same (Pruitt 1968).

Guilt and reparative altruism   Guilt can be seen as an internal warning of the likely negative responses of others to your own cheating, and feelings of remorse clearly motivate attempts at reparation where the damage has already been done. Such feelings need not be interpreted in terms of group benefit alone; they can be seen as adaptations to modulate and control individual responses in a social species where others are likely to punish cheating if they detect it. Many studies support the notion that public transgressions, whether intentional or not and whether immoral or not, lead to acts of reparation (Krebs 1970). For example, experimental subjects who thought that they had broken an expensive machine were more likely to volunteer for a painful experiment than those who did not, but only if they had been discovered to have broken it (Wallace and Sadalla 1966).

The evolution and detection of mimics   Trivers observes that once psychological mechanisms like friendship, guilt and gratitude have evolved, selection will favour mimicking these traits in order to get their benefits without necessarily paying the costs. Apparent generosity, sham guilt or simulated remorse may induce genuine responses in others to the advantage of the mimic. However, selection should fa-vour the detection of subtle cheating and the unmasking of mimics. Individuals should not be selected to be too trusting of others, and should be suspicious when occasion arises. For example, individuals who compensate for a misdeed without showing genuine emotion may be distrusted for that reason alone: their behaviour may suggest a cold, calculating attitude that doesn't inspire confidence in their future reli-ability as co-operators. Trivers concludes that one of the reasons why human beings attach so much importance to motivation in considera-tions of altruism is that such a concern makes sense in terms of self-protection from cheats.

Setting up altruistic partnerships   Given the importance of reciprocal relationships to humans, selection will probably favour mechanisms for establishing such relationships. Like TIT FOR TAT in iterated pris-oner's dilemma, it might pay to be nice, if being nice is defined as starting with a co-operative move, and not being the first to defect. As Trivers puts it, this amounts to 'do unto others as you would have them do unto you.' For example, American schoolchildren in the third grade were found to be more likely to give a valuable toy to a stranger than to a friend, and some said that this was because they were trying to make friends with the stranger (B. Wright 1942). Another study found that reciprocity is reduced after receiving many trinkets from a friend, but that after receiving many such gifts from a neutral or dis-liked individual, more gifts tend to be given in return. However, re-ceiving few gifts from a neutral or disliked individual results in reduced reciprocity. This has been interpreted to mean that generous friends are taken for granted, as are stingy non-friends. It also suggests that generosity from a non-friend is taken as an overture of friendship, and stinginess from a friend as evidence of a deteriorating relationship which is in need of repair (reviewed in Krebs 1970).

Multi-parity interactions   In the small, presumably close-knit com-munities in which humans first evolved, selection would probably favour more complex interactions than simply two-party ones. Spe-cifically, selection might encourage:

- learning from and about others, in particular about others' atti-tudes, behaviour and reputation where co-operation or non-co-operation are concerned;
- helping in dealing with cheats, where co-operation against cheats and in response to them would obviously be beneficial;

- generalized altruism, where individual co-operation was judged within the context of a multi-parity group;
- rules of exchange, which modulate and control interactions in complex groups;
- developmental plasticity in those traits regulating both altruistic and cheating tendencies.

Trivers concludes, 'Given the psychological and cognitive complexity the system rapidly acquires, one may wonder to what extent the importance of altruism in human evolution set up a selection pressure for psychological and cognitive powers that partly contributed to the large increase in hominid brain size during the Pleistocene' (Trivers 1981).[2]

Cognitive adaptations for social exchange

According to Leda Cosmides and John Tooby, 'humans have a faculty for social cognition, consisting of a rich collection of dedicated, functionally specialized, interrelated modules (i.e., functionally isolable subunits, mechanisms, mental organs, etc.), organized to collectively guide thought and behavior with respect to the evolutionarily recurrent adaptive problems posed by the social world.' After summarizing some of the findings relating to prisoner's dilemma set out above, Cosmides and Tooby argue that these insights suggest that 'If having a particular mental structure, such as a rule of inference, allows a design to outreproduce other designs that exist in the species, then that mental structure will be selected for.' They point out that 'Traditionally, cognitive psychologists have assumed that the human mind includes only general-purpose rules of reasoning and that these rules are few in number and content-free.' Instead, they conclude that 'natural selection is also likely to have produced many mental rules that specialize for reasoning about various evolutionarily important domains, such as cooperating' (Cosmides and Tooby 1992). Their example is the *Wason Selection Task* (named after Peter Wason, its inventor).

Imagine that you have the job of checking that documents have been sorted correctly. You have to make sure that *if a person has a 'D' rating on one side of a card, they have the code '3' on the other*. You suspect that the documents have not been completed in accordance with this rule. The four cards below have to be checked to see if they conform. The question is, which card or cards do you definitely have to turn over in order to see if it violates the rule?

Less than one in four people get this right. Most people either choose D and 3, or D alone. The correct answer is D and 7. The reason is that the rule says simply that a card with a D on side must have a 3 on the other, *not* that a card with a 3 must have a D on the other side. So whether the 3 has a D on its back or not is irrelevant. However, it is important to know what is on the other side of the 7, because if that were a D, the rule would be violated, and the correction would have to be made.

Now consider a second situation. You are serving at a bar and have to enforce the rule that *if a person is drinking beer, he or she must be over 20 years of age.* The four cards below have information about people sitting at a table. One side of the card tells you what a person is drinking and the other side tells their age. Which card or cards must you turn over to see if the rule is being broken?

| beer | coke | 25 | 16 |

The correct answer is the cards with 'beer' and '16'. However, about 75 per cent of people get this one right. Why is this so when only one in four get the previous version right?

Peter Wason originally designed the test to see if people applied logic that would disprove a hypothesis by falsifying it. In both these cases, subjects are required to test a conditional hypothesis *if P then Q*. In the first case, *P* is having a D on one side of the card, and *Q* is having a 3 on the other. The correct logic is to check the *P* to see if the *then Q* consequence follows, and most people get this right. However, three-quarters of people tested fail to see that they must also check the *not-Q* term – the card with a 7 – because this card would also violate the rule *if P*, were there to be a D on the other side. Instead, they often misinterpret the rule to mean not only *if P then Q* but also *if Q then P*, which is not what it says, and so they make the mistake of turning over the card with the 3.

Cosmides and Tooby claim that both tests are logically exactly the same, but that in the second one a 'cheat detection' mental module kicks in which helps people to get it right most of the time. They argue that the problem with enforcing the law about drinking age is a 'social contract' problem which mobilizes the cheat detection module of the mind to get the answer right in the majority of cases. However, if cheat detection is not involved, as it isn't with the card checking problem, most people get the answer wrong (Cosmides and Tooby 1992).

What does the Wason Selection Task actually test?

Nevertheless, there is an alternative explanation. This is that in the second case, it is immediately apparent that a person who is 16 years old may be violating the rule. However, in the first case, it is not obvious until you think about it that the rule says that *a card with D on one side must have a 3 on the other* also means that *a card with any number other than 3 must be checked to see if the letter on its other side violates the rule*. Sperber, Cara and Girotto, along with other authors, claim that it is blatantly not the case that the two versions of the test given above are logically equivalent and differ only by irrelevant aspects of their content. On the contrary, they argue that in spite of a superficial similarity, these are simply different tasks (Sperber et al. 1995: 83).

Indeed, some believe that reasoning is not involved in the selection task at all, and that it is much more a question of judging the relevance of the information presented. (See box 3.6, 'Another Wason Selection Task', for a case in point.) Others claim in various ways that it is the understanding and context of the task that explain the findings, not the factor of detecting cheating, and offer experimental results to prove it (Green and Larking 1995; Love and Kessler 1995; Liberman and Klar 1996). According to another critic of their methods, the theory of reasoning set out by Cosmides and Tooby founders because of notions that are ill-described, ill-defined and above all ill-fitted to the discovery of how humans reason in genuine real-life social exchange situations (Davies et al. 1995).

The interpretation of the Wason Selection Task by Cosmides and Tooby is an instance of their reverse-engineering methodology discussed in chapter 1 (see above, pp. 16–19). Indeed, it is often cited by writers on evolutionary psychology as if it were one of the major triumphs of the subject. However, enough has been said here to suggest that things are not so simple and that, far from vindicating Cosmides and Tooby, much of the evidence – some would say, most of the evidence – is against them. By contrast, Trivers's earlier but much more wide-ranging and broadly based work on psychological adaptations for social exchange summarized earlier in this chapter is much less often cited. Why this should be so may puzzle many readers, particularly when, as we shall see, Trivers's work is much more directly in the tradition of Darwin's own writing on evolutionary psychology. However, Darwin's approach to evolutionary psychology as contrasted with that of modern evolutionary psychologists is a subject that demands a chapter of its own, and it is to this that we must now turn.

Box 3.6

Another Wason Selection Task

Below is a version of the Wason Selection Task that is logically the same as that given in the main text (p. 106). However, there are two versions, which differ as indicated between version A and B:

The City Council of Padua in Italy has asked for volunteers to take care of visiting English schoolchildren. Volunteers have to fill in a card. Mr Rossi and Mrs Bianchi, two clerks of the City Council, are about to sort the cards.

Version A

Mrs Bianchi: I am sure that only women will volunteer. Men won't want to be bothered with children!
Mr Rossi: You are wrong. There are male volunteers!
Mrs Bianchi: Well, if that is so I bet you that they are all married.

Mr Rossi accepts the bet. Cards filled in by the volunteers show sex on one side and marital status on the other. In front of the clerks on the table are four cards. Two of them show the sex of the applicant, and two show the marital status. Because sex and marital status are on different sides of the card, it is impossible to find out if Mrs Bianchi has won her bet without turning over one or more cards.

Your task is to decide which card or cards it is absolutely necessary for Mr Rossi to turn over in order to see if Mrs Bianchi has won her bet that if a volunteer is male, then he is married.
The four cards are:

Version B

Mrs Bianchi: Men with dark hair love children!
Mr Rossi: Do you think so? Can you prove it?
Mrs Bianchi: Yes I can. I bet you anything that any man who has volunteered has dark hair.

Mr Rossi accepts the bet. Cards filled in by the volunteers show sex on one side and hair colour on the other. In front of the clerks on the table are four cards. Two of them show the sex of the applicant, and two show their hair colour. Because sex and hair colour are on different sides of the card, it is impossible to find out if Mrs Bianchi has won her bet without turning over one or more cards.

Your task is to decide which card or cards it is absolutely necessary for Mr Rossi to turn over in order to see if Mrs Bianchi has won her bet that if a volunteer is male, he has dark hair.
The four cards are:

1 Male	2 Female
3 Married	4 Unmarried

1 Male	2 Female
3 Black hair	4 Fair hair

Thirty-six undergraduates at the University of Padua took part in the experiment, and were randomly assigned version A or B. The correct answers are cards 1 and 4 in both versions. However, only 16% got the right answer in version B, while 65% got it right in version A. Sperber, Cara and Girotto (1995) interpret this finding to prove that the relevance of information to the selection task is more important than any other factor. For example, in this case, marital status is often relevant to child-care, whereas hair colour usually isn't.

However, these findings also cast doubt on Cosmides and Tooby's (1992) claim that a specific 'cheat-detection module' is involved because there is no question of deception in either case, and both versions are logically and semantically the same.

Suggestions for further reading

Axelrod, R. (1984)   *The Evolution of Cooperation.*
Hamilton, W. D. (1996)   *Narrow Roads of Gene Land.*
Maynard Smith, J. (1982)   *Evolution and the Theory of Games.*
Ridley, M. (1996)   *The Origins of Virtue.*
Trivers, R. (1981)   Sociobiology and politics. In *Sociobiology and Human Politics*, ed. E. White.

4

Mind, Emotion and Consciousness

The mind is the subject of psychology, and the evolved mind that of evolutionary psychology. Yet, as we shall now see, for much of the twentieth century academic psychology denied the mind and held that psychology was the study of behaviour. As we shall also see, evolutionists often took much the same view, perhaps partly explaining why biological determinism was so easy to identify with evolutionary thinking at that time: there was little or no discussion of the mind as the entity that is pre-eminently best suited to fill the explanatory gap between genes and behaviour. However, the appearance of evolutionary psychology has changed all that, and today the mind and some of the mental states that inhabit it – such as consciousness – are once again regarded as serious subjects of scientific interest.

Anti-mentalism

Mid-twentieth century academic psychology was dominated by behaviourism. Behaviourism derived its name from its dogmatic assertion that the mind was like a 'black box' that could not be opened and whose internal workings science could not speculate about. All that could be studied objectively was what went into it in the form of stimuli and what came out of it as observed behaviour. Nothing else could be said. Behaviourism was the study of behaviour, not of the mind – mindless psychology, if ever there was.[1]

Such an attitude epitomized *anti-mentalism*: the belief that the mind was a redundant, unscientific, purely subjective phenomenon that had no proper place in scientific psychology. Nor were behaviourists alone in such denials. George Williams, an authority on modern Darwinism and, along with William Hamilton and Robert Trivers, one of those who did more than most to shape our present view of the subject, took the same, anti-mentalist view. According to Williams,

> only confusion can arise from the use of an animal-mind concept in any explanatory role in biological studies of behaviour. . . . Mind may be self-evident to most people, but I see only a remote possibility of its being made logically or empirically evident. . . . I feel intuitively that my daughter's horse has a mind. I am even more convinced that my daughter has. Neither conclusion is supported by reason or evidence. Only if it violates physical laws would mind be a factor that biologists would have to deal with. . . . There is no such evidence for mind as an entity that interferes with physical processes, and therefore there can be no physical or biological science of mind. . . . no kind of material reductionism can approach any mental phenomenon. (1985: 2, 21, 22)

Williams concludes that the 'solution to the non-objectivity of mind' is 'to exclude mind from all biological discussion'. Elsewhere Williams castigates what he calls 'lubricious slides into discussions of pleasure and anxiety and other concepts proper to the mental domain' as nothing other than 'flights of unreason' on the part of authors who 'claim to have provided a physical explanation of mental phenomena' (Williams 1996). Clearly, to the extent that evolutionary psychology attempts to be a biological science of mind, this leading Darwinist appears to rule it out completely.

Anti-mentalism was typical of most twentieth-century Darwinists and students of animal behaviour. Similar comments to those of Williams quoted just now can be found in the work of the ethologists **Niko Tinbergen** (1907–1988) and **Konrad Lorenz** (1903–1989). These writers contrasted sharply with behaviourists in stressing the importance of innate over conditioned factors, but, like the behaviourists, concentrated on observed behaviour and mistrusted mental terms, which were often dismissed as 'anthropomorphic' (that is, committing the error of attributing human thoughts and feelings to animals). So, while ethologists recognized instinct and behaviourists denied it, both were at one in concentrating on behaviour and disparaging the purely mental. Either way, it seemed the mind was an unacceptable concept to scientific study, and evolutionary psychology therefore an impossibility.

The result of such views was what you might call evolutionary, genetic or ethological behaviourism: 'explanations' of behaviour that went directly from the evolutionary, genetic or ethological factors proposed to the observed behavioural result. Such an approach neglected the mental level of explanation altogether – and at times left you wondering why organisms that have them have minds at all, so irrelevant did they seem to behaviour. Where human beings were concerned, evolutionary, genetic or ethological behaviourism prompted understandable protests that such an approach was 'reductionistic' and reduced people to the status of mindless robots, controlled by their genes or evolutionary programming to act in ways essentially no different from the way in which an ant or an amoeba might behave.

Darwin was a mentalist

Ironically in view of Williams's Darwinism, his condemnation of mentalistic thinking includes Darwin himself, who claimed that 'the lower animals, like man, manifestly feel pleasure and pain, happiness and misery.' Indeed, we shall see later in this chapter that he saw such feelings as the principal form in which natural selection affected their behaviour. Far from avoiding mental concepts where animals were concerned, Darwin openly proclaimed that his aim was to 'shew that there is no fundamental difference between man and the higher mammals in their mental faculties', and attributed disappointment, dejection, fear, affection, servility, joy, courage and even sulkiness to them. Where dogs were concerned, he was even prepared to add some measure of conscience and self-consciousness (Darwin 1871, 1998).

Autism and theory of mind

According to Premack and Woodruff, who originated the term, *theory of mind* describes the ability to infer that other people experience mental states like our own. They claim that such a capacity may properly be viewed as a theory because mental states are not directly observable, and because it can be used to make predictions about the behaviours of others (Premack and Woodruff 1978).

Conversely, the inability to attribute such states to others that is seen, for example in *autism*, has been graphically described as 'mindblindness'. Autistic people are distressed by their inability to understand what other people are thinking or feeling. For example, one young autistic man complained that he couldn't 'mind-read'. He explained that other people seem to have a special sense by which they can read other people's thoughts and anticipate their responses and feelings. He knew this because they managed to avoid upsetting people whereas he was always 'putting his foot in it': not realizing that he was doing or saying the wrong thing until after the other person became angry and upset (Baron-Cohen and Howlin 1993).

People with autism tend to be insensitive to other people's feelings, are poor at interpreting others' intentions, beliefs and knowledge, and often fail to anticipate the reactions that other people will have to their behaviour. They have difficulty dealing with misunderstandings, and are often unable to practise, detect or understand deception. The result is that their behaviour often seems bizarre, callous or childish to others.

Experiments suggest that normal children acquire a theory of mind between the ages of three and five, but that autistic children are notably lacking in this respect. For example, autistic children do not differ from others in their ability to understand the functions of an internal organ like the heart. Nor are they deficient in their knowledge about the location of organs such as the liver or brain. However, whereas other children are able to understand that the brain has purely mental functions, autistic children tend to associate it only with behavioural functions, so that it appears that specifically mental, unobservable events are beyond their comprehension. As Simon Baron-Cohen puts it, 'Lacking a theory of mind is in one sense akin to viewing the world as a behaviorist' (Baron-Cohen 1989).

Again, experiments also suggest that although other primates closely related to ourselves such as chimpanzees possess many of our mental abilities in rudimentary form and can certainly perceive things like the direction of gaze, they probably lack understanding of the mental states of others, an understanding that can be clearly demonstrated in children as young as two-and-a-half (Povinelli and Preuss 1995).

There is some evidence for thinking that introspective knowledge of our own mental states makes it possible for us to ascribe such states to others. If this were true, we would expect autistic people to suffer from a primary deficit in their own ego's perception of itself. A hint that this may indeed be the case comes from a study of language in autistic children which compared them with children with Down syndrome, matched for age and level of language development. The autistic children all made pronoun reversal errors, referring to themselves as 'you' and their mothers as 'I' or 'me'. None of the children with Down syndrome made this error. If these were just verbal slips resulting from poor language skills, you would expect the children with Down syndrome to make them as often as the autistic children did. The fact that they didn't suggests that these confusions about the self may go deeper and be among the factors contributing to autistic mindblindness (Baron-Cohen 1989).

Autistic people are not totally mindblind

Nevertheless, it is by no means the case that all internal states are beyond the understanding of autistic people. For example, they may have an intact understanding of desire and the link from desire to the simpler emotions of happiness and sadness. Other internal states that they are predicted to understand include hunger and thirst, because such states, like desires, can be understood without an ability to represent others' mental representations in your own mind (Baron-Cohen 1989). Desire, happiness, sadness, hunger and thirst are all emotional brain functions, whereas the characteristic deficit in autism appears to affect social cognition. Autistic people have also been described as 'desire psychologists', and when autistic children were compared with children with Down syndrome, matched for age and language competence, autistic children used significantly more words related to desire, but far fewer to do with cognition (Tager-Flusberg 1993).

The implication of these findings is that the possession of a theory of mind is a distinctively human characteristic and is probably yet another unique attribute rooted in our species' enormously developed brain. Another is that, if possession of a theory of mind is an evolved attribute of human beings, evolutionary psychology should be able to explain it and to make explicit what is otherwise implicit in our behaviour. Here lies a major contrast with the older generation of Darwinists and ethologists: whereas they shared the anti-mentalist bias of behaviourism, evolutionary psychology is distinguished by a new interest in purely mental matters. To put it another way, you could say that evolutionary psychology represented a recovery from the mindblindness of mid twentieth-century Darwinism and a return to something much closer to Darwin's own mentalistic views.

Darwin's three principles of the expression of the emotions

Nevertheless, evolutionary psychology still appears to be blind – or at best, partially sighted – where one aspect of the mind is concerned, and the irony is that it is the very aspect that most concerned Darwin: the emotions. Darwin's pre-eminent work on evolutionary psychology was his *The Expression of the Emotions in Man and Animals*, published in 1872. Darwin's book is organized around three fundamental principles.

1   Serviceable associated habits   According to Darwin, 'Certain complex actions are of direct or indirect service under certain states of the mind, in order to relieve or gratify certain sensations, desires, etc.; and whenever the same state of mind is induced, however feebly, there is a tendency through the force of habit and association for the same movements to be performed, though they may not then be of the least use' (Darwin 1998: 34).

An example would be scratching your head when in doubt or perplexed about something. You can't actually relieve such feelings by directly stimulating your brain or thoughts, but Darwin's deduction is that you are acting *as if* you could, and thereby attempting to remedy the feeling of being perplexed. Such an action is serviceable only by way of association. Serviceable associations become *habitual* by normally being expressed in such situations. According to Darwin, a man

> rubs his eyes when perplexed, or gives a little cough when embarrassed, acting in either case as if he felt a slightly uncomfortable sensation in his eyes or windpipe. . . . A man . . . who vehemently rejects a proposition, will almost certainly shut his eyes or turn away his face; but if he accepts the proposition, he will nod his head in affirmation and open his eyes widely. . . . I have noticed that persons in describing a horrid sight often shut their eyes momentarily and firmly, or shake their heads, as if not to see or to drive away something disagreeable; and I have caught myself, when thinking of a dark or horrid spectacle, closing my eyes firmly. (Darwin 1998:14, 37–8)

Modern brain research has confirmed Darwin's belief that such expressions are functionally related to stimuli that might occasion them. For example, brain scans of subjects presented with an expression of disgust reveal a reaction in a part of the brain that normally reacts to offensive tastes and smells (the anterior insular cortex). According to the researchers, 'This suggests that our responses to others' disgust have, perhaps through associative learning between visual stimuli and taste, become closely linked to the appraisal of distasteful stimuli' – just as Darwin proposed (Phillips et al. 1997).

2   Antithesis   To illustrate his second principle, Darwin asks us to consider the dog illustrated in figure 4.1:

When a dog approaches a strange . . . man in a savage or hostile frame of mind he walks upright and very stiffly; his head is slightly raised . . . his tail is held erect and quite rigid; the hairs bristle . . . the pricked ears are directed forwards, and the eyes have a fixed stare. These actions . . . follow from the dog's intention to attack his enemy, and are thus to a large extent intelligible. As he prepares to spring with a savage growl on his enemy, the canine teeth are uncovered, and the ears are pressed close backwards on the head . . .

But now, Darwin continues,

suppose that the dog suddenly discovers that the man he is approaching, is not a stranger, but his master; and let it be observed how completely and instantaneously his whole bearing is reversed. Instead of walking upright, the body sinks downwards or even crouches, and is thrown into flexuous movements; his tail, instead of being held stiff and upright, is lowered and wagged from side to side; his hair instantly becomes smooth; his ears are depressed and drawn backwards . . . and his lips hang loosely.

Figure 4.1   Hostility in a dog
Source: From Charles Darwin, *The Expression of the Emotions in Man and Animals*, 1872

Figure 4.2 Friendliness in a dog
Source: From Charles Darwin, *The Expression of the Emotions in Man and Animals*, 1872

In other words, the reactions of a friendly dog like that illustrated in figure 4.2, unlike those of a hostile one, 'are explicable . . . solely from being in complete opposition or antithesis to the attitude and movements which . . . are assumed when a dog intends to fight, and which consequently are expressive of anger' (Darwin 1998: 56). This constitutes the principle of *antithesis*. Essentially, it expresses *not-X*, understood as a denial, rebuttal or converse of X. An example from human behaviour that Darwin gives is the shrug of the shoulders, which expresses 'impotence or an apology' by doing the opposite of what the arms, shoulders and hands would do if we were asserting ourselves (Darwin 1998: 65). (For a further example, see box 4.1, 'Antithesis in homophobia'.)

3   **Direct action of the excited nervous system on the body independently of the will**   According to Darwin, 'The frantic and senseless actions of an enraged man may be attributed in part to the undirected flow of nerve-force.' Darwin gives many other examples of this third principle, including a lot more from human experience, ranging from trembling with fear, to perspiration, palpitation, blushing, laughter and crying. Although many of these expressions involve elements of the first two principles, their particular intensity often derives from what Darwin called 'nerve force generated in excess' (Darwin 1998: 69–87).

Box 4.1

Antithesis in homophobia

Homophobia, defined as 'irrational fear, hatred, and intolerance by heterosexual individuals of homosexual men and women', was established in a sample of 29 men by means of psychological tests. A control group of 35 heterosexual
men was similarly rated non-homophobic. Each man was then placed in a cubi-
cle with a strain gauge (or plethysmograph) attached to his penis to measure
erection, and shown three separate four-minute erotic videos of consensual sex
between a man and a woman, two women, and two men. The videos featured
foreplay, oral–genital contact, sexual and anal intercourse. Levels of sexual
arousal as measured by the plethysmograph were compared with each man's
subjective rating of his degree of erection after having seen the video.

For both the heterosexual and the lesbian videos, there was a fairly similar
degree of erection in both the homophobic and non-homophobic group. However, only the homophobic group showed a significant degree of erection during the male homosexual video: 20% showed no significant tumescence; 26%

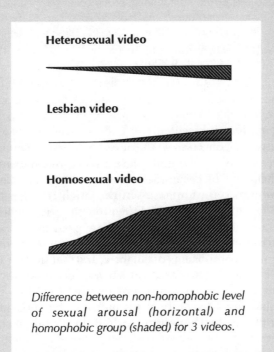

*Difference between non-homophobic level
of sexual arousal (horizontal) and
homophobic group (shaded) for 3 videos.*

showed moderate tumescence; and 54% showed definite tumescence. The figures for the non-homophobic group viewing the male homosexual video were: 66% no tumescence; 10% moderate tumescence; and 24% definite tumescence. Subjective assessments of degree of arousal as indicated by erection were largely accurate for both groups where the heterosexual and lesbian videos were concerned. But in the case of the male homosexual video, the homophobic group significantly underestimated their true degree of arousal.

The study concludes that 'the reports of subjective arousal were not consistent with penile responses with the male homosexual video. These data appear to be due to underestimates of arousal, particularly by homophobic men, to the homosexual stimuli.' A separate questionnaire measuring levels of aggression failed to show any significant contribution to the reactions of either group. The authors conclude that their data are consistent with psychoanalytic views of homophobia which explain it as 'a threat to the individual's own homosexual impulses causing repression, denial, or reaction formation' and which see homophobia as 'one type of latent homosexuality where persons either are unaware of or deny their homosexual urges' (Adams et al. 1996).

To the extent that a phobic attitude towards homosexuality suggests aversion to it and the plethysmograph results indicate attraction, the strikingly contradictory reactions of the homophobic group could be seen as evidence of antithesis in human behaviour, comparable to what Darwin described in *The Expression of the Emotions in Man and Animals*. These findings also illustrate the fact that it is in psychoanalysis rather than anywhere else that Darwin's principles have been developed and explored, in this case in the concepts of denial, reaction formation, and repression.

A literal case of excitation of the nervous system independent of the will was recently demonstrated when a conscious patient burst into laughter when part of her cortex was electrically stimulated by surgeons. The duration and intensity of the laughter increased with the level of the stimulation current. However, the patient herself attributed her amusement to whatever she happened to be looking at or thinking at the time, suggesting a close link between the motor, affective and cognitive components of laughter, and that smiling and laughter appear to be closely associated on a single continuum (Fried et al. 1998). Other cases are known where a brain lesion caused a man to begin laughing uncontrollably at his mother's funeral, or in which a woman literally laughed herself to death (Ramachandran and Blakeslee 1998).

Nor are such findings limited to laughter. Doctors treating a patient with Parkinson's disease found that an electrode implanted into a particular part of her brain while she was fully conscious caused her to feel intensely depressed. The patient reported that she didn't want to live any more and was 'disgusted with life'. She had no history of depression, and her despair disappeared less than 90 seconds after the stimulation ended, but could be reproduced in a similar way on subsequent occasions. However, suggestion that the stimulation was occurring when no current was flowing produced no such effect, indicating that the depressive reaction was indeed directly caused by the electrical stimulation of the brain (Boyce 1999).

Modern research has vindicated Darwin's belief in the universality of emotional expression

In *The Expression of the Emotions* Darwin commented that 'it seemed to me highly important to ascertain whether the same expressions and gestures prevail, as has often been asserted without much evidence, with all the races of mankind, especially those who have associated but little with Europeans.' By way of finding out, in 1867 he sent a questionnaire to his many correspondents abroad, asking 16 or 17 specific questions on the subject, and got 36 replies (Darwin 1998: 22–3).

In pursuit of these questions, Darwin distinguished between gestures, which he conceded were in the main socially learnt conventions, and emotional expressions, which he claimed were universal and the product of evolution.[2]

However, the question of the universality of the emotions became embroiled in the nature/nurture controversy, and influential twentieth-century social scientists like **Margaret Mead** (1901–1978) and her husband, **Gregory Bateson** (1904–1980), insisted that emotional expressions were nurtured, rather than being innate as Darwin had believed. 'We are forced to conclude', wrote Mead, 'that human nature is almost unbelievably malleable, responding accurately and contrastingly to contrasting cultural conditions.' Bateson and Mead objected to the view that emotions were expressions of internal, psychological states, and instead they insisted that they were communications. However, the idea of using multiple observers, of gathering quantitative data, of building safeguards against the influence of the researcher's commitments, which are standard in experimental psychology, were foreign to Mead and Bateson (Ekman 1998). (For a different example of Mead's methodology, see box 7.2, 'Margaret Mead and Samoa', p. 231 below.)

Most modern writers on emotions agree that human beings express at least five distinct emotions: anger, fear, sadness, disgust and enjoyment. If the more extreme claims of the emotions-are-nurtured school were correct, the expression of these emotions should vary as much in human cultures as the words used to describe them. But manifestly they do not. In modern, scientific studies, photographs of facial expressions representing fear, anger, sadness, disgust, happiness and surprise were shown to subjects in 21 countries, and their interpretations recorded. In every case, the majority in each country agreed about the pictures that showed happiness, sadness and disgust. For surprise, there was agreement by the majority in 20 out of 21 countries; for fear 19 out of 21; and for anger 18 out of 21. Further research with peoples in Papua New Guinea who had never been exposed to Western media produced similar results, but showed that fear and surprise were not always clearly distinguished (Ekman 1998).

Such studies are sometimes criticized on the grounds that the researchers may influence the outcome, so it is particularly interesting to note that when Heider and Rosch set out to disprove these findings of Ekman's in Papua New Guinea, they in fact got the same results. The exception was that the people studied did not differentiate between anger and disgust, something Heider had predicted, having observed that the people in question avoided the expression of anger by masking it with disgust (cited in Ekman 1998: 381–3).

Of course, these findings do not deny that cultural conventions can influence the way that emotions are expressed. Further studies by Ekman showed that neither the culture of an observer nor the culture of the expresser of an emotion mattered in the accurate judgement of whether facial expressions were reactions to a stressful or neutral film. High correlations were found between the particular facial movements by Japanese and American students when viewing such films, but only when the subject was alone. When an observer was present while the subject viewed the films, the Japanese smiled much more than the Americans during the stressful film – presumably to mask anxiety.

Most scientists now consider the universality of the facial expression of emotions to be proved. The group of emotions for which there is some evidence of universality includes most, but not all, the emotions studied by Darwin: surprise, sadness, anger, enjoyment, contempt, disgust, shame and fear. Modern research concludes that Darwin's central point is well established: a number of emotions do indeed have a universal expression. The evidence shows that when people are experiencing strong emotions and are not making any attempt to mask them, the expression of these basic emotions will be the same regardless of age, race, culture, sex or education (Ekman 1998).

Evolutionary psychology and *The Expression of the Emotions*

Given the vindication that Darwin's work has recently found, and given the fact that *The Expression of the Emotions in Man and Animals* is Darwin's most important single work on evolutionary psychology, you might have expected evolutionary psychologists to celebrate its importance – or, at the very least, to cite it. But one of the most revealing and astonishing facts about evolutionary psychology is that Darwin's pioneering book on the subject has been almost completely ignored by most modern Darwinists. Even in *The Adapted Mind* (Barkow et al. 1992), a 666–page collection of papers on evolutionary psychology that clearly regards itself as the manifesto of the movement, Darwin's major work on psychology is never discussed. It is only cited twice in bibliographic references to the 18 chapters, and both times the title is wrong (1992: 127, 424)! There is certainly no discussion of Darwin's book or its contents anywhere in the volume. Again, there is no mention whatsoever of Darwin's book on the emotions in Buss's textbook of evolutionary psychology, nor is it even listed in the bibliography or cited in the introductory chapter entitled 'Landmarks in the history of evolutionary thinking' (Buss 1999).

Contrary to Darwin's emphasis on the emotions, the editors of *The Adapted Mind* self-consciously adopt the approach of cognitive science, defining all psychological processes as *cognitive*:

> An account of the evolution of the mind is an account of how and why the information-processing organization of the nervous system came to have the functional properties that it does. Information-processing language – the language of cognitive psychology – is simply a way of getting specific about what, exactly, a psychological mechanism does. In this volume, most psychological mechanisms are described in information-processing terms, either explicitly or implicitly. (Barkow et al. 1992: 8)

Although they mention 'affective reactions' later, it is clear that emotion is not central to their approach in the way that it was to Darwin. Echoing the anti-mentalistic nostrums of behaviourism, two of the editors, John Tooby and Leda Cosmides, state elsewhere in the book that 'things such as beliefs and desires are inherently unobservable hidden variables used to explain observations that could be explained by any of an infinite set of alternative theories . . . Therefore, a belief in beliefs and desires cannot be justified by observations alone.' What they disparagingly term 'belief-desire folk psychology' has no place in the brave new science of evolutionary psychology (Tooby and Cosmides 1992: 90).

Indeed, with the exception of the one and only chapter on evolution and psychoanalysis (Lloyd and Nesse 1992), drives, instincts and emotion are seldom if ever mentioned, and have no entries in the index. On the rare occasions when Cosmides and Tooby do use the word 'instinct' in the book, it is placed in inverted commas (Cosmides and Tooby 1992: 220). In their writing elsewhere, they insist on qualifying instincts as 'cognitive', and, although they admit that 'instinct blindness has been crippling for psychology', they add that such blindness to instinct is 'sanity for the individual' (Baron-Cohen 1995: xii)! A similar emphasis on cognition is found in nearly all writing on evolutionary psychology (Cosmides and Tooby 1987; Pinker 1994, 1997; Wright 1994; Buss 1995, 1999; Crawford and Krebs 1998 and, within it, Wells 1998).

Is there a prejudice against emotion in cognitive psychology?

Cognitive psychology, with which the evolutionary psychology of *The Adapted Mind* has so much in common, has often been described as the 'new science of the mind'. But as the neuroscientist Joseph LeDoux commented recently, in reality cognitive science was only about part of the mind – the part having to do with thinking, reasoning and intellect. He points out that cognitive science treats minds like computers and has traditionally been more interested in how people and machines solve logical problems or play chess than in why they are sometimes happy and sometimes sad. It left emotions out, and minds without emotions are not really minds at all. They are what he calls 'souls on ice' – cold, lifeless things devoid of any desires, fears, sorrows, pains or pleasures. Indeed, he adds that this shortcoming has been corrected in an unfortunate way – by redefining emotions as cognitive processes, stripping them of their passionate qualities. Why would anyone want to conceive of minds without emotions, he asks. How could such a field focused on emotionless minds be so successful (LeDoux 1996: 20, 25)?

LeDoux is not alone in expressing amazement at this state of affairs. According to another leading neuroscientist, Antonio Damasio, we may never understand why emotion was given the cold shoulder of science for almost a hundred years. He points out that by the last quarter of the nineteenth century, the nature of emotion, the possible biological mechanisms behind it and the ways in which it could be disturbed had been brilliantly described by Charles Darwin, William James and Sigmund Freud. The British neurologist John Hughlings Jackson had even made a first stab at discerning the anatomy of human emotion by correctly locating it in the right cerebral hemisphere. There would have been every reason to expect that the budding brain sciences would take up emotion in much the same way as they had been concerning themselves with language or visual perception. But curiously, it never came to pass. Emotion was consistently left out of the mainstream of what became neuroscience and cognitive psychology. A handful of psychologists carried on important studies on emotion; psychiatrists and pharmacologists concerned with mood disorders developed and applied drugs that gave indirect information on the mechanisms of emotion. But, by and large, neuroscience and cognitive science neglected emotion until very recently. Emotion was not trusted in real life or in the laboratory – it was too subjective, too elusive, too irrational for the likes of modern science (Damasio 1997).

In a momentary lapse into greater candour about their personal prejudices than most neuroscientists would normally allow themselves, Simon LeVay admits that there has been a tendency to avoid the hypothalamus, which is a key component of what LeDoux would call the 'emotional brain' (see above, pp. 25–6). He confesses that most brain scientists including himself until recently prefer 'the sunny expanses of the cerebral cortex' to the 'dark, claustrophobic regions at the base of the brain'. Although they would never admit it, they think of the hypothalamus as 'haunted by animal spirits and the ghosts of primal urges'. They suspect that it houses, he says, 'not the shiny hardware of cognition, but some witches' brew of slimy, pulsating neurons adrift in a broth of mind-altering chemicals' (LeVay 1993: 39).[3]

The pleasure principle

Writing in his *Autobiography*, Darwin comments that 'an animal may be led to pursue that course of action which is most beneficial . . . by suffering, such as pain, hunger, thirst and fear; or by pleasure, as in eating and drinking and in the propagation of the species.' It was his view that

> pain or suffering . . . is well adapted to make a creature guard itself against any great or sudden evil. Pleasurable sensations, on the other

hand . . . stimulate the whole system to increased action. Hence it has come to pass that most or all sentient beings have been developed in such a manner, through natural selection, that pleasurable sensations serve as their habitual guides. (Darwin 1958: 89)

At much the same time that Darwin was writing these words, Herbert Spencer expressed the same opinion in another founding work of evolutionary psychology, his *Principles of Psychology*. According to Spencer,

> pleasures are the incentives to life-supporting acts and pains the deterrents to life-destroying acts. Not only do we see that among inferior sentient creatures this guidance is undeniably efficient, but also that it is undeniably efficient in ourselves, so far as regards the functions on which life immediately depends. (Spencer 1878: 284–5)

What Darwin and Spencer are describing here is what today might be called an epigenetic rule: namely, a naturally selected tendency for an organism to prefer one outcome to another (see above, pp. 68–9).

Furthermore, it is easy to understand how such a general purpose epigenetic rule could evolve. If you imagine a population of organisms with their pleasure/pain principles randomly arranged, it is easy to see that those who indulged in pleasurable activities that enhanced their ultimate reproductive success while avoiding those that reduced it because of the pain attached to them would tend to be selected over those whose pleasure/pain principles were not so favourably fixed. Indeed, long before modern evolutionary psychologists had begun to labour the point, Spencer explicitly drew attention to the assumptions that need to be attached to such adaptive arguments: that the pleasure/pain principle need only be effective 'on average' and 'that, by natural selection, the guidance of pleasure and pains can be adjusted only to the circumstances of the habitat within which the special type has been evolved' (Spencer 1878: 280–1) (see above, pp. 10–11).

Until recently, neurophysiologists have largely ignored the importance of reward in shaping behaviour (Nichols and Newsome 1999). However, a study of monkeys' responses to visual stimuli and associated rewards showed that experimental animals preferentially select one target over another in proportion to the relative reward associated with it. Specifically, the study found that the reward expected by the monkey modulates activity of neurones in the relevant part of the cortex (the lateral interparietal area, concerned with transforming visual signals into eye-movement commands). Additionally, it showed that the activity of the neurones in question was sensitive to the probability that a particular response would result in a gain (Platt and Glimcher 1999). This is much as you would expect the pleasure principle to work in practice and suggests that the mechanism is indeed a fundamental – even if somewhat neglected – one.

An example of the way in which evolution can affect behaviour through the pleasure principle might be the consumption of alcohol. The extent to which a person feels pleasure or otherwise in relation to drinking is critically determined by whether they carry an efficient allele of the gene for *alcohol dehydrogenase*, an enzyme (or biological catalyst) that detoxifies alcohol and disposes of it. Most Westerners have this gene, and so can indulge the pleasure they may feel in consuming alcohol. However, many people in the East don't have the same allele and feel distinctly ill on consuming alcohol because their bodies can't deal with its toxic effects. Indeed, the drug given to alcoholics in the West to dissuade them from drinking produces symptoms of a very similar kind to those felt by drinkers who lack the alcohol dehydrogenase gene. Effectively, it exploits the pleasure/pain principle by spoiling the pleasure that the drinker would otherwise feel as a result of consuming alcohol (Jones 1993: 191–2).

The discovery of the brain's pleasure centres was a critical step in understanding brain mechanisms in motivation and reward. For example, an area near the hypothalamus, the *septum*, appears to contain a primary pleasure centre related to sex. This was demonstrated by a neurological patient who had electrical implants placed there which he stimulated 1,500 times in a single three-hour session, bringing himself to orgasm on one occasion (Forsyth 1997).

Today there is increasing evidence that a whole range of addictive disorders from alcoholism, drug abuse, smoking and over-eating to hyperactivity and compulsive gambling can be traced in many cases to genes implicated in the brain's pleasure and reward system. The common factor is craving, stimulus-seeking and impulsiveness. The biochemical cascades involved in the feelings of pleasure and relief of anxiety produced by the thrills associated with gambling, by bingeing on carbohydrates and by consuming drugs and alcohol are now being worked out and begin with serotonin secretion in the hypothalamus triggering the release of natural opiates (encephalins) and dopamine in various parts of the brain. Serotonin, dopamine and the encephalins are *neurotransmitters*: that is, chemicals that transmit nerve impulses across the gaps between nerve fibres. Alcohol, drugs and carbohydrates all cause release of dopamine in the primary reward area of the brain just above the hypothalamus. So too does winning in a computer game – the first behaviour ever to be directly linked to dopamine release in humans (Koepp et al. 1998). A gene on chromosome 11 for the D_2 dopamine receptor appears to be implicated in all of these reactions and to play a central role in what is now being called *reward deficiency syndrome*. The association of this gene with another compulsive disorder, Tourette's syndrome, which is known to have a genetic basis, suggests that reward deficiency syndrome is also heritable and is often prefigured in behavioural disorders in childhood, again centring on impulsiveness, hyperactivity and cravings (Blum et al. 1996).

Recent insights suggest that 'liking' something and 'wanting' it are mediated by different components of the mammalian reward system: liking sweet foods, for example, is mediated by particular opioid forebrain systems and by the brain stem, whereas wanting seems to be mediated by the dopamime neurons in the limbic system. The liking system is activated by receiving a reward, while the wanting system anticipates reward and motivates behaviour: 'The separate neural mediation of "wanting" may have evolved so that disparate "likes" for food, sex, and other incommensurate incentives could be compared in a common currency of utility' – or, in Darwin's and Spencer's term: pleasure (Nesse and Berridge 1997).

'Darwinist' evolutionary psychologists prefer to cite William James rather than Darwin or Spencer

Strangely in view of what Darwin himself had to say about pleasure and pain and the fact that Spencer's *Principles of Psychology* is a far more obvious source of inspiration for modern evolutionary psychology, evolutionary psychologists prefer instead to quote a passage by **William James** (1842–1910). Here James asks: Why do hens undergo the tedium of incubating eggs? Why do men prefer soft beds to hard floors? Why do they sit around a stove on a cold day? Why do people prefer champagne to pond water? Why do young women interest young men? His answer is that

> Nothing more can be said than ... that every creatures *likes* its own ways, and takes to following them as a matter of course. Science may come and consider those ways, and find that most of them are useful. But it is not for the sake of their utility that they are followed, but because at the moment of following them we feel that that is the only appropriate and natural thing to do. Not one man in a billion, when taking his dinner, ever thinks of utility. He eats because the food tastes good and makes him want more. (Pinker 1997: 184–5)

Notwithstanding the emphasis on 'likes' in the first sentence, this passage, when compared with the earlier quotations from Spencer and Darwin, is nothing more than a watered-down statement that the pleasure/pain principle is the prime motivator for much human and animal behaviour. Why evolutionary psychologists should prefer this bowdlerized expression of the basic principle by someone they describe as a 'follower' of Darwin to Darwin's own words will puzzle many readers who have done their homework on Darwin and Spencer.

A clue may lie in the fate of Darwin's original comment. The account of the pleasure/pain principle I quote above was edited out of Darwin's *Autobiography* by members of his family after his death, and not restored in published editions until 1958. However, there are no personal references, no embarrassing errors or other ostensible justifications for expurgating this passage as an obvious blemish or affront to the family. Nor does it say anything outlandish, obscene or foolish. On the contrary, it simply endorses a fairly obvious point that Spencer had made independently and at much greater length. Could it be that its honest acknowledgement of the power and primacy of the pleasure/pain principle offended Victorian prudery, and could it be that it continues to offend the cognitive prejudices of modern evolutionary psychologists? Given that pleasure and pain centres lie in the lower brain close to the hypothalamus, could this be another example of the point we saw Simon LeVay making earlier: one of a prejudice in favour of the shiny hardware of cognition and against the slimy, pulsating depths of the brain?[4]

Freud and Darwin

The Expression of the Emotions in Man and Animals appeared when **Sigmund Freud** (1856–1939) was still undergoing his secondary education and at a time when Darwin's theories were being widely popularized in the German-speaking world. Writing much later in his *Autobiographical Study,* Freud remarks that 'the theories of Charles Darwin, which were then of topical interest, strongly attracted me, for they held out hopes of an extraordinary advance in our understanding of the world' (Freud 1959). By contrast to the main stream of twentieth-century psychology, which ignored Darwin and continues to ignore the principles he employed to interpret emotions, Freud applied Darwin's principles directly in his treatment of *hysteria* – essentially a state of disordered emotions. Freud found that

In taking a verbal expression literally and in feeling the 'stab in the heart' or the 'slap in the face' after some slighting remark as a real event, the hysteric is not taking liberties with words, but is simply reviving once more the sensations to which the verbal expression owes its justification. How has it come about that we speak of someone who has been slighted as being 'stabbed to the heart' unless the slight had in fact been accompanied by a sensation in the region of the heart which could suitably be described in that phrase and unless it was identifiable by that sensation? What could be more probable than that the figure of speech 'swallowing something', which we use in talking of an insult to which no rejoinder has been made, did in fact originate from . . . sensations which arise in the throat when we refrain from speaking and prevent ourselves from reacting to an insult? All these sensations and innervations belong to the field of 'The Expression of the Emotions', which, as Darwin has taught us, consists of actions which originally had a meaning and served a purpose. These may now for the most part have become so much weakened that the expression of them in words seems to us only to be a figurative picture of them, whereas in all probability the description was once meant literally. (Breuer and Freud 1955: 181)

Where Darwin's second principle, antithesis, was concerned, Freud observed something similar in one of his hysterical patients. This was a woman among whose symptoms were '*tic*-like movements, such as clacking with the tongue and stammering, calling out the name "Emmy . . . Keep still! Don't say anything! Don't touch me!"' Freud found that these symptoms were the result of 'the putting into effect of antithetical ideas. . . . Our hysterical patient, exhausted by worry and long hours of watching by the bedside of her sick child which had at last fallen asleep, said to herself: "Now you must be perfectly still so as not to awaken the child."' According to Freud, 'This intention probably gave rise to an antithetical idea in the form of a fear that she might make a noise all the same that would wake the child from the sleep which she had so long hoped for.' Furthermore, 'In our patient's state of exhaustion the antithetic idea, which was normally rejected, proved itself the stronger. It is this idea which put itself into effect and which, to the patient's horror, actually produced the noise she dreaded' (Breuer and Freud 1955:91–2). (See box 4.1, 'Antithesis in homophobia', for another Freudian example.)

Abreaction is a derivative of Darwin's third principle

However, Freud's chief insight into the mystery of hysteria was a direct extension of Darwin's third principle of the expression of emotion. Freud thought that it was an excess generation of nerve-force independent of consciousness that underlay the symptoms of hysterics. 'Some of the striking motor phenomena' exhibited by the patient mentioned above

> were simply an expression of the emotions and could easily be recognised in that light. Thus, the way in which she stretched her hands in front of her with her fingers spread out and crooked expressed horror, and similarly her facial play. . . . Others of her motor symptoms were, according to herself, directly related to her pains. She played restlessly with her fingers or rubbed her hands against one another so as to prevent herself from screaming. This reason reminds one forcibly of one of the principles laid down by Darwin to explain the expression of the emotions – the principle of the overflow of excitation. . . . We are all of us accustomed, when we are affected by painful stimuli, to replace screaming by other sorts of motor innervations. A person who has made up his mind at the dentist's to keep his head and mouth still and not to put his hand in the way, may at least start drumming with his feet. (Breuer and Freud 1955: 91)

The overflow of nervous excitation independent of the will provided not only Freud's most characteristic insights into hysterical symptoms, but also laid the foundation of the psychoanalytic therapy. *Catharsis* was the classic method of early psychoanalysis, and was in fact discovered not by Freud, but his associate, **Joseph Breuer** (1842–1925), and his patient, Anna O., now known to have been **Bertha Pappenheim** (1859–1936). It involved *abreaction*, the discharge of repressed emotions attached to symptoms, and resulted in unconscious mental conflicts being brought to consciousness, and – ideally at least – resolved in reality (what Bertha Pappenheim called 'chimney sweeping' and 'the talking cure'). To this extent, the cathartic method in particular, and abreaction in general, were therapeutic applications of Darwin's third principle, and today have become clichés of psychotherapy – indeed even an advertising slogan for telephone companies ('It's good to talk!').

These examples show that Freud, by contrast to most twentieth-century psychology, was heavily indebted to Darwin. It has been the Freudian tradition in psychology, rather than any other, that has followed Darwin's example of observing infants (Darwin 1877). Indeed, psychoanalysis has institutionalized it to the extent that today observation of infants is a requirement of psychoanalytic training, and a whole subdiscipline of child psychoanalysis has emerged. Darwin also suggested that a prime insight into the expression of the emotions could be gained through studies of the insane. Here no one could deny that Freud and his followers in the psychoanalytic movement have been at the forefront of attempts to understand mental illness and to establish new standards of humane treatment. Freud had a unique opportunity to observe the mind in both its normal and abnormal states, as recommended by Darwin. Indeed, Freud's study of Michelangelo's *Moses* fulfilled Darwin's disappointed hope of also enlisting 'the great masters in painting and sculpture, who are such close observers' (Darwin 1998: 21). Anyone familiar with *The Expression of the Emotions* would immediately recognize that study as precisely what Darwin had in mind, concerned as it is with the interpretation of the complex emotions expressed in that great work of sculpture (Freud 1955).

Finally, Freud more than any other twentieth-century psychologist, developed and defended the pleasure principle, affirming that 'what decides the purpose of life is simply the program of the pleasure principle. This principle dominates the operation of the mental apparatus from the start. There can be no doubt about its efficacy' (Freud 1961a: 76). To put the matter in modern terminology, you could say that, agreeing with Darwin and Spencer but notably differing from today's evolutionary psychologists, Freud saw the pleasure/pain principle as a prime epigenetic rule governing human behaviour (see above, pp. 68–9).

Trivers's evolutionary psychodynamics of consciousness

Adding to his analysis of subtle cheating that I summarized at the end of the previous chapter (see above, pp. 102–6), Trivers points out that

> Of particular importance to cheating is the self-deception that it automatically tends to generate. Since it is useful to maintain a facade of morality and public beneficence, cheating must be disguised – increasingly, even to the actor himself. The actor becomes less and less conscious of the true nature of his actions, and this self-deception induces a range of impaired learning that may have costs far removed from the initial acts generating the impulse towards self-deception. (1981: 26)

He adds that

> With the advent of language in the human lineage, the possibilities for deception and self-deception were greatly enlarged. If language permits the communication of much more detailed and extensive information –

concerning, for example, events distant in space and time – then it both permits and encourages the communication of much more detailed and extensive misinformation. A portion of the brain devoted to verbal functions must become specialized for the manufacture and maintenance of falsehoods. This will require biased perceptions, biased memory, and biased logic; and these processes are ideally kept unconscious. (1981: 35)

If lying can pay – and what honest person doubts it can? – detecting lies becomes critical. Research by Paul Ekman and others has shown that lying can often be detected by so-called *leakage cues*. He points out that the voice is tied to the areas of the brain involved in emotion, so that it is very difficult to conceal some of the changes in the voice that occur when emotion is aroused. According to Ekman, the best-documented vocal sign of emotion is the pitch of the voice. For about 70 per cent of people who have been studied, pitch becomes higher when the subject is upset. Studies show that pitch also rises when the subject is lying, probably as a result of the anxiety about detection that the deception induces. However, unusual flatness in the voice can also conceal deception, perhaps by way of compensation for this effect.

But the sound of the voice is not the only source of clues about the truth or falsity of what a listener is hearing. The face can also give away a lot. Here smiles are an excellent example. Ekman points out that there is a subtle difference between a false and a genuine smile. In the genuine smile, muscles around the eye contract, causing visible creases, as Darwin noted (Darwin 1998). But the muscles in question cannot be voluntarily contracted in a false smile. The result is that insincere smiles tend to be somewhat exaggerated by way of trying to produce the wrinkles around the eyes characteristic of a sincere one through stretching the mouth into a more emphatic smile than would be the case if it were sincere.

Body language is also a good source of clues to deception. Ekman argues that, unlike the face or voice, most body movements are not directly tied to areas of the brain involved in emotion. Monitoring of body movements need not be difficult because people can feel and often see what their bodies are doing. Concealment of body movements can be much easier than concealing facial expressions or voice changes in emotion, and people are rarely held accountable for what they reveal by their body language. He concludes that 'Liars usually do not monitor, control and disguise all of their behaviour. They probably couldn't even if they wanted to. It is not likely that anyone could successfully control everything he did that could give him away, from the tips of his toes to the top of his head' (Ekman 1985).

If this is so, Trivers's point is that the most effective liars are likely to be those who do not know that they are lying. Totally unaware of their own deception because they believe their own lies, they are less likely to give the truth away in leakage cues:

> As mechanisms of spotting deception become more subtle, organisms may be selected to render some facts and motives unconscious, the better to conceal deception. In the broadest sense, the organism is selected to become unconscious of some of its deception, in order not to betray, by signs of self-knowledge, the deception being practised. (Trivers 1981: 35)

Trivers concludes that 'The mind must be structured in a very complex fashion, repeatedly split into public and private portions, with complicated interactions between the subsections.'

Divided consciousness

While psychology was still dominated by the anti-mentalistic thinking epitomized by behaviourism, any consideration of consciousness – and more particularly, unconsciousness – was regarded as 'unscientific' and unacceptable, in part because it was alleged that no hard evidence for unconscious mental processes existed. But however that may have been, today there is an increasing body of evidence that the mind is indeed split into parts that have different levels of consciousness, just as Trivers suggests.

Blindsight   A condition in which a person can be proved to have seen something, but at the same time lacks all consciousness of having done so, is called blindsight. One of the most notable cases is an individual known as DB, who lost most of his sight on the left-hand side of his visual field following surgery to remove part of his visual cortex in order to relieve migraine and other symptoms. In dozens of experiments carried out under rigorous laboratory conditions over many years, DB repeatedly demonstrated that he could see images projected on to the 'blind' part of his visual field but without any conscious awareness of being able to do so. Time and time again the experimenters report tests in which DB was able to sense visual stimuli in his blind field with an accuracy much better than chance, yet constantly he insisted that he was 'just guessing'. For example, despite being 92.5 per cent correct over 40 trials, DB insisted that 'it was 100 per cent guess-work. I was not aware of anything.'

Persuasive evidence that these remarkable findings can't be explained by internal reflections of light within the eye or by any other such means is provided by the experiments in which DB was asked to judge his reactions to images which fell both on the defective area of his visual field and on the blind-spot that everyone has where blood-vessels and nerves exit through the retina. In all these cases he felt he saw nothing, and said he was 'just guessing'. Yet objectively his test scores showed him performing worse than chance when the image was on the blind-spot (43 per cent correct – chance being 50 per cent), but much better when the image was displaced from it, but still within the area of his impairment (77–97 per cent correct: Weiskrantz 1986).

These findings can't be dismissed as anecdotal or limited to pathological cases, because recent experiments have reported similar findings in people with normal vision. As in the case of DB, experiments show that in certain circumstances subjects can 'guess' the correct answer just as well when they are unaware of having perceived a visual stimulus as when they are aware of having done so (Kolb and Brain 1995). There are good reasons for thinking that blindsight can be explained by the fact that in humans and other primates only about half of nerve fibres run directly from the eye to the visual cortex. Other connections are to the midbrain and subcortical regions, and one of these contains about 100,000 fibres, which means that it is larger than the whole of the auditory nerve (Weiskrantz 1986).

Nor are such findings limited to sight. In every major class of deficit in which patients apparently lose some particular cognitive ability through brain damage, examples of preserved capacities can be found of which the patient is unaware. This range extends from perception, to meaning, to memory and to language, with several different subtypes within each of the categories. Along with blindsight, there are reports of 'blind touch' and even 'deaf hearing'. A patient who could not consciously feel anything in her right arm could nevertheless point to the approximate area where she had been touched on it. Again, a brain-damaged patient could say whether the written name of a country belonged inside or outside Europe, whether the name of a person was that of an author or a politician, or whether a name was that of a living or non-living object. All this, even though he could not read or identify the word aloud or explicitly give its meaning (Weiskrantz 1997).

Readiness potentials   Laboratory research on normal subjects has established that conscious, voluntary acts are preceded by electrophysiological *readiness potentials* in the brain that can be measured
objectively and which suggest that 'cerebral initiation of a spontaneous voluntary act begins unconsciously.' However, it was found that
the final decision to act can still be consciously controlled during the
150 milliseconds or so remaining after the specific conscious intention
appears. In other words, subjects can 'veto' motor performance during a 100–200 millisecond period before a prearranged time to act.
According to these findings, 'The role of conscious will would be not
to initiate a specific voluntary act but rather to select and control the
volitional outcome.' It appears that, rather than initiating an act, 'conscious will can function in a permissive fashion, either to permit or to
prevent the motor implementation of the intention to act that arises
unconsciously.' In other words,

> the brain 'decides' to initiate . . . the act before there is any reportable
> subjective awareness that such a decision has taken place. . . . The present
> experimental findings provide direct evidence that unconscious proc-
> esses can and do initiate voluntary action and point to a definable cer-
> ebral basis for this unconscious function. (Libet 1985: 536)

Unconscious processing in normal subjects   Other recent research
using brain imaging has shown that semantic data and appropriate
motor responses can be processed unconsciously by everyone. Subjects reliably responded to a cue number by pressing a button despite
being consciously unaware of seeing the number, which was projected
for only 43 milliseconds and masked by other data. The study concluded that when subjects engage in an overt semantic comparison
task with a clearly visible target numeral, measures of covert motor
activity indicate that they also unconsciously apply the task instructions to an unseen masked numeral. A stream of perceptual, semantic
and motor processes can therefore occur without consciousness. The
authors conclude that a large amount of cerebral processing, including perception, semantic categorization and task execution, can be
performed in the absence of consciousness (Dahaene et al. 1998).

Knowledge of true facts inaccessible to consciousness can be demonstrated in perfectly normal people. For example, an experiment with
a gambling game showed that players had a cognitive equivalent of
blindsight where making the best bets was concerned. Players had to
select decks from which winning or losing cards could be drawn. They
were not told that half the decks gave occasional large wins, but over-

all incurred greater losses for those who chose them, or that the other half gave lower single wins, but were better overall. The experimenters found that long before they were consciously able to say so, emotional reactions in the players showed that they were unconsciously aware of which decks to avoid. Indeed, some of the players never consciously realized what was happening, but still tended to make the right choices based on their feelings. Like DB in the blindsight experiments, they were choosing on nothing better than hunches or intuition, but they were nevertheless choosing correctly (Bechara et al. 1997).

Split-brain research   This term refers to a situation in which surgeons have separated the right hemisphere of the brain from the left by cutting the nerve fibres that link them (*cerebral commissurotomy*, usually as a treatment of last resort for otherwise uncontrollable epilepsy). Within each hemisphere of the cortex there are about ten billion nerve cells, each with at least a hundred connections (and many with thousands). However, the two hemispheres are connected by only about 800 million nerve fibres, which means that only a fraction of what happens in one hemisphere can be communicated to the other. In split-brain patients, the fibres connecting the two halves of the cortex have either been wholly or partially cut, so that each half of the brain is even less connected to the other than normal, and consequently even more independent (Bogen 1990).

Nerves from one side of the body are, in the main, connected to the opposite side of the brain. Normally, we don't notice this because the two sides of the cortex communicate with one another. For example, although only one side of the visual field from each eye is directly linked to the hemisphere on the opposite side, the other half of what is seen is also relayed to that hemisphere from its partner, so that the brain sees a complete picture. However, in split-brain patients the differences between left and right become dramatically apparent. The one extraordinary defect revealed by these studies, quite unlike anything seen in animals, is that subjects are unable to give a verbal description of experiences of the left half of the visual field or of the left hand. Though both hemispheres of the brain register awareness, only the left can write or speak (Trevarthen 1990a: xxxii).

In experiments, a split-brain patient was found to be able to reliably report emotive reactions to visual stimulus words that were presented as images only to his right, non-verbal hemisphere. When the right hemisphere saw the word 'mom', the left hemisphere rated it 'good', and when the right side saw the word 'devil', the left rated it 'bad'. The equivalence with blindsight comes out in the fact that the left hemisphere had no idea what the stimuli were. No matter how hard the experimenters pressed, the patient could not name the stimulus that had been presented to the right hemisphere. Nevertheless, the left hemisphere was consistently right in its emotional ratings. In some way the emotional significance of the stimulus had leaked across the brain, even though the identity of the stimulus had not. The patient's conscious emotions, as experienced by his left hemisphere, were, in effect, being influenced by stimuli that he claimed he had never seen (LeDoux 1996: 14). (See box 4.2, 'Seeing with a split brain'.)

The alien hand   The fact that both hemispheres of the brain are contained within a single head and are part of the same body might tempt you to assume that co-operation between them is obvious and inevitable, irrespective of what differences there might be in their particular functions and consciousness. But once again, split-brain patients show that, at least for a while after their surgery, such co-operation can't necessarily be assumed.

Conflict rather than co-operation between the hemispheres sometimes shows itself in the so-called *alien hand*. In right-handed people this is typically the left hand, which acts not merely independently of the right as in some of the experiments above, but actively against it. For example, a patient repeatedly pulled a plate of food towards himself with one hand, only to push it away with the other. Another patient was reported by his wife to sometimes pull up his trousers with one hand and to push them down with the other while dressing; or the left hand, having helped the right to tie the belt of his dressing gown, would promptly untie it again. On one occasion the left hand tried to push away his wife while the right hand beckoned her; once it seemed to threaten her and had to be restrained by the right hand. Indeed, there is even a case in which the left hand slapped a split-brain patient to wake him when he overslept, and another in which it repeatedly attempted to strangle its owner (Ramachandran and Blakeslee 1998)! These findings are strong evidence for the existence of conflicting intentions in the left and right hemispheres. Indeed, some have even drawn the conclusion that they are evidence of multiple minds: one in each hemisphere (Puccetti 1973, 1981).

Anosognosia   An affliction that accompanies a left-side stroke, anosognosia usually disappears within a few weeks, but on rare occasions can be permanent. Strokes often paralyse one side of a person's body, but in anosognosia the paralysis goes with complete denial by the patient that the paralysis has occurred. A striking characteristic of

Box 4.2

Seeing with a split brain

In the experiment illustrated below, the left eye of a split-brain patient – that is, the one connected to the right side of the brain – sees a scene that shows a log cabin under heavy snow. His right eye – connected to the left side – sees a chicken's claw. He is asked to point to a corresponding object in an array below the scenes. The left hand/right hemisphere is offered a choice between lawn-mower, rake, shovel and axe, and correctly points to the shovel as the tool you would most need to clear the snow. The right hand/left hemisphere is offered an apple, toaster, hammer or chicken to pair with the chicken's claw, and of course points to the chicken.

When asked why he pointed to the chicken and to the shovel the patient replied, 'Oh, that's simple. The chicken claw goes with the chicken, and you need the shovel to clean out the chicken shed.' Because conscious awareness is largely restricted to the left, verbal hemisphere, the patient was unaware of having seen the snow scene with his left eye, yet he clearly did so, as his correct answer with his left hand showed. In a way very reminiscent of blindsight, the subject of this experiment showed that he had seen the snow-bound log cabin,

but had no conscious knowledge of having seen it, despite the fact that his left hand had made the most appropriate choice of tool to clear the snow.

Unconscious, left-side perceptions also produce revealing rationalizations. If a stimulus word like 'laugh' is flashed up on a screen only seen by the left eye (and therefore by the right hemisphere), the response will be to laugh: one patient laughed and when asked why replied, 'You guys come up and test us every month. What a way to make a living!' Patients will respond to similar left eye stimulus words such as 'walk' and will provide various explanations when asked why they did so – such as wanting to go to get a drink. According to the experimenter, 'However you manipulate this type of test, it always yields the same kind of result.' (Redrawn and quoted from Gazzaniga 1994).

anosognosia is the extent to which patients attempt to rationalize and not simply deny their disability. For example, when asked to perform an action with her paralysed left arm, one patient would usually rationalize her failure with statements such as, 'My shoulder hurts a lot today; I have arthritis, you know,' or 'I didn't really want to point that time.' Although the patient could be induced to admit that she was paralysed after several such trials, just ten minutes later she not only reverted to denial – insisting that her left hand was fully functional – but also claimed that she had successfully used that hand during the preceding testing session! This was despite the fact that her memory for other details of that session was completely accurate.

Vilayanur Ramachandran, who described this case, reports that it was almost as if she had 'forgotten' or selectively repressed the memory of her failed attempts as well as her verbal acknowledgement of her paralysis. He adds that such responses are 'classic examples of Freudian rationalization' and that anosognosic patients have a whole arsenal of such defence mechanisms at their disposal. Ramachandran suggests that 'what one is really seeing in these patients is an amplified version of Freudian defence mechanisms caught *in flagrante delicto*; mechanisms of precisely the same sort that we all use in our daily lives' (Ramachandran 1995).

Further evidence that anosognosic patients do indeed know unconsciously that they are paralysed but repress the realization comes from the astonishing discovery that the condition can be temporarily cured by pouring icy water into the patient's left ear. Given that anosognosia is linked to paralysis only on the left side of the body, it seems plausible to suppose that irrigation of the left ear with cold water stimulates the right hemisphere, and in particular the *vestibular system*, which is

Box 4.3

Conversations with an anosognosic

BM is an anosognosic patient who has a paralysed left arm. Vilayanur Ramachandran (VR) is her doctor:

VR: Mrs M., can you use your arms?
BM: Yes.
VR: Can you use both hands?
BM: Yes, of course.
VR: Can you use your right hand?
BM: Yes.
VR: Can you use your left hand?
BM: Yes.
VR: Are both hands equally strong?
BM: Yes, they are equally strong.
VR: Mrs M., point to my student with your right hand. (*Patient points.*) Mrs M., point to my student with your left hand. (*Patient remains silent.*) Mrs M., why are you not pointing?
BM: Because I don't want to.
BM: (*Looking at her paralysed hand*) Doctor, whose hand is this?
VR: Whose hand do you think it is?
BM: Well, it certainly isn't yours!
VR: Then whose is it?
BM: It isn't mine either.
VR: Whose hand do you think it is?
BM: It is my son's hand, Doctor.

It is important to add that BM was completely normal where everything other than the paralysed arm was concerned. A series of experiments in which she was given the choice of a task that involved two hands or just one resulted in her choosing the two-handed tasks. However, her response to the box of candy which was offered as a reward for success was, 'I am a diabetic, Doctor – I can't eat candy. You should know that!'

Irrigation of the left ear with cold water produces a temporary remission:

VR: Do you feel OK?
BM: My ear is very cold but other than that I am fine.
VR: Can you use your hands?
BM: I can use my right arm but not my left arm. I want to move it but it doesn't move.
VR: (*holding the paralysed arm*) Whose arm is this?
BM: It is my hand, of course.

VR: Can you use it?

BM: No, it is paralysed.

VR: Mrs M., how long has your arm been paralysed? Did it start now or earlier?

BM: It has been paralysed continuously for several days now.

But eight hours later a colleague (EX) spoke to her again:

EX: Can you use both arms?

BM: Yes.

EX: Can you use your left arm?

BM: Yes.

EX: This morning, two doctors did something to you. Do you remember?

BM: Yes. They put cold water in my ear; it was very cold.

EX: Do you remember they asked some questions about your arms, and you gave them an answer? Do you remember what you said?

BM: No, what did I say?

EX: What do you think you said? Try to remember.

BM: I said my arms were OK.

Ramachandran comments that her admission that she had been paralysed for several days suggests that even though she had been continuously denying her paralysis, the information about the paralysis was being continuously laid down in her brain. He tentatively concludes that at some deeper level she does indeed have knowledge about her paralysis. He draws attention to the fact that the insight gained during the caloric stimulation seemed to last half an hour after the stimulation ceased, but that when she was questioned eight hours later, she not only reverted to denial, but also repressed the admission of paralysis that she had made during her stimulation (Ramachandran 1995).

connected to the semicircular canals of the ear and is concerned with maintaining balance and a sense of the orientation of the body. Irrigation of the left ear with resulting stimulation of the vestibular system's links with the affected right hemisphere appears to temporarily restore whatever function of the right brain is compromised in anosognosia and to allow a remission during the treatment and for about 30 minutes afterwards. During this time, the patient not only openly admits to the paralysis, but shows evidence of having laid down memories consistent with this realization throughout the previous period of denial. Ramachandran comments that it is almost as if the irrigation treatment had revealed two separate conscious human beings who are mutually amnesic: a 'cold water' person who is intellectually honest and acknowledges the paralysis, and an anosognosic one who completely denies it (Ramachandran 1996)! (See box 4.3, 'Conversations with an anosognosic'.)

Prosopagnosia Individuals affected with this disorder can't recognize faces – even of members of their own family whom they have known all their lives. Typically, a person with prosopagnosia will fail consciously to distinguish between the face of a close relative and that of a stranger when shown photographs of both. However, a detector which measures changes in skin conductance will register a response to the relative, but not to the stranger. These findings suggest that, like DB above, prosopagnosics can be unconsciously aware of something while lacking conscious knowledge of it. Skin conductance responses are known to be controlled by the unconscious limbic brain, whereas conscious visual perception occurs in the cortex. This suggests that in prosopagnosic patients a perceptual link to the cortical brain that is critical for the recognition of well-known faces has been severed, but that other links to the emotive brain are still open and that it is on these that the unconscious perception relies (Tranel and Damasio 1985).

Gur and Sacheim's voice recognition experiments Prosopagnosics can often consciously identify well-known people by the sound of their voices, even when they cannot do so by sight. Nevertheless, experiments have shown that even in quite normal people with no brain dysfunction, the equivalent of blindsight can be demonstrated where perception of voice is concerned. Normally, skin conductance response rises on hearing your own voice, but tends to remain flat on hearing someone else's. Experimental subjects were wired up to a lie detector and asked to verbally identify voices as they heard them. Some subjects were found to reliably identify their own voices by evidence of their skin responses, while failing to do so consciously. As Robert Trivers comments, 'for most mistakes, the part of the brain controlling speech got it wrong, while the part controlling arousal got it right (Trivers 1985: 417).

In a variation on this experiment, the subjects' self-esteem was manipulated by randomly telling them that they had either done very well or very poorly on a test of verbal comprehension. The experimenters found that after being told that they had done well, subjects were more likely to consciously recognize the sound of their own voices, and even sometimes to misattribute their own voice to others. However, subjects whose self-esteem had been manipulated downwards by being told that they had done badly did the opposite: they tended to deny their own voices more often and to attribute their own voice to others much less. Furthermore, when questioned after the experiment, those with lowered self-esteem reported enjoying hearing their own voice less and rated their own voices as less pleasant than the successful group did. Here the implication is that if your self-esteem is high, you are more likely to want to be aware of yourself than if it is low, in which case you would probably prefer not to notice yourself, let alone be noticed by others (Gur and Sacheim 1979).

Mental topography and brain lateralization

Ramachandran suggests that located in the left hemisphere there is a mechanism for imposing consistency in the form of small rationalizations, repressions and so on. When an anomaly is detected, the left hemisphere tries to impose consistency by ignoring or suppressing the contrary evidence, for example by Freudian defence mechanisms. However, he also suggests that there is an 'anomaly detector' in the right hemisphere whose sole purpose is to serve as a 'devil's advocate' that periodically challenges the left hemisphere's 'story', and detects anomalies or discrepancies. He speculates that when the anomaly reaches a critical threshold, an interaction with the right hemisphere forces a complete change in one's worldview. Ramachandran adds that you could think of the anomaly detector 'as a mechanism for preserving intellectual honesty or integrity. . . . I might be willing to engage in some minor rationalization, i.e., make some small false assumptions to get on with my life, but when the false beliefs become too far removed from reality, my anomaly detector kicks in and makes me re-evaluate the situation' (1995: 39).

Evidence for this interpretation comes from an experiment in which an anosognosic patient's paralysed left hand was put inside a box with hidden mirrors which allowed the experimenter to make it appear to move. This was done by making the patient wear a glove on the hand and contriving the mirrors in such a way that a hidden accomplice's gloved hand looked as if it were the patient's. The patient was first tested by being asked to clap, and proceeded to do so Zen Buddhist style, with only one hand, but claimed to be clapping normally! When asked to move her paralysed hand – placed within the box – to the sound of a metronome, the patient was not surprised to see it moving, despite the fact that it was of course the accomplice's hand which she saw in motion. But when the accomplice's hand was kept still like the patient's real hand, the patient also nevertheless claimed to see it moving. According to Ramachandran,

When confronted with the contradictory information from her different sensory systems, her left hemisphere tries to impose consistency by simply inserting the required evidence, i.e., the visual appearance of a moving right hand. Since she has a malfunctioning anomaly detector in her right hemisphere, this bizarre delusion goes unchecked and, consequently, she reports that she can actually see her hand moving even though this belief is contradicted by the visual appearance of a stationary hand. (1995: 48)

Clearly, Ramachandran's model of the mind and Trivers's suggestions about the evolutionary foundations of the conscious/unconscious division are compatible (Ramachandran 1996). If Ramachandran's right hemisphere devil's advocate is indeed concerned with honesty, it is easy to see why it should be repressed by the verbal, left hemisphere's public relations department in situations where telling the truth would not promote an individual's ultimate reproductive success. The 'false assumptions' that Ramachandran suggests that the left hemisphere might maintain for 'getting on with life' could clearly include the 'facade of morality and public beneficence' that Trivers specifically mentions as a predictable screen for subtle cheating.

'Consciously,' suggests Trivers, 'a series of reasons may unfold internally that accompany action, so that when actions are challenged a convincing alternative explanation is at once available, complete with an internal scenario ("But I wasn't thinking that at all, I was thinking . . . ").' Split-brain research leaves little doubt that in the majority of people such conscious, verbal scenario-building occurs more or less exclusively in the left hemisphere. Trivers continues by pointing out that 'Of course it must be advantageous for the truth to be registered somewhere, so that mechanisms of self-deception must reside side by side with mechanisms for the correct apprehension of reality' (Trivers 1981). Ramachandran's model suggests that indeed they do, and that while the left hemisphere indulges in self-deception, the right hemisphere anomaly detector tracks the truth, and challenges the left's 'story' if the discrepancy becomes too great, too painful, or too dangerous.

Trivers's view of consciousness is close to Freud's

If Ramachandran's view of consciousness is comparable to that of Trivers, both are certainly strongly reminiscent of that of Sigmund Freud. Long before Ekman or Trivers, Freud had noticed and analysed leakage clues: 'He that has eyes to see and ears to hear may convince himself that no mortal can keep a secret. If his lips are silent, he chatters with his finger-tips; betrayal oozes out of him at every pore' (Freud 1953: 77–8).

At the time he put them forward and for long afterwards, Freud's discovery that the unconscious mind was both *topographical* (that is, divided into different levels of consciousness) and *dynamic* (structured by conflicting forces) was widely ridiculed and rejected. However, previous parts of this chapter have shown that today there is unassailable evidence for both propositions in blindsight, measurements of readiness potentials, prosopagnosia, split-brain research, anosognosia and the Gur and Sacheim experiments. The latter demonstrated that consciousness was topographical in the sense that the subjects could be proved to have two, completely contradictory pieces of information about the same thing – the sound of their voice – entered in different regions of their awareness (consciousness, which denied it was their own voice, and the unconscious which by their skin conductance indicated that the voice was recognized as their own). The second experiment, in which subjects' self-esteem was artificially raised or lowered, demonstrated that repression is dynamic to the extent that their motivation to repress or recognize their own voices was shown to be affected by their feelings about themselves.

Agnosia was a term coined by Freud in the early, neurological phase of his career, and it is still in use today, defined as 'an impairment in the higher-order recognition of objects not due to a deficit in the sensory pathway' (Miller 1991: 167). As Ramachandran points out,

> Even though Freud's own interests shifted from hard-core neuroanatomy to 'soft' psychology, he never lost sight of his initial goal of providing a neural explanation for psychological phenomena and he continued to pay lip-service to this goal until the end. Surely, were he alive today, he would have been delighted with what we now know of the syndrome of anosognosia. . . . Contrary to the frequently expressed view that memory repression is not a real phenomenon, my findings provide compelling experimental/clinical evidence that it is indeed a robust psychological process. (Ramachandran 1995)

He adds that Freud's 'basic idea – that consciousness is simply the tip of the iceberg and that our behaviour is mostly governed by a cauldron of emotions and motives of which we are largely unconscious ("the unconscious mind") – is still a perfectly valid concept that is sure to have a tremendous impact on both psychology and neurology' (Ramachandran 1996). Joseph LeDoux agrees that 'Freud was right on the mark when he described consciousness as the tip of the mental iceberg' (LeDoux 1996: 25).

Split-brain research has had to adopt Freud's topographical terminology distinguishing between the conscious, preconscious and unconscious (Trevarthen 1990b). Freud defined the *conscious* as that which occupies current awareness; the *preconscious* as that which describes anything that can voluntarily be recalled to consciousness; and the *unconscious* as that which can't be recalled under any circumstances (Freud 1958b).

These topographical distinctions between different states of consciousness nicely fit the findings of split-brain research, because Freud also found that mental contents had to be linked to verbal representations in order to be fully conscious in the sense just defined (Galin 1974). As Freud put it, 'the conscious presentation comprises the presentation of the thing plus the presentation of the word belonging to it, while the unconscious presentation is the presentation of the thing alone' (Freud 1957c). Freud in his turn appears to have acquired this way of thinking from **John Hughlings Jackson** (1835–1911), who directly related object-consciousness and word-consciousness (if we may call them that) to the two halves of the brain (Harrington 1985). As we have already seen, in most people sophisticated verbal ability does indeed go with consciousness in the left cerebral hemisphere. What is preconscious could presumably normally be found in either hemisphere, but could only become conscious by being communicated to the left, verbal one – something that we saw can't happen in split-brain patients if stimuli are limited to registering only in the right hemisphere.

According to Freud, the mechanism of *repression* acts essentially to keep mental contents away from consciousness (Freud 1957b). In practice, repression might simply be a question of the right hemisphere being denied access to the speech centres of the left hemisphere – perhaps by blocking the neural pathways between them. Freud discovered the repressed unconscious mainly thanks to his use of *free association*, which encouraged patients to talk at random, without they or the analyst exercising censorship of any kind on what they said. (This is how blindsight was investigated in DB: by insisting that he should guess even though he could not consciously see anything. He was being asked to produce material in essentially the same, unconstrained way as that encouraged by free association. 'Just guess!' is a psychoanalyst's stock response when a patient claims not to consciously know the answer to a question.)

With the new insights from split-brain research in mind, it would be tempting to see the success of free association and of the psychoanalytic 'talking cure' to which it gave rise as a result of the finding that access to consciousness in the left hemisphere also implies access to the primary speech centres. Clearly, if you encourage the left hemisphere to relax its vigilance and allow free and unfettered access to speech, it follows that much more might cross the cerebral commissures from the right, unconscious half of the brain – both explaining the therapeutic success of psychoanalysis and the remarkable new insights it gave into human psychology.

Brain lateralization might also explain what was once known as *Charcot's rule* (after **Jean-Martin Charcot** (1825–1893), one of Freud's most important mentors). This was the finding that hysterical symptoms tend to be more frequently found on the left side of the body than the right (Harrington 1985). As **Sándor Ferenczi** (1873–1933, an associate of Freud's) noted, 'It is possible that – in right-handed people – the sensational sphere for the left side shows from the first a certain predisposition for unconscious impulses, so that it is more easily robbed of its normal functions and placed at the service of unconscious libidinal fantasies.' According to Freud, hysterical symptoms (that is, physical symptoms with purely psychological causes) represent the return of the repressed in a disguised form. If the right hemisphere corresponds more to the repressed unconscious than the left, the finding that hysterical symptoms predominate on the left side of the body would be exactly what we should expect, given that each hemisphere is connected to the opposite side of the body. More recent research broadly confirms this expectation, also finding that 73 per cent of patients suffering from 'hypochondriacal states' who have symptoms limited to one side of the body have them on the left side (Galin et al. 1977).

Suggestions for further reading

Barkow, J., L. Cosmides and J. Tooby (eds) (1992)   *The Adapted Mind: Evolutionary Psychology and the Generation of Culture.*
Baron-Cohen, S. (1995)   *Mindblindness: An Essay on Autism and Theory of Mind.*
Darwin, C. (1998)   *The Expression of the Emotions in Man and Animals* (1872).
Ramachandran, V. S. and S. Blakeslee (1998)   *Phantoms in the Brain.*
Weiskrantz, L. (1997)   *Consciousness Lost and Found.*

5

Sex, Mating and Parental Investment

In 1871, Darwin published his second great contribution to our understanding of evolution, *The Descent of Man, and Selection in Relation to Sex*. Sometimes sexual selection is represented as an afterthought to the discovery of natural selection. The following quotation dates from Darwin's earliest essay on evolution in 1842, and shows that sexual selection was clearly in his mind from the beginning:

> Besides selection by death, in bisexual animals . . . the selection in time of fullest vigour, namely struggle of males; even in animals which pair there seems a surplus and a battle, possibly as in man more males than females, struggle of war or charms. Hence that male which at that time is in fullest vigour, or best armed with arms or ornaments of its species, will gain in hundreds of generations some small advantage and transmit such characters to its offspring. (Darwin 1909)

Here Darwin succinctly sets out the basic idea that was to be the subject of his great, two-volume book of 30 years later. This is that, besides the effects of natural selection (what he aptly calls 'selection by death'), you can discern those of sexual competition among organisms of the same species for reproductive success.

Sex and parental investment

In modern biology sex can be objectively and unambiguously defined. Despite the fact that in the vast majority of all sexually reproducing species, male and female donate the same amount of genetic material to the nucleus of the sex cell, or *gamete*, the gametes they produce are dramatically different. In the human case, the largest cell found in the body is the ovum and it is almost visible to the naked eye. The smallest, by contrast, is the sperm. And this is typical. Throughout nature, in animals, plants and fungi where sexes exist there is almost always a massive, relatively immobile gamete, the ovum or egg, always regarded as the distinctive attribute of the *female*; and a minute, relatively mobile sex cell, the sperm of the *male*. Furthermore, there is no question of one being only marginally larger, or of the two being almost equal in size. Almost always, as in the human case, the disparity spans many orders of magnitude and is vast and unmistakable. This difference is sometimes called *gametic dimorphism* (meaning that the sex cells of each sex are characteristically different in shape and size), or simply, *anisogamy* (meaning that sex cells are not identical). In the few cases where no discernible difference is found, as in some fungi and algae, the sex cells appear to be indistinguishable and are arbitrarily labelled *plus* and *minus*.

Although the egg and sperm typically differ by orders of magnitude, this difference still fails to reflect the true difference in organisms such as birds or mammals, where much more is at stake. In the case of a bird, the true disparity in terms of what male and female contribute is not the difference between the sperm and ovum so much as that between the sperm and the egg as it is laid, containing as it does, not merely the developing embryo, but all that it needs in the way of nutrients to bring it to a live birth some time later. The contrast in size at this level is truly staggering. Sperm cells are tens of billions of times smaller than any bird's egg, and a male mammal's sperms are even more negligible by comparison with the newborn offspring. In the human case, a newborn baby is a hundred billion times heavier than the fertilized egg from which it hatches, and all of this additional weight is provided exclusively by the mother, who also contributes all the cytoplasm and slightly more than half the genes of the original egg (Coen 1999).

The key concept is parental investment

In order to understand the different contributions of the sexes clearly we need a much more fundamental concept than mere size difference, one which will include not simply the provision an organism makes in the form of sex cells, but all the other factors involved in producing an offspring, such as warmth or shade, protection, instruction, transportation, food, and so on. The concept we need is that of *parental invest-*

Box 5.1

Penis-fencing and darts in the battle of the sexes

You might have thought that if you were a hermaphrodite – that is, an organism that contained both male and female sex organs in the same body – sexual conflict would not apply to you. How could there be a 'battle of the sexes' if you were both sexes at one and the same time? Surely, your female sex would make you at one with the female part of your fellow hermaphrodites, and your male sex would put you at peace with their male aspect. Foreplay would presumably be harmonious and equitable, with both partners being identically matched. You would think that being a hermaphrodite was the ultimate guarantee of equality between the sexes, and a sure safeguard against conflict.

But however obvious that may seem, the flatworm, *Pseudoceros bifurcus*, shows that it simply isn't true, and that the battle of the sexes is as intense – if not more intense – in hermaphrodites than it is in single-sex organisms. When two of these worms meet, bouts of so-called 'penis-fencing' begin, which can last for up to an hour. The two rear up, erect their hypodermic syringe-like penises, and literally try to stab each other with them. If one succeeds in penetrating the skin of the other, it ejaculates sperm, but only about one in six strikes results in successful insemination. Even if both animals inseminate each other, the first to penetrate achieves a longer insemination time. Both animals are usually left severely wounded, with many prominent punctures. Effectively, it is an attempt at mutual rape with penises that resemble weapons.

What on earth is going on? This form of mating has been described as 'brutally inefficient', and it is yet another illustration of the way that natural selection – and in this case, sexual selection too – can be prodigiously perverse, wasteful and destructive.

The explanation lies in the fact that even when organisms are both male and female at the same time, differences in cost still attach to the male and female aspects of their bodies and behaviour. In the case of penis-fencing flatworms which use hypodermic insemination, the worm that gets injected with sperm has to bear the cost of healing the wound and loses control over the fertilization of its own eggs. The winner of the bout has claimed use of the other's eggs for its own reproduction, while keeping its own eggs free. As the researchers conclude, 'Hypodermic insemination . . . allows hermaphrodites to skew sexual interactions in favour of sperm donation, fuelling an evolutionary arms race between strike and avoidance behaviour' (Michiels and Newman 1998).

Something similar happens in garden snails, which are also hermaphrodites. Instead of penis-fencing, they throw darts at their partner during the foreplay that precedes several hours of mating. The sharp, calcareous needles that each partner shoots into the other's body don't carry sperm, but they are coated in a mucous that makes the snail equivalent of the vagina more accessible to sperm, and shuts down defences against it. Because matings with a number of different partners are common before egg-laying, the active substances in the mucous are clearly designed to give an advantage to the dart-thrower's sperm, making it more likely that it will be the father of its partner's offspring.

ment defined as *any benefit to an offspring's reproductive success at a cost to the remainder of the parent's reproductive success* (R. A. Fisher 1930: 142–3; Trivers 1972).

Immediately we can rephrase our earlier definition of the difference between the sexes in terms of this definition and say that, where gametes differ in size as they do in the overwhelming majority of cases, the female is the sex whose investment in the sex cell is the larger, and the male is the sex whose investment is the smaller. This establishes a fundamental, objective and quantitative distinction between the sexes based on the inequality of their respective investments in gametes. (See box 5.1, 'Penis-fencing and darts in the battle of the sexes'.)

Variance of reproductive success

If we ask what consequences follow from the fundamental difference between the sexes defined in terms of parental investment, we could immediately predict that if one sex produces many more sex cells and invests much less in them than the other, that sex ought potentially at least to be able to engender many more offspring. A striking example of the cumulative effect of male, as opposed to female, reproductive success is provided by the members of the modern Saudi Arabian royal family who now number several thousand but are all descended from Ibn Abd al-Rahman al-Saud (1880–1953) and his brother Faisal (1906–1975). Both monarchs had hundreds of official wives and an unknown but large number of concubines.

The Saudi example may, admittedly, be exceptional, but it is nevertheless a simple fact of arithmetic that where individual men number their wives in tens, their offspring may number hundreds by the end of their lives, and where they have wives by the hundred there is nothing to stop them having offspring numbered in thousands. Nor is this effect limited to royalty. In modern Ghana, where men often marry several wives, the average father has twice as many children as the average mother (Konotey-Ahulu 1980). In other places where polygyny is common the same effect can be measured in terms of genetic diversity on the Y chromosome. This is because the Y chromosome is only inherited by males from the father (see above, pp. 47–9), and so the number of Y chromosome genes present in a population measures the number of fathers. In central Africa, Y chromosomes are very similar, suggesting relatively few fathers (Lucotte et al. 1994). In the Sinai Peninsula, Y-chromosome genetic diversity is low while diversity of mitochondrial genes – which are inherited solely from the mother – is high. This reflects the fact that in such societies there are many more mothers than fathers (Salem et al. 1996).

Males have greater variance of reproductive success than females

The most important single behavioural consequence of all this as far as selection is concerned is that, thanks ultimately to their small and numerous sex cells, males can be vastly more reproductively successful than females. In the case of a species like elephant seals, for example, most offspring in any one breeding season are fathered by between 2 and 5 per cent of the males. In the case of red deer, more than half the young were sired by 12 per cent of the adult males in one closely studied population. But these figures also reveal the inevitable corollary of the generalization above: if a male can have vastly greater reproductive success than can a female thanks to his small and numerous sex cells, then equally he can have considerably less success than she can. This is because the figures quoted immediately above also show that in the case of the elephant seals 95 per cent of the male population had little or no reproductive success, and in that of the red deer the other half of the offspring in the season in question had to be fathered by 88 per cent of the remaining males, many of whom fathered none at all. Facts such as these show that we must modify our assertion above and conclude that it is not safe to say that males have greater reproductive success than do females, but that males almost always show a greater *variance* of reproductive success than do females. By this we mean that whereas a male may be more reproductively successful than a female, he may also be much less successful, and that we must take note of both possibilities. But because of her typically greater degree of parental investment, and because females will almost always be in short supply where males ready to mate with them are

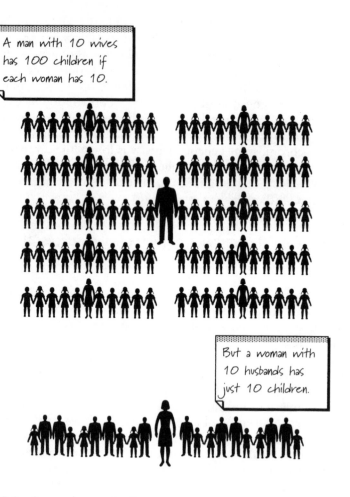

Figure 5.1   Sex and reproductive success

concerned, female reproductive success will vary much less than that of the male. (See figure 5.1.)

A study of 18,876 British men and women aged 16–59 carried out in 1990–1 revealed that variance of reproductive success translates directly into observable differences in sexual behaviour even in a modern population partly emancipated from traditional sex roles:

- women were twice as likely to have had only one sexual partner during their lifetime than were men;

- whereas 24.4 per cent of all men had had ten sexual partners or more, only 6.8 per cent of women had done so;
- 1 per cent of men accounted for 16 per cent of all female partners in the previous five years.

Similar findings from even larger samples have been reported in France (Johnson et al. 1992).

Sometimes people argue that there can't be any variance in numbers of partners, because every male is partnered by a female in every act of heterosexual intercourse: 'statistically, for heterosexual pairings, the numbers of partners simply have to even out. The discrepancy ... arises from men's tendency to exaggerate and women's fear of derogatory labelling' (Taylor 1996).

But imagine a community of couples where just one of the women has affairs with all of the men, but all the remaining wives are faithful. The number of male partners of all the women except one would be one, and this would indeed be less than the corresponding number of female partners of all but one of the men, which would be two. In society at large, a very few women may account for a vast number of male partners: for example prostitutes. But prostitution caters overwhelmingly for men, and the same is true of homosexuals who partner members of their own sex: men do this more than women and with many more partners (as the AIDS epidemic showed). Again, some people may have no sexual partners whatsoever. Theory predicts that there should be more men in this category than women, and the survey quoted above did find that 6.6 per cent of all men surveyed reported no sexual partners whatsoever in their lifetime compared to 5.7 per cent of women. (Here misreporting may indeed be an important feature, and men may be suspected of it more than women where admitting to no partners in a lifetime is concerned.) Certainly, where marriage is concerned, a uniform, worldwide finding is that fewer men than women ever marry, and this appears to be even more pronounced in traditional societies (Lopreato and Crippen 1999: 172).

Mating systems

Mating systems can be classified in terms of the number and sex of the individuals concerned: we can have uni-female, multi-female, uni-male and multi-male units combined in four possible ways. In a multi-female system, a number of females can be mated to one, or to a number of males. If it is the former, a number of females mated to one male,

Table 5.1   Four fundamental mating systems

	Uni-male	Multi-male
Uni-female	**Monogamy**	**Polyandry**
Multi-female	**Polygyny**	**Polygamy/Promiscuity**

we have *polygyny* (Greek for 'many females'). If it is the latter, a number of females mated to a number of males, we could call it *polygamy* ('many mates'), or, if there is little in the way of systematic contact among mating partners, *promiscuity*. As far as uni-female systems are concerned, there are again two possibilities: one female may be mated to one male – what we know as *monogamy* ('one mate'); or one female may be mated to many males – what is termed *polyandry* ('many males') (see table 5.1).

Polygyny   The majority of human societies – approximately 84 per cent of the total – are either generally polygynous or allow polygyny to those men wealthy or powerful enough to be able to practise it (although there are wide regional variations). The remainder are mostly monogamous, with fewer than 1 per cent polyandrous (Murdock 1967; but see also White 1988).

Monogamy   Despite the large number of societies that allow polygyny, most human marriages are monogamous: that is, they are marriages of one man to one woman. This is partly because there are almost always many more men in a polygynous society who can only afford one wife as compared to those who can manage two or more. Because women are always in short supply in a mating system which allows men more than one each, it follows that there will usually be a large number of monogamously married men – as well as quite a few unmarried ones – in a society where some men have many wives.

Polyandry   A system of one female simultaneously mated to many males is rare in nature as it is in the human case, and presumably for the same reasons. Among these are the fact that only one male is needed to fertilize a female at any one time, and that female reproductive success, unlike that of most males, is not directly linked to the number of a female's sexual partners (figure 5.1 above). Of course, where males contribute more than mere fertilizations, more of them may be useful to a female. For example, there are some birds who find that even two parents are barely enough to raise offspring, and so sometimes a second male is recruited by a female. If neither he, nor the other male, knows who is the father of the offspring, both may be induced to invest and support the female in raising young who are certainly hers.

Among mammals polyandry is extremely rare, and in human societies it is normally found only where males are too poor to be able to afford a wife of their own, and so club together with others to support one. The classic examples come from the Himalayan region where high-altitude farming imposes exacting limits on both the minimum size of holding that can be viable and the numbers of people needed to farm it. In order to prevent the break-up of farms, families with sons tend to contract only one marriage per generation, while those with daughters can ensure that by marrying a number of husbands she and her offspring will be adequately supported. Normally the males concerned in sharing a wife are brothers. Although such brothers might in theory have equal access to a shared wife, their age distribution almost always means that polyandry benefits older brothers more than younger ones, and that for the latter monogamy ought to be a better option wherever economically possible. However, quantitative data show that completed polyandrous families have more children than monogamous ones and that marrying daughters polyandrously does indeed pay. Nevertheless, the fact that males typically do not invest as much as females in offspring and that selection will not reward those males who invest in the offspring of others to whom they are not related means that polyandry can't be expected to be a common mating strategy, and almost always reflects some degree of exceptional circumstances (Crook and Crook 1988).

Polygamy Understood as group marriage of a number of men to a number of women, this was once believed to have been characteristic of primal human beings and to be the origin of the classificatory kin terminology of many traditional societies (that is, the application of kinship terms like 'mother' or 'brother' to entire groups of relatives, rather than simply to individuals). However, the existence of formal polygamy has never been established in any known society, and if it ever has existed among human beings as an institutionalized mating system, it is certainly even rarer than polyandry. On the few occasions that it has been experimented with in utopian or sectarian communities, it has always broken down to the extent that such communities have reverted to more traditional forms of marriage, or simply dissolved. Presumably the reason is that polygamy carries all the costs of a multi-male mating system for men, along with all the costs of a multi-female system for women, without the individual benefits that a male polygynist or the sole wife of several husbands enjoys.

Promiscuity   Understood as socially accepted mating of a number of men and women without any further formal relationship, this is also rare, presumably because it implies no parental commitment by men whatsoever, and so is normally not in women's interests. Again, the fact that we regard covert copulation as natural and desirable suggests that we are not adapted for the open, public copulation that true promiscuity implies. (Indeed, this is all the more telling because our nearest evolutionary relatives, the great apes, show no such inhibitions about copulating in public, which suggests that we are much less comfortable about promiscuity than they are.)

Admittedly, all matings outside formalized monogamy, polygyny or polyandry could be called promiscuous – and to some extent they are. But, as a species-typical mating system, promiscuity is the least widely observed, and in many respects the most marginal among humans. Nevertheless, it is important to recognize that, although marginal, aspects of it are always present, and that whatever the formal mating arrangements of a society may be, promiscuous matings of one kind and another are almost always going on, often – thanks to covert copulation – on a much greater scale than is supposed.

Divorce and remarriage

Although many modern Western societies might give the appearance of being monogamous thanks to allowing an individual to be married to only one partner at a time, divorce allows men to remarry and effectively become serial polygynists, particularly if a divorced and remarried man has to continue to contribute to the support of his divorced wife and her children. Of course, a divorced and remarried woman might also have to support her divorced husband, and perhaps even his children, and so would effectively be a serial polyandrist by the same argument. However, such outcomes are rare, and in the main it is men who find themselves supporting two or more families at once. Men are certainly more likely than women to remarry, and to do so soon after a divorce. Again, whereas high status men are more likely to remarry than lower status ones, such status differences are not found in remarrying women. And whereas divorced men who remarry are much more likely to find mates who are considerably younger than their former spouses and who have not been previously married, divorced women more frequently remarry men who are closer to their own age and who have been divorced themselves (Lopreato and Crippen 1999).

Because a man's reproductive life can last considerably longer than can a woman's and be much less critically affected by his health and physical capacity than is a woman's, divorced and remarried men are more likely to have more children as a result of their divorce and remarriage than are women. And of course, if we extend the argument to include all sexual partners and not just official ones, from the point of view of their lifetime reproductive success men can almost always be much more polygynous than women can be polyandrous.

According to a study by Helen Fisher based on comparative data from 58 modern societies found in the United Nations demographic yearbooks, divorce generally occurs early in marriage, peaking in or around the fourth year after the wedding, and gradually declining thereafter. This appears to be a worldwide pattern, irrespective of varying traditions of marriage, myriad different opinions about divorce, and diverse procedures for terminating relationships. 'Marriage', Fisher concludes, 'has a cross-cultural pattern of decay'.

In the 24 societies for which data are available in the United Nations yearbooks, divorce risk for men is highest in the age group 25 to 29, while for women it is about equal in both this age group and the younger, 20 to 24–year-old one. Divorce then becomes less common until by middle age it is uncommon: 81 per cent of all divorces occur before age 45 in women; and 74 per cent of all divorces happen before this age in men. Fisher points out that if boredom, sexual satiety, or ageing were the explanation, divorce would increase with length of marriage, rather than decrease. However, if you consider the fact that the twenties are a period of peak fertility for both sexes, separation could make sense from an evolutionary point of view if it indicated a failed attempt at satisfactory mating.

Another pattern that emerges from the United Nations data is that, among hundreds of millions of people in 45 societies between 1950 and 1989, 39 per cent of all divorces occurred among couples with no dependent children, 26 per cent with one dependent child, 19 per cent with two, 7 per cent with three, and 3 per cent with four; while couples with five or more dependent children rarely split up. In other words, the more children a couple have, the less likely are they to divorce. This finding also fits evolutionary expectations because mating is a means to successful reproduction, and the more children a couple have, the more successful they have been. By the same argument, fewer or no children indicate less success, and therefore a greater expectation that in a couple one or both might want to try another mating relationship.

This interpretation is also consistent with the finding that 80 per cent of all divorced American men and 75 per cent of all divorced American women remarry within an average of three years (with the median ranging from three to four-and-a-half years, depending on age). As evolutionary theory would predict, the peak age category for remarriage of divorced American women was 25 to 29, lower than the corresponding peak age for divorced American men of 30 to 34. The percentage of men and women in other cultures who remarry is not provided by the United Nations census data, but among 98 cultures surveyed between 1971 and 1982, the peak ages for remarriage of divorced men and women were the same as in the US.

Fisher concludes that like many other species that mate only through a breeding season, human pair-bonds originally evolved to last only long enough to raise a single, dependent child through the first four years of infancy (unless a second infant was conceived). The modern pattern of serial monogamy – with a peak marriage duration of four years – appears to conform to what could be the traditional period between successive births. Human serial monogamy may have evolved in the hominid lineage to raise successive cohorts of highly dependent young. The 'seven year itch' – recast as a four-year reproductive cycle – may be an evolved, biological phenomenon (H. Fisher 1991, 1992).

Human sexual adaptations

You could dispute the findings about human mating, marriage and divorce on the grounds that they could be culturally-determined. However, there are a number of pieces of physical evidence that point in the same direction as the considerations above.

Sexual dimorphism   This is just Greek for 'two sexual forms' and describes regular physical differences between the sexes, apart from the primary sex organs. In the case of elephant seals, by far the greatest element of sexual dimorphism is size, with males being up to seven times heavier than females. Since elephant seal males rear up and use their great bulk in attempting to knock over opponents in sexual contests, it is not surprising that natural selection has rewarded the largest and heaviest males with the greatest degree of reproductive success.

Indeed, it is in general true that where size, muscularity and sheer brute force are important factors in winning fights among males over females, such attributes will tend to become typical of males merely because the males who best possessed those attributes in the past left the largest number of descendants to inherit them. Other adaptations such as enlarged teeth, horns, antlers or claws may also be preferentially selected in males for the same reason, and the degree to which a species is sexually dimorphic in characteristics such as these will normally be a good guide as to how intense the sexual conflict is among its males.

If, bearing these general principles in mind, we now look at the facts regarding human beings, we find that our species is indeed sexually dimorphic. This is true in the general sense that adult men and women are usually easily distinguished, regardless of culturally dependent factors, such as hair length. Here human beings are unlike many birds, whose degree of sexual dimorphism is so slight that it sometimes takes an internal, post-mortem examination to sex them. The features that make men and women easily distinguishable are female attributes such as breasts, rounded hips and generally fuller buttocks, more youthful complexion and markedly less body hair; males, by contrast, have broader shoulders, more muscle development and body hair, beards and deepened voices. (See box 5.2, 'Waist-to-hip ratio'.)

Although Japanese and European subjects of both sexes prefer more feminine female faces, enhanced masculinity in a male face produces a reaction of increased perceived dominance along with negative attributions, such as coldness and dishonesty. This may be because masculine face shape (larger size, square jaw, etc.) is induced by testosterone, high levels of which are also associated with higher incidence of infidelity, divorce and violence (Booth and Dabbs 1993). However, although women generally have a preference for slightly feminized male faces, they nevertheless prefer somewhat more masculine ones at the time in their sexual cycles when they are more likely to conceive by contrast to when they are not. This effect may be explained by the fact that more masculine features appear to correlate with disease resistance in men, and hence with the genetic quality of a woman's potential mate. These findings suggest that men's faces are subject to complex and even conflicting selective forces whose overall effect is to keep sexual dimorphism within definite limits: too much masculinity may be as bad as too little, with the optimum amount depending on a woman's preferences at the time in question (Perrett et al. 1998; Booth and Dabbs 1993; Penton-Voak et al. 1999).

In terms of overall size and weight, the difference between men and

Box 5.2

Waist-to-hip ratio

Standards of physical attractiveness vary quite widely, tempting many to conclude that they are culturally determined. However, research into waist-to-hip ratio (WHR) suggests that it is a universal standard of attractiveness, and one that applies to both sexes. WHR is defined as the ratio of the narrowest measurement around the waist to the largest measurement at the greatest protrusion of the buttocks, and correlates strongly with fat content of the body. Body fat distribution differences between men and women are at a maximum during early reproductive life. After puberty oestrogens stimulate women to deposit adipose fat (which is critical for fertility) on the buttocks, thighs and breasts. Testosterone in men, by contrast, causes them to lose fat from buttocks and thighs after puberty, and begin depositing it on the stomach, shoulder and nape of the neck. WHR also reflects pelvic size, so that the volume of the body below the waist in women is ±40% larger than in men. WHR is similar for the sexes before puberty, but afterwards women's range from 0.67 to 0.8, whereas men's range from 0.85 to 0.95.

Photo Nigel Stead

WHR is an accurate measure of reproductive and endocrinological status. Women with higher WHR and lower body weight are less fertile than those with the contrary indications. Risk factors for obesity-related diseases such as diabetes, hypertension and heart disease vary with WHR, so that it is also a good indicator of health in this respect: higher WHR indicates increased risk of death in women independently of weight.

Studies in which subjects were asked to judge the attractiveness of female body profiles with differing WHRs showed that, contrary to previous studies not involving WHR, men and women were largely in agreement. Although women tended to prefer thinner profiles to men, both preferred profiles with low WHR (0.7). A comparison of older and younger mens' preferences showed that, although younger men had more of a preference for the thinnest profiles, neither age group inferred the reproductive capability of a woman from weight or fatness alone. No subject found female profiles with WHRs typical of men (0.9–1.0) attractive. Subjects rated heavier profiles as older, independent of WHR, perhaps explaining why normal weight profiles were generally preferred to lower or higher weight ones (Singh 1993).

Nevertheless, prehistoric figurines like the Dolní Vestonice Venus illustrated here suggest that even though judgements about total body weight may be influenced by environmental factors, WHR remains an independent factor. The WHR of this figurine is estimated to be 0.7, suggesting that even in what may be cold-adapted conditions where extra body fat may have been positively valued and perhaps associated with youth rather than age, ideal WHRs fell within the same range as they do today.

women is significant, with men standing on average between 5 and 12 per cent taller than women, with the figure being higher in traditionally polygynous cultures where, presumably, some degree of conflict or competition among men for women occurs. As far as weight is concerned, women are on average about 20 per cent lighter than men. But this figure is more significant than it seems if one also notices that the body weight of the sexes is not constituted in exactly the same way. On the contrary, it seems to be independently dimorphic in the sense that, whereas women have about one-quarter of their body weight in the form of fat, men on average have only about half that amount.

In other words, although women on average have about twice as much fat as men, they nevertheless weigh on average almost a fifth less than men. Clearly, the difference is not explained by how well fed the sexes may be but by the fact that males have larger skeletons on average, with heavier bones, and considerably more muscle than most females have. In women, the degree of fat deposits is critical to reproductive success in primal conditions, but in men muscle, bone

Box 5.3

Fat is a fertility issue

Because maternal investment in the developing foetus is principally in the form of nutrients, it is not surprising that research has shown that it is the level of such nutrients stored in the mother's body—fat, in other words—which is critical to fertility and that a baby's weight correlates most with its mother's pre- rather than post-pregnancy weight. Human females are unusual among mammals in the large amount of fat they can carry. Body fat increases prior to menarche (the beginning of menstruation) by a factor of 120% and in so doing reaches a critical level of 24% body fat by weight. A further increase in body fat proportion to a typical 28% is achieved by age 18, at which point full fertility is normally achieved. So sensitive is the female body to body weight variations that some women athletes can turn their sexual cycles on and off at will with just a 3lb pound change in weight.

In the case of the Ache hunter-gatherers, the mean age at which women first gave birth was found to be the same as that at which they first reached mean weight for adult females in the population. Heavier women were also found to have more children, to have them more closely spaced, and to have children who survived better than did the offspring of lighter women. Sheep have long been known to be much more likely to give birth to twins if ewes are fed a high-calorie diet for a week or two prior to mating. In what seems to be a close human parallel, the rate of fraternal twins was found to decline during the wartime food shortages in a number of Western European countries, but returned to normal levels afterwards. The fact that the incidence of identical twins (who develop from a single egg) remained the same suggests that it was an increase in the number of eggs released during the cycle that accounted for the change.

The finding that emotional stress can interrupt or disturb the sexual cycle is understandable if we make the not unreasonable assumption that such stress would normally indicate unfavourable social or psychological circumstances for starting a pregnancy. Indeed, according to a recently proposed model, anorexia nervosa, an eating disorder predominantly found in young women and involving severe loss of weight with the resulting suppression of the sexual cycle, may be explicable as an extreme example of this. Its occurrence at the beginning of a woman's reproductive life and often after her first sexual experiences, along with its effect of suppressing her fertility, suggest it may be seen as a means whereby young women who are not yet ready to begin their reproductive lives bring about a postponement.

If this were true, we would expect anorexia to be more common where the costs of delaying reproduction were lower thanks to increased life expectancy, decreased child mortality and generally high standards of health and welfare. The fact that it is indeed found in the affluent societies of the West, but hardly at all in the Third World, bears out the prediction that anorexia should occur predominantly where life is most secure and a woman's reproductive life is the longest. Again, anorexics often come from family backgrounds with above average social, economic or psychological stress, or have dominating, manipulative parents who wish them to postpone their reproductive lives in the interests of educational, social or career achievement. This finding, too, argues the case for seeing anorexia as motivated by stresses of various kinds which a young woman might implicitly interpret as evidence of the undesirability of embarking on her reproductive life at that particular time (Voland and Voland 1989; Anderson and Crawford 1992).

and height are critical in aggressive encounters with other men. These facts alone suggest that in human beings, as in many other species, sexual dimorphism of this kind on the part of males is an indicator of the fact that sex and conflict often go together. (See box 5.3, 'Fat is a fertility issue'.)

You could explain some human sexual dimorphism in terms of the different food-gathering activities of men and women in primal hunter-gatherer societies and see male brawn as an adaptation for hunting, rather than competition for women. However, hunting may be an activity that is as much to do with sex as it is with obtaining food. Research suggests that, in some hunting-and-gathering cultures at least, men use meat in part for sexual conquest, and in most such societies, being a good hunter is a trait highly valued by women in men (Hill and Kaplan 1988; Hawkes 1990). So in practice the two interpretations of male sexual dimorphism may come to much the same thing.

According to Laura Betzig, the evidence suggests that in virtually all societies women are a significant cause of male conflicts of interest in general and of violence in particular (Betzig 1986). Data on the proportion of male murders of other males as compared to female murders of other females from 35 different societies throughout the world show an immense contrast. On average, out of every 100 murders of a person of one sex by a member of the same sex, 95 will be murders of males by other males. Put another way, you could say on the basis of these figures that a man is 20 times more likely to be murdered by another man than is a woman likely to be murdered by another woman. Furthermore, since the figures just quoted ignore male deaths at the hands of other males in war and similar conflicts, and count female murders which do not relate to conflict between mature women such as female infanticides, they probably underestimate the true extent of homicidal violence among males and exaggerate that among females.

In the case of the polygynous Yanomamö indians of South America, approximately 30 per cent of deaths among adult males were attributable to violence, and almost half of all men aged 25 or more had participated in a killing; while nearly 70 per cent of all adults over 40 years of age had lost a close relative because of violence. Among the Mae Enga, Huli and Dugum Dani of highland New Guinea the figures for violent death of adult males were 25 per cent, 19.5 per cent and 28.5 per cent respectively. That such violence can contribute significantly to the reproductive success of a man is suggested by the Yanomamö findings which show that killers have on average two-and-a-half times as many wives and three times as many children as non-killers (Chagnon 1988). A recent study of the available data concluded that there is no known human society in which the level of lethal violence among women even begins to approach that among men, and added that competition is far more violent among men than among women in every human society for which information exists (Daly and Wilson 1988).

Sperm competition   Although an important one, sexual dimorphism is not the only indicator of inter-male competition in a species, and thereby of its characteristic mating strategy. Another, only recently appreciated, is the relative size of the male's testes. A glance at figure 5.2 shows that the relative size of the testes to body weight in men, gorillas and chimpanzees reveals some interesting similarities and differences. It also indicates the average degree of sexual dimorphism in each species. As one might expect, gorillas, which are highly polygynous, show the highest degree of sexual dimorphism, but also the smallest relative testis size. Chimpanzees, by contrast, who are markedly less sexually dimorphic than are gorillas, have testes which are proportionately much larger (and, like those of gorillas, but unlike those of men, are largely retained within the body).

From the evidence of reduced sexual dimorphism we might conclude – correctly as it happens – that chimpanzees are nothing like as polygynous as gorillas. This is indeed the case because, although dominant adult males will pair off with a female during the period when she is likely to conceive, the generally much more fluid and variable nature of chimpanzee groups means that single males cannot monopolize entire harems of females as do gorillas. The consequence of this is that, because any one chimpanzee male cannot exclude all others from a female as can a gorilla, male chimpanzees must carry on the fight by other means than merely physical aggression and social dominance. This they do by means of *sperm competition*: letting their sex cells

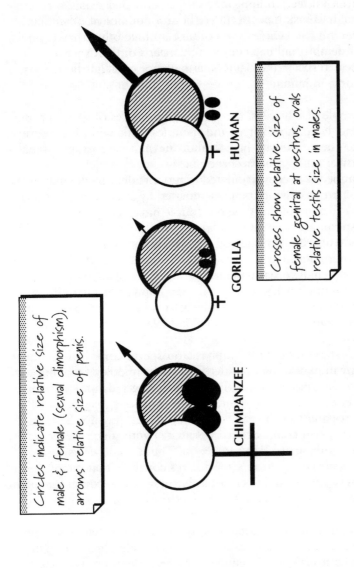

Figure 5.2 Sexual dimorphism, relative testis size and genital size in three primate species

Source: Modified and redrawn from Short 1979: 152–3

continue the struggle for greater reproductive success within the female's reproductive tract. Here, obviously, the male who deposits the largest quantity of sperm at the same time as others is likely to win, and so natural selection appears to have rewarded males with large testes. Similar effects have been found in a number of other species, such as grey whales, where males cannot exclude others from copulation with a female, but can compete by means of their sperm.

According to Baker and Bellis, sperm competition has been a major selective force in human evolution. They claim that:

- in a sample of 28 males, those with higher rates of sperm production ejaculated more often, and spent less time with their partner, who was more likely to be polyandrous than the partners of males with lower rates of sperm production;
- the number of sperm ejaculated is proportional to the risk of the female partner having been inseminated by another male as measured by the amount of time the couple have been apart;
- more sperm are ejaculated in larger females;
- masturbation in men is timed to increase the viability of sperm at the next copulation;
- timing of female orgasm determines number of sperm retained;
- sperm retention is higher in extra-pair copulations than in-pair;
- timing of masturbation in women affects likelihood of conception at next copulation (Baker and Bellis 1995).

However, Baker and Bellis's emphasis on sperm competition fails to explain why human testis size falls right in the middle of the range for ground-dwelling polygynous primates such as gelada and hamadryas baboons (both of whom are intensely polygynous), suggesting that, like the latter and like the gorilla, human males may not be as much adapted for sperm competition as primates with much larger testes, such as the chimpanzee (Dixson 1987). The latest reviews of the literature on sperm competition in primates conclude that relative testis size in man is modest and does not indicate strong selection for sperm competition (Gomendio et al. 1999; Dixson 1999).

Sexual bimaturism   This describes the tendency of females in polygynous species to mature sexually earlier than males. In a typical mammalian polygynous species, females mature earlier because their total lifetime reproductive success is critically dependent on the number of pregnancies they achieve in their reproductive lives, and therefore on its length. Since male reproductive success, by contrast, is dependent on how many females a male has access to in competition with other males, maturation may be slower if, as is usually the case, mature males compete better than younger ones, for example by virtue of being bigger or better armed.

Although the growth rates of girls and boys are almost identical in infancy and childhood, a noticeable difference occurs at about age ten, when girls start to grow faster than boys, achieving the maximum rate by age 12 and completing their growth by the age of 15. Boys, by contrast, do not start their growth spurt until two years later than girls, and do not achieve full growth until approximately 17–18. Four-fifths of the mean height difference of 10 cm between adult men and women is accounted for by the delayed onset of the growth spurt in boys which allows them a longer growing time, and only one-fifth by the increased magnitude of that growth (Short 1980).

Menopause   This is the term given to the cessation of the sexual cycle that normally occurs in modern human females round about age 50. The key evolutionary question is: why? After all, if reproductive success is the bottom line for evolution, why don't women see their fertility decline much more gradually with no obvious cut-off point like men do? This is especially puzzling because usually menopause occurs earlier than other impairments associated with ageing, such as heart failure, senile dementia or osteoporosis.

According to one view, menopause is simply an early effect of senescence. Genes that might promote reproductive success in early life but have adverse effects after most of an organism's reproductive period is over might not have been selected out, particularly if a large proportion of the population dies before that point is reached (see above, p. 20). In the case of men, for example, this is exactly what testosterone does (see box 1.1, 'Testosterone and fitness', pp. 8–9). Effects of ageing in general are almost certainly mainly to be accounted for this way, so why not menopause? However, this theory can't explain why female fertility ceases so abruptly compared to male fertility in our species.

A second theory holds that menopause evolved because a point might be reached where ancestral women's reproductive success later in life would be greater if, rather than risking further pregnancies of their own, they terminated their own fertile periods so as to be able to help daughters raise more grandchildren. Some anthropologists have claimed that the presence of grandmothers indeed promotes the survival of grandchildren in some hunter-gatherer societies. Lionesses tend to live long lives (thanks to having few other animals to fear), and typically live in matrilineal groups of mothers, sisters, and their daughters. Nevertheless, in their case reproductive cessation reduces an older female's ability to feed her grandchildren, because she needs to have a litter of her own to produce milk for them. Indeed, in both lions and baboons, fertility of females is constant for many years, but then shows a steep decline, and terminates before eventual death, much as it does in women. In neither species do 'menopausal' females promote the reproductive success of their daughters. In baboons, a living mother does not affect age of puberty, birth frequency, success of pregnancy or survival of offspring in their first year. In lions, litter size and survival of cubs in their first year are the same regardless of whether their grandmother is alive or dead.

However, the different degree of parental investment between the sexes may explain why fertility declines so steeply in mammals like lions, baboons and humans. In one baboon population, infants were much more likely to die if they were orphaned prior to their second birthday, and this may explain why a typical baboon female has an average life expectancy of about five years after the age of 21, at which point reproductive senescence first appears. In lions, maternal survival only matters during the first year of a cub's life, and from the age of about 14, when reproductive senescence first becomes really apparent, an average female has less than two years to live – but enough to raise her last cub. If these findings are reliable, they suggest that a similar effect may explain menopause in human females. But the period during which maternal survival would be critical for an offspring would be more like ten years, and this would explain the earlier onset of reproductive senescence in our species (Packer et al. 1998).

Concealed ovulation   Figure 5.2 above illustrates how much bigger a female chimpanzee's external genitalia get at the point in her cycle when she ovulates (*oestrus*) as compared to those of a woman. The reason for this massive genital engorgement in female chimpanzees is that it serves to advertise the time at which females are most likely to conceive, and to motivate males to mate with them then. Yet although closely related to chimpanzees in terms of evolutionary descent, modern women are totally unlike their chimpanzee sisters, not merely in not advertising the time at which they are going to ovulate and possibly conceive, but in actually hiding it so effectively that it was not until the 1930s that medical science definitely established when it occurred.

There are a number of different theories that attempt to explain concealed ovulation (cryptic oestrus) in human beings. According to one, in primitive societies (and, by implication, in primal ones) females attempted to control their childbearing activities in ways that are not biologically adaptive to themselves or to their spouses. As a result, natural selection countered this trend by suppressing cues of ovulation to the point where women themselves had no idea when it occurred, and as a result found it much more difficult to avoid conception (Burley 1979).

However, advertising or concealing the time of ovulation also has important implications for *certainty of paternity*: a male's ability to know if a female's offspring are his or not. Because females produce eggs which are either laid by them or give rise to offspring that are born from them, maternity is almost always certain. Paternity, however, depends on a microscopic sperm fertilizing a particular ovum inside the female's reproductive tract, and the origin of the sperm in question can be doubtful if a female has copulated with more than one male.

This fact has given rise to two other theories of cryptic oestrus in human beings, one emphasizing certainty and the other uncertainty of paternity. According to an influential theory first put forward by Richard Alexander and Katharine Noonan, cryptic oestrus evolved in humans because it enabled females to force desirable males into 'consort relationships' with them. They argue that a male who lacked any indication of when a female was about to ovulate would have to mate with her over a considerable span of the sexual cycle if he was to make her pregnant with his own offspring. The same effect would, they think, heighten a male's confidence that his female consort's offspring were indeed his because 'only a male who tended her more or less continuously could be sure of the paternity of her offspring' (Alexander and Noonan 1979).

However, you could turn the argument about certainty of paternity on its head and argue that advertisement of ovulation would increase certainty of paternity even more because a male who mated with the female at the critical time could be much more certain that the offspring were likely to be his. This way of looking at the matter is suggested by studies of polyandrously mated hedge sparrows which show that males allocate their investment in relation to the likelihood of offspring being theirs as a result of having had access to the female during the mating period, which DNA fingerprinting confirms is a good predictor of paternity (Burke 1989).

But according to another theory put forward by Sarah Hrdy, cryptic oestrus evolved in human beings because it ensured *uncertainty* rather than certainty of paternity. Vervet monkeys also conceal ovulation and females continue to copulate with males throughout the sexual cycle, and even halfway through pregnancy. Vervets mate promiscu-ously in groups of up to seven males and ten females, and this, com-bined with the long period of sexual activity by females, means that paternity is highly uncertain (Andelman 1987). The advantage as far as females is concerned is that their offspring are not as vulnerable to males as they might otherwise be. Clearly, males who are not the fa-thers of a female's offspring have no genetic incentive to value them, and often destroy them if, for example, they are preventing their mother from conceiving by being breast-fed. Single males who take over polygynous groups from other males in species such as langur mon-keys routinely murder all existing offspring, and continue to do so until it becomes likely that those being born are their own (see box 3.1 above, p. 75). Similar findings have been reported in a large number of other mammalian species and are not without a tragic human parallel (see above, pp. 87–8). In the light of such an infanticidal danger to their offspring, Hrdy believes that cryptic oestrus evolved in our spe-cies for the same reason as it appears to have done in vervets: as a defence against infanticide by males (Hrdy 1979).

Which of these theories is correct? A comparative analysis of 68 species of anthropoid primates revealed that almost a half also feature concealed ovulation, including one species of ape: the orang-utan. Sev-eral others, such as the gorilla, show only slight signs of oestrus. The remainder, 18 species out of a total of 68, advertise ovulation clearly in the way that chimpanzees do. However, no monogamous species advertises oestrus, and most have no visual ovulatory signs. Neverthe-less, although the preponderance of sexual swellings is found in multi-male species, ovulatory signs are also absent in many others. The species were also classified by mating system. If certainty of paternity is criti-cal for the evolution of cryptic oestrus, you would expect it to corre-late with uni-male mating, monogamy or polygyny; whereas if uncertainty of paternity is what drives the concealment of ovulation, it should go with multi-male mating systems, polyandry or polygamy/ promiscuity.The results show that monogamy, polygyny and multi-male breeding systems are associated with the absence of visible oe-strus, but in different ways. The researchers infer that signs of ovulation have disappeared many times in the evolution of multi-male breeders, but at the most once in a monogamous context, indirectly supporting Hrdy's paternity confusion theory (Sillén-Tullberg and Møller 1993).

If this is so, modern women conceal ovulation because their ances-tors ran a significant risk of having their children abused or killed by males who were not their fathers. Nevertheless, according to a recent critique, absence of signs of ovulation has been accorded too much significance in terms of sexual selection, and environmental and cultural factors may account for many of the findings, along with an increased reliance on sexual communication through a largely unconscious sense of smell (Pawlowski 1999).

Mating preferences

The largest study ever undertaken of human mating preferences covered all major religious, racial and ethnic groups in 37 samples drawn from 33 countries and surveyed 10,047 people in all. It found that in 36 out of the 37 samples, women place roughly twice as much value as men do on good financial prospects in a partner. But there are cultural variations: women in Nigeria, Zambia, India, Indonesia, Iran, Japan, Taiwan, Columbia and Venezuela value good financial prospects more than women from the Netherlands and Finland and among the Zulu in South Africa. In Japan, for example, women value financial prospects roughly 150 per cent more than men do, whereas women from the Netherlands do so only 36 per cent more. The one exception is Spain, which showed the predicted direction of the sex difference, but not significantly so (Buss 1997). According to David Buss, who carried out this research:

> These findings provide the first extensive cross-cultural evidence supporting the evolutionary basis for the psychology of human mating. Because ancestral women faced the tremendous burdens of internal fertilization, a nine-month gestation, and lactation, they would have benefited tremendously by selecting mates who possessed resources. These preferences helped our ancestral mothers solve the adaptive problems of survival and reproduction. (Buss 1994: 25)

Evolutionary theory predicts characteristic age differences between an individual and their mate because youthfulness will be more critical to the reproductive success of a woman than to that of a man. As we saw above, the length of fertile life has much more bearing on a woman's ultimate reproductive success than on a man's. For example, a man with ten wives for just one year could have the same reproductive success (ten children) as a woman with ten husbands could manage in ten years (assuming one child per year for ten years). Female fertility peaks at about age 25, and the study found that the preferred age of a female mate was approximately 25 years across the 37 samples. Males were found to prefer a mean age seniority for themselves over their mates of 2.66 years, whereas females preferred a larger age difference: 3.32 years seniority in males. Overall, these sex differences were statistically the most significant found in the study (above the 0.0001 level in each of the 37 samples). However, age preferences varied strikingly between the samples, with polygynous cultures showing the greatest age differences in preferences, but always in the predicted directions. If actual age differences at marriage are compared with these preferences, differences range from 2.17 years (Ireland) to 4.92 years (Greece) in 27 countries sampled. The preferred average age difference was 3.04 years, which compares with a difference of 2.99 years in actual average differences between husband and wives (Buss 1997). Nevertheless, the issue is a complex one, and not all data have such a clear fit to the model presented by Buss (Davis 1998; for a discussion see Kenrick and Keefe 1992).

Consistent with these findings is the fact that men rate youthfulness, physical attractiveness and healthiness more highly than women do in their preferences for a mate. Women, by contrast, rate wealth, industriousness and ambition as more important in a potential mate than do men. Both sexes rate intelligence and attractive personality roughly equally (Buss 1994).

Predicted sex differences are also found in sexual fantasy

You could argue that sexual fantasy provides a unique insight into evolved human sexual psychology simply because it is not constrained by reality. Being largely internally generated, you could see fantasy as reflecting the innate tendencies of the mind where sex is concerned, rather than reacting to the external environment. Evolutionary psychology would predict important differences between the sexes, which ought to be reflected in fantasy. For example, with millions of sex cells at his disposal, and with little or no obligatory parental contribution after fertilization, a human male

- should be much less discriminating in his choice of fantasized sex object;
- should take a much more superficial view of it;
- should be much more easily and more frequently aroused;
- should play a more active role in his fantasy than a woman.

Studies of sexual fantasy confirm that this is so. Men are more likely than women to have sexual fantasies, and are more likely to be physically aroused by them. American teenage boys are nearly twice as likely to fantasize about sex than girls. Other studies in the US, Great Britain and Japan indicate twice as much sexual fantasy in men compared to women in the same countries, while other studies show that men are more likely to have explicitly sexual dreams. Men's fantasies treat others as objects of sexual arousal, whereas women are more likely to view themselves as objects of other's desire, and to find the situation arousing. Although passive fantasies are found in both sexes, they are more common in women. Women's fantasies have been found to contain more affection and commitment, and are more likely to emphasize themes of tenderness and emotion. Male fantasies, by contrast, are more explicitly sexual, more concerned with the sexual organs, and more likely to involve more partners. A recent survey concludes that male sexual fantasies tend to be more ubiquitous, frequent, visual, specifically sexual, promiscuous and active. Female sexual fantasies tend to be more contextual, emotive, intimate and passive – just as theory would predict (B. J. Ellis and Symons 1997).

Because paternity is much less certain than maternity, but can still be critical to a man's reproductive success, men should be more concerned with the biological details of insemination than women, who should instead be more concerned with a man's level of emotional commitment. This difference is reflected in jealousy, where men are much more disturbed by the physical details of their partner's activity with another male than are women in the corresponding situation. Women, by contrast, are much more disturbed by the emotional dimension of infidelity and its implications about their partner's feelings for them (Daly et al. 1982).

Sex, scent and the selfish gene

Despite the tendency of evolutionary psychologists to ignore him (see above pp. 129–32), Sigmund Freud strikingly anticipated the most fundamental and important aspect of the modern evolutionary view of sex when he observed that

> The individual himself regards sexuality as one of his own ends; whereas from another point of view he is an appendage to his germ-plasm, at whose disposal he puts his energies in return for a bonus of pleasure. He is the mortal vehicle of a (possibly) immortal substance – like the inheritor of an entailed property, who is only the temporary holder of an estate that survives him. (Freud 1957a: 78)

It is notable that Freud's English translators use the very term 'vehicle' that Richard Dawkins, author of *The Selfish Gene*, was to adopt 60-odd years later to describe the view of the organism as little more than the temporary repository of its DNA (see above pp. 54–5). As David Barash pointed out in an early work on evolutionary psychology: 'much of being human consists of contributing to the success of our genes just as being a kangaroo, or even a dandelion involves contributing to the success of kangaroo and dandelion genes. Freud was right: much of our behavior has to do with sex' (Barash 1979: 40).

One important way in which an organism can contribute to the success of its genes is to ensure that they are teemed up with the right partners in sexual reproduction. Although the evolutionary origins and rationale of sex are still not completely understood, much evidence supports the so-called Red Queen theory (named after the Red Queen in Lewis Carroll's *Through the Looking Glass*, who had to keep running to stay in the same place). This holds that sex evolved to promote genetic diversity in offspring challenged by disease micro-organisms which could evolve much more quickly than their hosts. Given that complex organisms like human beings have generation times measured in decades but that many of the pathogens that attack them produce new generations in minutes, hours or days, it follows that such parasites have a major advantage in the evolutionary arms race that they run with their victims. Sex can redress the balance to the extent that it produces genetically unique individuals in each and every generation, so that pathogens seldom if ever encounter exactly the same adversary twice (Hamilton and Zuk 1989; Ridley 1993).

The *major histocompatibility complex*, or MHC for short, is part of the genome that contains the genes for the recognition molecules that the immune system uses to distinguish self from alien, and so plays a key role in the immunological response to pathogens. Mice who are genetically identical save in their MHC genes can be distinguished by other mice, despite an outward appearance of being clones. Indeed, a single mutation in just one gene is enough to make a difference: the clue lies in a smell that can be detected in the mouse's urine (J. L. Brown and Eklund 1994). Even more significantly, mice who have been infected by a protozoan parasite (as compared to those who have not) are discriminated against by female mice, again on the evidence of nothing other than the smell of their urine (Kavaliers and Colwell 1995).

Such subtle genetic discrimination is not limited to mice. Human beings can detect difference in MHC genes in mice from the smell of their urine just as easily as mice themselves can. This not only shows that the human nose has a highly rated power of discrimination, it also proves that very minor genetic differences are discernible to it (Stoddart 1990).

For women, smell is the most important factor in sexual attraction

Further evidence that human beings can accurately detect small genetic differences was found by Wedekind, who invited women to rate the attractiveness of the smell of T-shirts worn by men for 48 hours. He compared the MHC of the men and the women, and found that women preferred the smell of men with the most dissimilar MHC genes to their own, just as the Red Queen theory would predict. Further force was given to this interpretation by the finding that women taking the contraceptive pill preferred the smell of shirts worn by men with the most similar MHC genes to themselves. The contraceptive pill works by mimicking pregnancy, and suggests that women taking it were reacting as they would if pregnant, when it is help and resources they need from men, rather than simply genes. As we saw in an earlier chapter, genetic relatedness encourages altruism and co-operation, probably explaining the finding (see above, pp. 79–88). The fact that both types of attraction were found, that MHC composition was critical to both, and that they work in opposite directions suggests that the effect is real and that women can indeed assess the genetic status of potential mates simply by smell (Wedekind et al. 1995; Wedekind and Füri 1997). Indeed, mice show the same preference: when given the choice, female mice prefer to mate with genetically dissimilar individuals but, when nest-building, prefer to work with relatives (Grafen 1992).

Other studies suggest that women rate a man's personal odour as most important in their estimation of his sexual attractiveness, but that men rate a woman's smell equally with her appearance. Additionally – and quite unlike men – women singled out body odour from other sensations as the most offputting when considering sexual activity. To the extent that you could interpret these findings as indicating that women are more selective than men, they nicely fit evolutionary theory: as we have seen, a woman has much more to lose by the wrong choice of a mate than a man normally has thanks to the reduced variance of female as compared to male reproductive success (Herz and Cahill 1997).

Taken together, these findings suggest that ultimately what matters most to both sexes in the choice of a mate – but especially to women – is not age, wealth or social standing, but more subjective feelings of sexual attraction. Although poets, lovers and psychoanalysts have always known this, it is only recently that the genetic basis of this universal fact has become known: not only are we the vehicles of our genes, we appear to be their epigenetic agents where finding a mate is concerned and our expertise evidently extends to invisible but critical genetic differences discriminated by our sense of smell.

Sex ratios

Because every future individual in a sexually reproducing species must have one mother and one father, it follows that if parents do not know who those mothers and fathers are likely to be, production of equal numbers of male and female offspring is the best strategy. Furthermore, this will even be true if the mating arrangements are not monogamous. Even in a species where, for example, only one in ten males may mate, each male who does mate is worth exactly ten times more to its parents' ultimate reproductive success than the nine who do not. As long as the parents have no way of knowing which particular males are likely to be particularly reproductively successful, they ought to invest in equal numbers of males and females irrespective of the actual outcome. Essentially, the situation is rather like producing nuts and bolts. Assuming that every nut needs exactly one bolt, and every bolt one nut, manufacturers should aim to produce equal quantities of both, because any that produced an excess of one or the other would not be able to sell them.

But one respect in which all other things may not be equal is the relative cost to the parents of producing the sexes. Whereas it might seem obvious to engineers that every bolt needs a nut, and that therefore equal numbers should be produced, accountants might point out that, if there is a difference in cost in producing nuts and bolts, and if profits are proportional to costs, production should be set to maximize profit, not necessarily to equalize the number of nuts and bolts.

If the cost of producing one sex is significantly different from that of producing the other, an analogous argument applies where parental investment is concerned, and here the equivalent of profit would be the return in terms of reproductive success per unit of parental investment. Suppose that a male costs twice as much to produce as a female, but that there is a 1:1 sex ratio. In this case, parents will find that the return on parental investment in males is only half that of females.

However, parents who produced more females would find that their reproductive success per unit of parental investment increased because they could produce two females for the cost of every male. Only when there were on average two females for every male in the breeding population would the incentive to produce extra females disappear, and the sex ratio would stabilize at 1:2 males to females (R. A. Fisher 1930).

An increasing number of empirical studies of birds, mammals and humans have endorsed the basic prediction that sex ratios should stabilize where parental investment in each sex is broadly equal. For example, an analysis of 14,420 births in 21 parishes in Finland between 1775 and 1850 revealed that more sons were indeed produced when males were rarer than females. This shows that human beings do indeed adjust the sex ratio of their offspring in response to local inequalities in order to maximize the reproductive success of their progeny. The research also suggests that a biased sex ratio in these parishes led to a decreased birth-rate and thus, presumably, to a lowered population growth rate. This in turn emphasizes the fundamental insight that, where setting the sex ratio is concerned, selection is acting at the level of individual parents, rather than favouring the interests of the population as a whole (see above, pp. 74–6) (Lummaa et al. 1998).

The exceptions prove the Trivers–Willard rule

However, if parents could predict the likely future reproductive success of individual offspring, the situation would be quite different. All that would be necessary is that mutations which favoured the correct choice of sex allocation would be reproductively successful, irrespective of what the exact mechanism might be.

A study of an isolated population of red deer on the Scottish island of Rum showed that the social status of mothers was strongly reflected in the sex ratio of their offspring: the highest ranking females produced about 70 per cent males as compared to the lowest ranking females' 30 per cent. Yet, lower ranking females nevertheless managed a higher survival rate for their female offspring than did those at the top. Red deer are a highly polygynous species, with stark differences in the reproductive success of males, as well as in that of males compared to females. In the population in question, for example, half the offspring were sired by only 12 per cent of the males. The consequence is that a female's ultimate reproductive success is likely to be greater if she invests preferentially in males who are going to enjoy high reproductive success themselves. Females who have high social status also command the best resources for parental investment in terms of access to food, and are themselves likely to be relatively more able to bear the additional costs which male offspring impose. Low status females, by contrast, ought to do the exact opposite and invest preferentially in female offspring since, unlike males, all females in a polygynous mating system will tend to be mated and most will enjoy some degree of reproductive success, albeit always more modest than that of the most successful males (Clutton-Brock et al. 1982). A similar situation has been described in roe deer (Wauters et al. 1995).

A number of species of insect also seem to act in conformity with theory in this respect. In the case of many bees and wasps, females are the larger sex because larger size means increased capacity to produce eggs. Larger adult body size is a function of feeding during development, and often the mother provides this in the form of a food supply immured with the eggs in a burrow or brood cell, or provided as a dead or immobilized host in which the parasite's eggs are laid. In the latter case, it is the size of the host which usually correlates with the sex ratio, and in that of some parasitic wasps, females will lay eggs with a strong male sex bias if the host in question has already been parasitized, but with a marked female-biased one if it has not. Such cases as these leave little doubt that where offspring sex can be manipulated, selection will produce parents able to do so in accordance with their ultimate reproductive self-interest.

Differential parental investment according to offspring sex is a consequence, then, of the fundamental inequality of the sexes which stems ultimately from the differences in the size of their sex cells. Trivers and Willard pointed out that because male reproductive success usually varies more than that of females, parents who have some way of reliably predicting the likely reproductive success of offspring should be selected to invest in males if the prospects are good, but in females if they are poor (Trivers and Willard 1973).

One of the most striking experimental confirmations of this prediction comes from studies of zebra finches, a desert-living species suitable for laboratory work because they will breed whenever sufficient food is available. An observant experimenter noticed that the coloured leg-tags used to identify individual birds seemed to affect their mating success. Red leg-tags promoted the attractiveness of males to females, whereas green reduced it. In the case of females, by contrast, black tags were preferred to red by males. But experiment showed that if either parent had had their attractiveness to the opposite sex artificially enhanced in this way, the sex ratio of that pair's offspring was

Box 5.4

Does the mother determine a child's sex?

According to the maternal dominance hypothesis (Grant 1998), the sex of an infant may be under the control of the mother through the hormones of reproduction. These hormones in turn appear to provide the biological basis for the personality trait known as *dominance*. This is one of the few personality measures that humans share with animals. Women whose scores on measures of dominance are in the top 20% are five times more likely to conceive sons than are women at the other end of the scale. Although the mechanism that brings this about is still unknown, the maternal dominance hypothesis suggests that individual differences in the female reproductive system may make it easier for either an X or Y chromosome-bearing sperm to fertilize an ovum. The theory is that the same hormonal influences that regulate reproductive processes and increase chances of an X or Y sperm fertilizing an ovum also provide the biological basis for a woman's personality, and influence the ways in which she responds to her social environment. At present, most scientific evidence supports the idea that testosterone is the relevant hormone, even though it is present in women in only tiny amounts. Individual differences between women in the amount of testosterone appear to underlie the potential both to behave in a dominant way and to conceive sons.

The evolutionary background to this hypothesis may be found in Trivers and Willard's suggestion that (all other things being equal) parents should produce male offspring when prospects for those offsprings' reproductive success are good, and female when they are poor (Trivers and Willard 1973). The maternal dominance hypothesis holds that since animals high in dominance rank have priority access to the best food and mates, rank ordering animals for dominance would be equivalent to rank ordering them for the likely reproductive success of their offspring. Several research teams have found that high-ranking females do indeed produce significantly more male offspring than female ones and that the sex ratio of offspring is related to maternal dominance rank. Because dominance makes men sexually attractive to women, but only half of males find dominance attractive in females, it could pay a dominant woman to pass on her dominance to sons, rather than to daughters. The maternal dominance hypothesis also explains why more boys than girls tend to be born in times of stress, such as famines, epidemics and wars. This comes about, according to this theory, because women respond to stress by producing more testosterone, which in turn predisposes them to giving birth to more sons.

More than a dozen developmental psychologists have found that mothers of male infants take the initiative more and are more active with their babies than mothers of girls, who are gentler and more responsive. This suggests that not only may dominant women conceive more sons, but those sons may be more frequently exposed to the interactive style of such mothers, making them more likely to be dominant in their turn. Because dominance in men has a number of positive effects on their reproductive success, it would clearly be wrong to conclude that styles of child-rearing were purely cultural, or that they could not be subject to selection. Ironically, it may be women themselves, by their very nature, who maintain psychosexual sex differences.

biased towards males. Correspondingly, a female bias among offspring was found when one of the pair was of artificially reduced attractiveness. Comparable effects have been reported in guppies fed a high protein diet and in wild populations of American opossums whose food supply was experimentally manipulated. Female wood rats fed a substandard diet preferentially nurse daughters, bringing about death by starvation in their sons (Trivers 1985). (See box 5.4, 'Does the mother determine a child's sex?')

Sex discrimination, abortion and infanticide in humans

In human beings, the unprecedented length of childhood dependency on parental investment and the high degree of that investment may well result in parents manipulating both their children's survival in general, and the survival of children of a particular sex.

One of the most extreme examples of the way in which sex may affect child survival is female infanticide in nineteenth-century India. A study by Mildred Dickemann showed that in some Rajput castes almost all newborn females perished. For example, early in the nineteenth century, in spite of public renunciations of female infanticide by chiefs, and in spite of public meetings and cash awards to fathers of daughters, only 20 females could be identified in one subcaste census. A few years later only 63 females (of whom all but three had been born after the initiation of the anti-infanticide campaign) could be found in an area whose population at the time must have been at least 4–5,000. Even as late as 1840, and with the inclusion of new districts in the census, a sex ratio of 420 males to every 100 females was reported. That such an enormous preponderance of males was not natural is proved by the fact that although the ratio for children under one year of age was still 225:100 males to females, at birth there was parity, 1:1. Nor were these figures exceptional. Subsequent inquiries uncovered the practice in numerous castes in Northern India, including Brahmins, Rajputs, Khatris, Jats, Gujars, Ahirs, Sikhs and Muslims, as well as in some tribal groups.

How are such extraordinary facts as these to be explained? Two factors in particular seem to be important. First, these were societies in which subcastes were both ranked in terms of social stratification and were exogamous. In other words, women had to marry out of their natal subcaste into one of different status. Secondly, women were meant to marry into a higher status group (*hypergyny*), and were expected to provide a payment (or dowry) to their husband for the privilege of doing so. As a consequence, female infanticide was positively correlated with social status, so that those at the bottom of the status hierarchy practised little or no female infanticide, while those at the top often destroyed all their females at birth. With less incentive to export females to superior groups and to pay dowries for the privilege of doing so, but much more incentive to acquire dowry-bringing daughters-in-law from lower castes, higher castes did the obvious thing and reduced their production of daughters, evidently sometimes to very near zero. The fact that these infanticidal castes were primarily dominant military elites in a feudal structure which had imposed their rule through conquest perhaps explains a great deal about how the system got going and how it was maintained, at least until the British tried to eradicate it (Dickemann 1979).

However, female infanticide was by no means confined to the nineteenth century. Data collected in an Indian hospital quite recently show, for instance, that of 92 pregnant women who had their amniotic fluid tested to determine the sex of the foetus, every female foetus was aborted and every male retained, even when the test also showed that there was a chance of a genetic defect in the male. In another hospital, 430 out of 450 women who were informed that they were carrying a daughter (95.5 per cent) had the foetus aborted. Again, every single one of 250 women who were diagnosed as carrying a son took the pregnancy to term, despite advice in some cases that the child was probably suffering from a genetic defect (Ramanamma and Bambawale 1980). Furthermore, female infanticide has not been confined to the Indian subcontinent. Dickemann quotes figures from traditional China showing childhood sex ratios of 430:100 and adult ratios of 2:1 males to females as late as the 1870s. She adds that infanticide is now known to have been practised in Europe from ancient times down to the late nineteenth century and that medieval British data show adult sex ratios as high as 133:100 (Dickemann 1979).

Historical data from a parish in Schleswig-Holstein suggest that preferential parental investment both in males and in females can sometimes be discovered. The parish in question was nothing like so highly stratified as the Indian castes, but did show a status gradient from wealthier farmers at the top to unpropertied farm labourers and tradesmen at the bottom. As evolutionary theory would predict, the lowest rate of male infant mortality and the highest rate of female infant mortality occurred among the highest social class, the farmers. As in the Indian castes, purely economic factors could not explain why daughters of the lowest social class survived better than those at the top, whereas sons survived worse. If child survival were purely an effect of affluence, one would expect children of both sexes to fare better at the top of the social scale and both to do worse at the bottom. The fact that the data in question show that they did not, but that a sex-specific effect of differential valuation appeared to apply in both cases, strongly argues that parental care and neglect may have been the operative factors. This is the most likely explanation of the discrepancy in rates of survival which the study found if deaths during the first 27 days of life were ignored. Figures for survival between day 28 and day 180 of an infant's life showed that just under 7 per cent of both girls at the top and boys at the bottom of the social scale died during this period, whereas the corresponding figure for their opposite-sex siblings was almost exactly 4 per cent in each case (Voland 1988).

A study of 1,314 Mormon women married to men born between 1821 and 1830 who emigrated to Utah before June 1851 is particularly significant as a test of the Trivers–Willard prediction because they were married at a time when polygyny was legal and because the population exhibited childbearing patterns suggesting uninhibited natural fertility. Another factor is the high reliability of Mormon demographic data, said to be superior to that obtainable from most historical records. The women belonged to 733 households that included up to 12 wives, with 39 per cent of households being polygynous at some time. The number of children per woman ranged from none to 18, with a mean of 7.3. At the time, men could hold one of five ranks in the church hierarchy, which were positively correlated with economic standing. Wives of men of the highest rank showed a significant bias towards male children compared to the overall sex ratio of the population. The effect was found when the analysis featured both the highest rank a woman's husband ever achieved and his rank at the time of the birth of a child. Although the study failed to identify the proximate cause of the sex ratio biases observed, it concluded that they are in line with the predictions of the Trivers–Willard model. Women of differing social status do bias the sex ratio of their offspring in a way that is consistent with maximization of reproductive fitness. Women of higher status produced relatively more sons that did women of lower status. (Mealey and Mackey 1990)

Parental favouritism towards daughters is much less widely documented than favouritism towards sons, but one particularly illuminating case has been recorded. The Mukogodo of central Kenya were once cave-dwelling hunters and gatherers, but have recently moved into sheep and goat herding. A birth census showed a clear excess of girls: in one year 32 girls but only 13 boys were born, and 98 girls but only 66 boys were found less than five years old. The explanation appears to be that the Mukogodo acquired the animals on which they now rely as bridewealths paid to them on the marriage of their daughters to men from wealthier neighbouring groups of pastoralists, such as the Samburu. Nevertheless, they have remained as the poorest group, so that Mukogodo men find it hard to raise the bridewealths necessary to marry, and a stigma attaches to them as a result.

As Lee Cronk, the ethnographer, points out, the Mukogodo case clearly fits the Trivers–Willard prediction that parents ought to invest preferentially in daughters in poor conditions. Although there is little evidence of male infanticide, Cronk found several cases where male children had died or suffered continuing illness because of the reluctance of their parents to take them to a dispensary or clinic. There was, however, a clear and statistically significant tendency for the Mukogodo to take daughters more often than sons for medical care when it was necessary; but no such discrimination against sons was shown by other ethnic groups in the area. For the Mukogodo, taking a child to a dispensary or clinic is a major expenditure of cash, time and effort. Mukogodo mothers also tend to breast-feed their daughters longer than their sons, and within the same family girls are often visibly better fed, healthier and happier than their brothers. Cronk suggests that similar facts may explain why Cheyenne Indians of nineteenth-century America, divided into high status 'peace bands' and lower status 'war bands', showed a female-biased sex ratio in the latter. Another example is the Kanjar people of Pakistan, who present one of the clearest cases of sex-role reversal thanks to the fact that women tend to dominate the society and earn most of the income from itinerant dancing, trading and prostitution (Cronk 1993). Yet another is Hungarian gypsies, who also invest more in daughters than in sons as measured by the duration of breast-feeding, interbirth interval and extent of secondary education. However, relatively wealthier native Hungarians invest preferentially in sons (Bereczkei and Dunbar 1997).

Trivers–Willard effects also have a cultural dimension

Fascinating findings are provided by a study of 3,700 members of the Portuguese nobility who were born between 1380 and 1580 and for whom remarkably detailed information regarding birth, death, marriage, fecundity, inheritance and even illegitimacy and concubinage has been preserved and recently analysed. Our basic theory would lead us to predict that the effect of differential parental investment according to sex and social status found among the relatively lowly farmers of the German parish discussed earlier (p. 184) would be amplified among the nobility of a highly stratified society like fifteenth- and sixteenth-century Portugal. This is because we would expect wealth and social standing to be an important factor in promoting the reproductive success of the sons of noble families, and this is precisely what we do find. But it is also interesting to note that a difference in total reproductive success could even be found between the higher as compared to the lower nobles, and that it was accounted for by the addition of illegitimate rather than legitimate offspring. For titled males as a whole, the number of serial marriages was a major factor in their overall reproductive success, and the probability of marrying more than once increased considerably with status.

As far as women were concerned, marriage to higher status males enhanced their reproductive success, and although, as basic theory would lead us to predict, the range of reproductive success was less for females overall, low status females nevertheless outreproduced low status males. Clear evidence was found that parental investment in girls was greater among the lower nobility than among the higher, with daughters of the lower nobility being more likely to marry than their brothers. It was also found that the probability of daughters of the lower nobility ever marrying also exceeded that of women of the higher nobility ever marrying. Since brides had to provide a dowry, enhanced parental investment in daughters was both significant and obvious among the lesser nobility as a result.

If women married more than men at the lower end of the social scale, despite having to provide dowries, then at the top men married more than women, with the surplus daughters tending to be sent to convents, rather as surplus sons in the case of the lower nobility were sent off to the wars, the colonies, or the church. Parental investment was concentrated in males at the top of the social scale by the means of inheritance through the male line and further by the practice of primogeniture, which gave priority to the eldest son (with excess sons always being a valuable back-up in an age of high infant and child mortality). Whereas dowries tended to represent modest, moveable wealth (often preferentially invested in the eldest daughter), male inheritances of the upper nobility tended to be much more substantial and to be in the form of landed estates and feudal rights. This meant that the more modest wealth of the lower nobility could be invested in marrying a daughter into a higher status family. Indeed, it may actually have had a higher reproductive value than the estate inherited by the son, again making preferential parental investment in daughters the natural choice among the lower nobility (Boone 1988).

However, it should not be assumed that Trivers–Willard effects can only be found in premodern, pre-industrial societies with traditional sex roles. On the contrary, a recent study of 906 mothers in the US showed a moderate Trivers–Willard effect. The study assumed that mothers with a larger available household income and with a co-resident male were in a position to make a greater parental investment in their children than those with the contrary indications. Longer interbirth interval was taken to indicate greater parental investment by the mother in the child subsequently conceived, and so was the duration of breastfeeding. The study found that mothers were more likely to nurse daughters in low income households, but were more likely to nurse sons in high income ones. Similarly, the interval was longer before the birth of a girl in a low income household, while it was longer before that of a boy in a high income one. For both these variables, there was more investment in daughters in poor conditions, and more investment in sons by mothers in good conditions. In addition, the duration of breastfeeding was longer for girls in households without an adult male but longer for boys in households with such a male in residence.

The authors emphasize that their findings do not indicate a simple sex bias in maternal investment: for example a tendency to invest in sons. On the contrary, their results indicate a sex bias that reversed at the extremes of the mothers' conditions, regardless of how these were measured. In accordance with the Trivers–Willard rule, this study found that mothers in poor conditions invested preferentially in daughters, while mothers in good conditions invested preferentially in sons. The authors insist that 'No simple model of sexist behavior can explain these findings' (Gaulin and Robbins 1991).

Suggestions for further reading

Betzig, L. (ed.) (1997)   *Human Nature: A Critical Reader.*
Buss, D. M. (1994)   *The Evolution of Desire: Strategies of Human Mating.*
Diamond, J. (1997)   *Why is Sex Fun? The Evolution of Human Sexuality.*
Fisher, H. (1992)   *The Anatomy of Love.*
Grant, V. J. (1998)   *Maternal Personality, Evolution and the Sex Ratio: Do Mothers Control the Sex of the Infant?*
Trivers, R. L. (1972)   Parental investment and sexual selection. In *Sexual Selection and the Descent of Man 1871–1971*, ed. B. Campbell.

6

Growth, Development and Conflict

Sex has a further consequence for evolutionary psychology that we have not yet considered. This is the fact that it creates offspring who are not clones of their parents. If offspring are not genetically identical to each other or to their parents, evolutionary conflicts of interest can arise because of the resulting genetic differences. This in turn means that co-operation between offspring and parents may be compromised by the resulting conflicts, particularly where the allocation of parental investment is concerned. Further conflict is likely if mating deviates from strict lifetime monogamy because, whereas a mother will always be related to all her offspring, a particular father might only be related to one or some of them (Haig 1999). In this chapter I shall review the basic theory of parent–offspring conflict and introduce some remarkable new findings that have extended it considerably. As we shall see in this and the concluding chapter, these discoveries have far-reaching significance for evolutionary psychology.

Parent–offspring conflict

From the point of view of the mother's genes, any child is a vehicle for half of them (see above, pp. 83–4). This means that a sacrifice by one child that confers a net benefit on another is worthwhile as far as her genes are concerned. The same could apply to the father. Half of his genes may also be invested in each child. Suppose that an elder child has a food item that it wishes to eat, but which a younger child also wants. The interests of the parents' genes are best served by them intervening and demanding that the elder gives it to the younger if there is any net benefit as a result. If the younger is smaller than the elder, as it usually will be, and if the item cannot be partitioned, it will almost certainly confer a greater benefit on the younger, merely because the younger has more growth to accomplish and because the item will make a proportionately larger contribution to it. So in this case the parents ought to transfer the food item to the younger child, despite the protests of the elder one.

At first sight you might think that even if we adopt the seemingly highly artificial view of looking at things from the point of view of an individual's genes, children and parents would agree about this. This is because siblings share the same proportion of genes with each other that parents do with them: one half. However, things are not so simple. The reason parents and children will not agree is that we are considering sacrifices by their children for one another, not parents' sacrifices for their children. As far as parents are concerned, any sacrifice by one of their children where the benefit to another of their children exceeds the cost is good news. This is because the parent has an equal number of genes invested in each child. So, on average and all other things being equal, a net benefit to one child at a cost to another is an overall benefit to the parents' genes invested in those children.

Reverting to the mathematical terms and definitions we used earlier, you could say that parents are selected to wish offspring to perform an act of altruism wherever $B>C$ (and B is the benefit to the gene for altruism in the recipient, while C is the cost to the identical copy in the altruist: see above, pp. 79–84). Suppose that a situation exists where one child might sacrifice itself to save other children with the same parents. From the point of view of the parents' genes, any child of theirs that sacrifices its life to save at least two other children will have conferred a net benefit (on average, all other things being equal). Fifty per cent of each parent's genes will have been lost in the child that sacrifices itself, but 100 per cent will have been saved in the two that survive as a result because each of them also contains 50 per cent of the parent's genes ($B>C$, see figure 6.1).

But now consider the same situation from the point of view of a gene in a child being asked to sacrifice itself to save brothers and sisters. If average relatedness between children with identical parents is a half or 50 per cent, the genes in the child contemplating the sacrifice will not be selected if they allow themselves to be lost for less than three siblings. This is because two siblings will amount to 100 per cent of the gene, an identical amount to that being sacrificed. So sacrificing itself for just two siblings confers no net benefit on the survival prospects of the gene. However, saving more than two is worth it, because

Figure 6.1 How parents and offspring disagree about self-sacrifice to save siblings

that way 100 per cent of the gene is lost in the sacrifice, but 150 per cent of it is saved in three siblings in each of whom it has a 50 per cent chance of being found. In other words, whereas parents are selected to want acts of altruism between offspring wherever $B>C$, offspring themselves apply Hamilton's inequality and only agree if $Br>C$, where r is the coefficient of relatedness (see above, box 3.3, p. 83, and figure 6.1). We can conclude that (on average, all other things being equal) parents will be selected to prefer twice as much co-operation among their children (or half as much selfishness, which comes to the same thing) as their children will be selected to prefer (Trivers 1974).

Maternal and paternal genes may be in conflict over the offspring's behaviour towards siblings

Maternal genes are certain to be present in all a woman's children, whereas paternal genes need not be paired with those from the same mother if a man mates with another woman. For a paternal gene, the 50 per cent chance that it is present in a sibling must be further discounted by the degree to which the brothers and/or sisters concerned share the same father. If they do indeed have the same father, their relatedness is 50 per cent, just as it is for a maternal gene in children of the same mother. However, if two siblings have different fathers, then the relatedness between a paternal gene in one and a paternal gene in the other is zero. If relatedness is zero, there is no situation in which a paternal gene in one would benefit from making any kind of sacrifice for the other – unlike the maternal gene in the same children. Conflict between maternal and paternal genes in such siblings would be maximized, and conflict between the wishes of the mother as to how her children should behave to one another and how their paternal genes would have them behave would be even more extreme. The mother would favour any sacrifice by one that conferred a net benefit on the other, no matter how small, simply because she has the same proportion of her genes invested in both. The paternal genes of paternally unrelated children (and those in the fathers they came from) would not favour any kind of sacrifice whatsoever because they are only present in one of the parties, and so could take a wholly selfish view.[1]

Genomic imprinting

Until quite recently such a conclusion as this would have seemed completely academic, because everyone thought that genes on 22 of the 23 pairs of chromosomes in a human being were indifferent to which parent bequeathed them because there was no way that they could be labelled (the exception, as we have seen, is the one pair of sex chromosomes: see above pp. 45–9). Furthermore, there seemed no reason why they should be, because a gene that a man had inherited from his mother he might pass on to his children as their father. Similarly, a gene a woman inherited from her father she would have to pass on to her children as their mother. So the same gene could be paternal in one generation, but maternal in the next, and vice versa. Indeed, the way that genes are shuffled each generation so that the single set that individuals pass on in their sex cells is a combination of the two sets that they inherited from their parents seemed to mean that the parent-of-origin was completely irrelevant to genes because they were being randomized in this respect every generation. In other words, any non-sex chromosome gene that a person transmits to an offspring in a sperm or egg cell might just as well have come from that person's mother or father.

However, today we know that although this remains true as far as the inheritance of genes is concerned, it is not the case if we consider a gene's expression. Here, surprisingly, there are differences in the way that genes are expressed which reflect which parent they came from. Some genes have been found to be expressed when they are inherited from one parent, but not when they come from the other. This effect is known as *genomic imprinting* (Ohlsson et al. 1995; Reik and Surani 1997).

An imprinted gene is expressed when inherited from one parent but is not expressed when inherited from the other. A gene that is expressed only when inherited from the father is said to be *paternally active* because it is the paternal copy only that is expressed, thanks to its maternal equivalent being imprinted. Similarly, a gene corresponding to a paternally imprinted one that is expressed only when inherited from the mother is termed *maternally active*. In other words, the imprints on genes are reset each generation, and a gene that is maternally imprinted in a male will be paternally imprinted when that male passes it on to his children, and vice versa.

At the time of writing, approximately 40 imprinted genes had been described in mice and humans. Current estimates put the total number of imprinted genes in mammals somewhere between 100 and 200, but no one knows for sure how many there may actually be (Falls et al. 1999). Most imprinted genes could be thought of as master control genes, which regulate many others downstream of them in the developmental cascade. For example, some produce growth factors which have effects throughout the organism and are expressed early in development, often with permanent consequences (Barlow 1995; John and Surani 1996).

IGF2 is a case in point. This gene produces the insulin-like growth

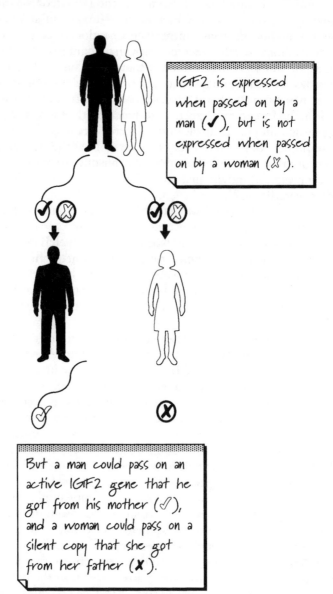

Figure 6.2 *IGF2*

factor number 2. Its effect is to stimulate the growth of the embryo. Its absence in mice results in pups that are 40 per cent smaller at birth than normal, but otherwise normally proportioned. In mice, as in most mammals, both parents tend to benefit from larger-sized offspring. In the case of human beings, larger, better grown babies live longer, suffer less from disease and have generally better health than smaller, less well grown ones (Barker 1996). Coronary heart disease, stroke and non-insulin dependent diabetes are particularly associated with low birth weight independent of lifestyle factors such as smoking, obesity and socio-economic status (Barker 1998, 1999). Research also suggests that taller men do better than shorter ones in many occupations and are preferred by women.

However, although the benefits of increased size of offspring may be similar for both parents, the costs are not. In mammals, larger offspring mean increased costs to the mother during gestation and lactation, but no necessary cost whatsoever to the father. This may explain why the *IGF2* gene in humans is only active when inherited from the father. The maternal copy is imprinted (figure 6.2). However, when the paternal *IGF2* gene is duplicated or when a mutant maternal copy is inherited that can't be silenced, the individual concerned receives a double dose of growth factor and Beckwith-Wiedemann syndrome results. The symptoms are large placenta, heavy birth weight, excessive growth during adolescence, large tongue, large liver, proliferation of insulin-producing cells and childhood tumours – in sum, overgrowth (Haig and Graham 1991; Reik and Maher 1997; Sun et al. 1997).

Under conditions of strict, lifetime monogamy, a paternal autosomal allele would be in the same position as a maternal one. It would 'need' the same mother in the same way to ensure its own reproductive success in the joint offspring of such a permanently mated couple. But among mammals as a whole only about 3 per cent of all species are monogamous, and even among those, DNA fingerprinting reveals that not all offspring are those of a female's apparent mate (Carter and Lowell 1993). Where ostensibly monogamously mated humans are concerned, estimates of the proportion of children who are not in fact the offspring of their official fathers vary from a fraction of 1 per cent in Switzerland to about 6 per cent in large urban centres such as London and as much as 30 per cent in particular tower blocks in northwest and southern England (Wenk et al. 1992; Sasse et al. 1994; Baker and Bellis 1995; Heyer et al. 1997). In plants, where imprinting is also found, a grain of pollen could come from practically any other plant within range of the one that it fertilizes, and so here even more than in mammals, multiple paternity is the rule and monogamy is unknown.

If a male mammal mates successfully with a female, the situation facing a paternal allele is different from that facing a maternal one. This is because there is no necessary reason why any of that male's genes should find themselves in further offspring of the same female. But maternity is certain in the sense that a foetus develops inside its mother and so is definitely hers. Any gene in the mother must have an equal chance of being in any and every foetus that occupies her womb.

The possibility that a man may not be the father of the rest of the children of his child's mother is not necessarily a remote or purely theoretical one. Indeed, it may have been as common in the evolutionary past as it is becoming today in modern Western societies, where frequent divorce, extramarital relationships and one-parent families produce this situation quite regularly. The result is that paternal genes don't have the same vested interest in not exploiting the mother that maternal ones have. In mating with many different females, a paternal gene that spared the mother at a cost to its own success would lose out in competition with other paternal genes that were less co-operative. If their greater demand on the mother promoted their own reproductive success, as it probably would do, the more rapacious paternal genes would become more common than the less exploitative ones.

Considerations of this kind almost certainly explain why imprinting is not found in birds, fish or reptiles, where the mother controls the production of eggs with a fixed amount of nutrients independent of the father. However, imprinting is found in classes of organisms where offspring are nourished directly from maternal tissues, such as mammals and flowering plants, and in which paternal genes can influence the allocation of resources to the offspring. The conflict of interest between maternal and paternal genes to which this gives rise probably explains the evolution of imprinting in such cases (Moore and Haig 1991; Trivers and Burt 1999).

Genetic conflict explains the findings

Igf2r (for *Igf2 receptor*) is imprinted contrariwise to *Igf2*: the mother's copy is expressed, while the father's is imprinted. *Igf2r* produces a sink for insulin-like growth factor 2, mopping it up before it can have much effect on the embryo (figure 6.3). Its success can be gauged by the fact that mice who lack this maternal gene are on average 16 per cent larger at birth than they otherwise would be (Haig and Graham 1991). *Igf2* and *Igf2r* illustrate the tendency for paternally active genes to make greater demands on the mother's resources, and for mater-

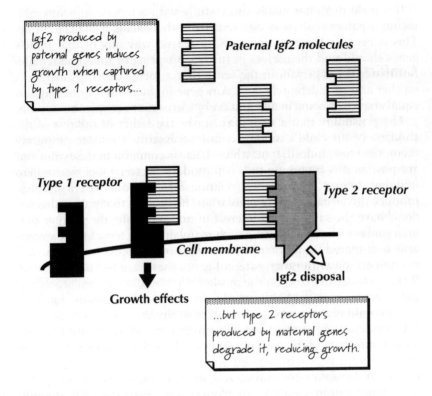

Igf2 produced by paternal genes induces growth when captured by type 1 receptors...

Paternal Igf2 molecules

Type 1 receptor

Type 2 receptor

Cell membrane

Igf2 disposal

Growth effects

...but type 2 receptors produced by maternal genes degrade it, reducing growth.

Figure 6.3 *Igf2r*
Source: After Haig and Graham 1991: 1045

nally active ones to make lesser demands on her. Paternal genes are usually associated with larger, faster growing or more active offspring, while maternal ones are correlated with the opposite effects. In maize, for example, paternal genes are associated with larger kernel size, while maternal genes produce smaller kernels (Domínguez 1995).

Such findings can't be explained by the view that parental contributions are complementary, because *Igf2/Igf2r* is a case of one gene sabotaging another: conflict and contradiction, not co-operation and complementarity. This is underlined by the fact that mice who lack both *Igf2* and *Igf2r* are of normal size. If co-operation between these paternal and maternal genes were essential for normal growth, knocking out both would be lethal, or at least, significant for growth and development. But if maternal and paternal genes simply counter each other in this instance, the finding that knocking out both makes little difference is exactly what you would expect (Jaenisch 1997).

Conflict in pregnancy

A consequence of conflict between imprinted genes in mammals is that paternal genes might be expected to be particularly prominent in the placenta because it is an organ specifically designed to extract resources from the mother and transfer them to the developing foetus in her womb. The placenta is genetically part of the foetus, not of the mother, and develops out of the fertilized egg cell. In the early stages of development the placenta dominates, comprising 85 per cent of combined weight with the foetus at eight weeks' gestation. Significantly, abnormal triploid human foetuses with a double set of their father's genes and a single set of the mother's (rather than a single set from each parent) are well grown except for the head and have a large placenta. By contrast, those with a double set of the mother's genes and one of the father's are small except for the head, show a retardation of growth and have small placentas. Even more tellingly, a double set of paternal genes without any genes whatsoever from the mother results in a massive proliferation of the placenta without any associated foetus to speak of.

The human placenta is the most invasive of all placentas, and in some cases can perforate the uterus, killing the mother. But the normal outcome is implantation *within* the lining of the uterus, not merely attachment to its surface. The foetus has direct access to its mother's blood, but the mother cannot regulate the flow of nutrients to the placenta without starving her own tissues. The fact that anaemic mothers have heavier placentas than non-anaemic ones despite giving birth to lower weight babies suggests that the placenta can actively respond to deficits in the mother's provision of nutrients. Indeed, as I mentioned earlier, adult diabetes, stroke and coronary heart disease linked to low birth weight may be a consequence of adaptive responses by the foetus/placenta to a lack of nutrients (Barker 1999: see above, p. 20).

The human placenta is an active protagonist in pregnancy, and it can come under attack itself from maternal cells in the lining of the womb that resemble the natural killer cells of the immune system. Indeed, these cells may function to limit the extent of placental invasion, and thus restrict the offspring's access to maternal resources (Haig 1996). Cells originating in the placenta appear to widen the mother's arteries that feed it by breaking down their walls and weakening them, so that they sag and distend, thereby increasing blood supply to the cavities that the placenta excavates to receive it. Fine, tree-like capillaries fill these spaces and directly absorb nutrients from the mother's blood and return wastes to it.

However, the mother has another line of defence. So aggressive is the attack mounted by the placenta at the very beginning of pregnancy that the heavy menstrual bleeding characteristic of our species may be explained by it. Each month the walls of the womb thicken by a factor of about two, and become filled with spiral arteries that grow longer and more elaborately coiled as time goes by. Greatly lengthening these arteries decreases the pressure of the blood flowing through them and so serves as an effective countermeasure to the activities of the foetal cells that are trying to widen them to improve the flow of blood. Indeed, in the absence of implantation, blood pressure in these arteries may be reduced to the point that the lining of the womb becomes starved of blood and necrosis sets in, necessitating its shedding during menstruation. Essentially you could see the spiral arteries as the vascular equivalents of tank-traps on a battlefield: designed to slow down and impede the enemy attack. Other cell changes that occur in the lining of the womb can be explained in a similar way. They too appear to be defences against invasion by the placenta (Haig 1993).

Although the loss of blood involved is normally trivial, menstruation is nevertheless surprisingly costly in terms of the energy required to sustain it. The increase in a woman's metabolic rate that occurs during the menstrual cycle has been estimated to be equivalent to nearly six days' food consumption over four cycles, and a year without any periods at all would probably save about two weeks of a woman's total energy needs (Strassmann 1996). In short, it looks as if menstruation may conceivably be the very considerable price that women pay for defence against the aggressive demands of paternally constructed placentas that want to implant deep in the lining of the womb. Like regularly maintained lines of defence along a border with a hostile nation, menstruation may be a symptom of conflict between a mother and paternal genes in a potential foetus, a conflict that is visible even before the pregnancy begins. (For a recent discussion of theories of menstruation see Gosden et al. 1999; Haig 1999.)

The fact that foetal cells have direct access to the mother's circulation as a result of their invasion of her tissues means that they can attempt to influence her by releasing hormones directly into her bloodstream. If this were merely a question of communication between foetus and mother serving the common interests of both, you would predict that only minimum amounts would be necessary – a whisper, so to speak. But in reality things are not so simple, and studies show an escalation of maternal and foetal hormone production more reminiscent of a heated argument than a quiet conversation – the hormonal equivalent of a shouting match. Levels of hormones produced by the placenta in pregnancy are typically hundreds or thousands of times higher than those produced by the mother herself in the non-pregnant state (Haig 1993).

The importance of these hormones is illustrated by the role that some of them play in maintaining the pregnancy. Some estimates put the number of conceptions that never come to term as high as 75 per cent. Most of these are believed to miscarry before the twelfth week of pregnancy, and many others before the first period. Other estimates suggest that 10 to 15 per cent of fertilized eggs will never be implanted, 42 per cent will fail to halt the sexual cycle and 28 per cent of all embryos will be spontaneously aborted (Bernds and Barash 1979).

Spontaneous abortions after the first couple of weeks often show chromosome abnormalities, suggesting that the mother actively discriminates against such embryos, thereby saving herself the very significant wasted effort of carrying offspring who are genetically malformed. Even when a viable baby is born, there is now evidence that in perhaps almost half of all cases a twin was present early in the pregnancy that subsequently vanished (Landy et al. 1986; Kelly et al. 1991; Rudnicki et al. 1991; Blumenfeld et al. 1992). In the case of sows, the mother always aborts if she is carrying fewer than five embryos by the twelfth day of the pregnancy – a clear case of the cost to the mother not being worth the return to her reproductive success (Wickler 1986).

The mother's readiness to spontaneously abort a foetus in her own interests creates an incentive for the foetus to defend itself from such a threat. In order to wrest control of the pregnancy from the mother, the placenta releases large quantities of a hormone of its own (chorionic gonadotropin) into her blood. This hormone makes the mother's ovaries produce oestrogens and progesterone, which stimulate growth of the womb and suppress ovulation; in the case of progesterone, it also quietens the womb. By the seventh week of pregnancy the placenta manufactures its own oestrogens and progesterone in sufficient quantities to maintain the pregnancy without the help of the mother. Progesterone output by the placenta reaches levels 20 times above those of the mother in the non-pregnant state. This in its turn may be exploited by the mother to gauge the quality of the offspring and its ability to thrive (Haig 1999). In sheep, the time of birth is decided by the foetus, not by the mother (Nathanielsz 1996). Although the situation in humans now seems more complex, a hormone produced by the placenta has been found to play a major role in determining the moment of birth (Smith 1999).

If the conventional, harmonious view of the relationship between foetus and mother were the correct one, you would expect the foetus to leave the management of the pregnancy to the mother, who could conduct it for the good of both. After all, the mother already has the hormone-producing machinery to do so in place, so why should the foetus duplicate it and try to do what its mother is already doing perfectly well? And surely the mother is in the best place to decide when to give birth, given that it is she who has to carry the burden of the pregnancy and that it is her body that has to maintain it. The fact remains that the foetus does not appear to be content to allow its mother to control the pregnancy. The reason is simple: mother and foetus are not always in agreement, and the foetus has only one life, whereas the mother usually has the option of starting another baby if the cost of carrying an existing one to term exceeds its benefit to her ultimate reproductive success.

Conflict also occurs over blood pressure and glucose level

There is evidence that the foetus heightens maternal blood pressure in order to decrease blood flow to the mother's peripheral circulation and to increase it to the placenta. The varicose veins, rosy cheeks, hot hands and similar symptoms that some women notice during pregnancy can be explained as the result of the mother's attempt to increase surface blood supply as a countermeasure to the hypertension induced by the foetus. Blood pressure in mothers appears to correlate with birth weight in both directions: women with lower than normal blood pressure during pregnancy tend to have lighter babies, and those with hypertension probably have heavier ones than they would otherwise. Furthermore, women with high blood pressure tend to lose fewer babies than average (Haig 1993).

A surprising finding is that the risk of high blood pressure in a pregnant woman appears to decline quite markedly with the amount of time she has lived with a particular man. This may be because the longer a relationship lasts, the more likely it is that future children borne by the same woman will share the father's genes. We noted earlier that conflict between paternal and maternal genes over exploitation of the mother is minimized in monogamy and maximized if every child a woman has is fathered by a different man. In the latter case, the father's genes have no self-interest in her reproductive future beyond the present pregnancy. However, if a man remains with a woman and fathers several of her children, he shares much more of a self-interest in her reproductive future, and so may be able to tone down demands on her by paternal genes in the foetus that result, among other things, in high blood pressure. Although a mechanism that could bring this about is currently unknown, hormones active in a male during a long-term relationship might deactivate genes in his sperm that would cause a foetus to pursue an aggressive strategy (Haig 1994).

The mother's glucose level falls during early pregnancy when the demands of the foetus are small, but stabilize at a new low level when its demands are rising. It seems that the mother is resetting her blood sugar level to be lower during pregnancy – in other words, providing less for herself and her baby than she does for herself alone! The mother's blood sugar level is determined by her output of insulin, which increases during pregnancy to produce the new, lower level. However, the mother also becomes more resistant to its effects – something which is especially puzzling in view of the increased output. Normally, blood sugar peaks after a meal, but returns to normal in response to insulin. After a similar meal in late pregnancy it remains elevated for longer, despite an exaggerated insulin response.

Genetic conflict between mother and foetus may explain these surprising findings. According to this way of looking at things, the mother reduces her glucose level in anticipation of an aggressive level of uptake by the foetus, rather as someone bidding at an auction might start off at a price much lower than the one they expected to have to pay. However, whatever the level, mother and foetus will compete for glucose after every meal. The longer the mother takes to consume her blood sugar, the more will be taken up by the foetus. Therefore the mother escalates her production of insulin so as to absorb it more quickly in late pregnancy when foetal demands are peaking.

The foetus, however, has an answer to this. It manipulates the mother's glucose economy by secreting human placental lactogen (hPL), a hormone that reduces the mother's sensitivity to her own insulin. This means that the mother's blood sugar level stays higher for longer, giving the foetus more time to consume the glucose despite the mother's best efforts to prevent this by escalating her output of insulin. The gene for hPL is paternally active and so is yet another instance of genetic conflict between maternal and paternal genes: in other words, a case of genes in the foetus exploiting the mother because they come from the father (Haig 1993). (See box 6.1, 'Morning sickness'.)

Box 6.1

Morning sickness

Pregnancy sickness (often called 'morning sickness' because it is more common then) normally coincides with the early stage of development during which the embryo is most vulnerable to poisons that cause deformities in development. Toxic substances that can cause damage to embryos are present in most things we eat, even seemingly innocuous ones such as apples, bananas, cabbage, celery, cherries, nutmeg, oranges and soya beans. These poisons were put there by natural selection when plants found themselves being eaten by animals and attacked by insects.

Normally, poisons in the food we eat are converted into less harmful water-soluble substances by enzymes in the liver and are then filtered out by the kidneys. This may explain why in early pregnancy the flow of blood to the mother's kidneys almost doubles and why the rate at which the kidney absorbs material from the bloodstream increases by up to 70%. It may also be a clue to one of the strangest symptoms of pregnancy sickness: cravings for bizarre foods such as earth or coal. Clay is mixed with potatoes in some cultures to detoxify them, and charcoal is widely used in filters to remove toxins and impurities from fluids.

Toxic substances in food and drink often betray their presence by their strong and/or distinctive taste and smell. Even when actual sickness is lacking, many pregnant women are nevertheless repulsed by certain foods and odours that they normally find attractive. Feelings of nausea and the vomiting reflex that goes with it are associated with a part of the brain stem called the chemorecep-tor trigger zone, or CTZ. Although blood does not normally cross the blood–brain barrier, it does to the CTZ, where it is sampled for toxins. Specialized receptor cells of the CTZ trigger nausea and vomiting when concentrations of specific toxic substances exceed a critical threshold. A possible explanation for the changed responses to foods that are associated with pregnancy sickness is that pregnancy hormones increase blood flow to the CTZ, effectively lowering its threshold of responsiveness by increasing the amounts of any substance sampled by it.

Numerous statistical studies suggest that women who experience severe preg-nancy sickness have significantly lower rates of spontaneous abortion than women who have little or no sickness. Women carrying a foetusless placenta produced by a double set of paternal genes experience severe morning sick-ness. This suggests that morning sickness could be a by-product of high levels of pregnancy-protecting hormones produced by the placenta in the interests of the foetus, rather than of the mother, whose genes are not present in these cases. In one particularly notable study of normal pregnancies almost a quarter of women with no or little sickness had spontaneous abortions, while those with severe pregnancy sickness had none whatsoever. These findings suggest

that morning sickness may be more than a mere side-effect of hormones that
protect the pregnancy and could provide a specific form of protection against
toxins. This would be a case of genetic conflict producing an effect on the
mother that is harmful from her point of view, but is beneficial from that of the
foetus (Profet 1992).

Imprinted genes and brain development

Prader-Willi syndrome is a developmental disorder in about one in
15,000 births, and is caused by the loss or silencing of paternally active genes on chromosome 15 through inheriting both copies of this
chromosome from the mother, or losing part of the paternal copy
(Nicholls et al. 1998). Significantly in view of the rule about maternal
genes having a self-interest in saving the mother's resources, symptoms include lack of appetite, poor suckling ability, a weak cry, inac-
tivity and sleepiness, high pain threshold and reduced tendency to vomit
– from the mother's point of view, an undemanding baby (Franke,
Kerns et al. 1995). Characteristic obsessive/compulsive behaviour is
also sometimes listed as a symptom in Prader-Willi syndrome, and as
the rule that maternal genes tend to favour smaller size would suggest,
Prader-Willi children also have small stature, hands and feet (Driscoll
1994).

By contrast to Prader-Willi, in Angelman syndrome only the paternal chromosome 15 is present in its entirety, and the critical maternal
genes involved in Prader-Willi syndrome are missing (Nicholls et al.
1998). Symptoms include prolonged suckling, hyperactivity and frequent waking – every mother's worst fear. Although both Prader-Willi
and Angelman children are retarded, Angelman retardation is usually
much more severe, and speech is absent. By contrast, 'exceptional
proficiency with jigsaw puzzles' has been mentioned as a diagnostic
criterion in Prader-Willi cases, and speech is usually present (although
articulation is often defective) (Holm et al. 1993). Whereas Prader-
Willi patients have a high pain threshold (and often damage themselves as a result), Angelman patients have a low pleasure threshold to
the extent that frequent 'paroxysms of laughter' are listed as a major
diagnostic feature and the condition is sometimes known as 'happy
puppet syndrome' (see box 6.2, 'Prader-Willi and Angelman syndromes').

Most imprinted genes will affect how much an offspring receives
from its mother, at the expense of siblings. Imprinting might be ex-

Box 6.2

Prader-Willi and Angelman syndromes

The characteristics of children with Prader-Willi syndrome (maternal additions and/or paternal deletions on chromosome 15) are

- poor suckling response;
- weak cry;
- inactivity/sleepiness;
- obesity;
- high pain threshold;
- reduced vomit reflex;
- temperature control abnormalities;
- exceptional skill at jigsaw puzzles;
- longer than normal heads, small mouths, hands and feet;
- obsessive-compulsive behaviour (Holm 1993).

The characteristics of children with Angelman syndrome (paternal addition and/or maternal deletion on chromosome 15) have a different pattern:

- prolonged suckling;
- frequent crying;
- hyperactivity/sleeplessness;
- low pleasure threshold ('happy puppets');
- severe retardation (no language);
- small heads;
- protruding tongue (Angelman 1965).

pected to affect genes that influence growth, suckling, neonatal behaviour, appetite, and nutrient metabolism (Moore and Haig 1991). The hypothalamus is an important part of the limbic brain that is concerned with basic drives and appetites such as hunger, thirst, sex and aggression, and with emotional responses such as pleasure, pain and anxiety (see above, pp. 125–8). Almost from the first, some kind of developmental defect in the hypothalamus was suspected in Prader-Willi and Angelman syndromes, in part because appetite, pain and pleasure threshold, vomiting and temperature control are all known to be functions of the hypothalamus (Franke et al. 1995).

Furthermore, such effects are not limited to offspring. A maternally imprinted gene expressed in the hypothalamus has recently been discovered that has a critical effect on maternal behaviour in mice, suggesting both that imprinted genes can affect adults, and that paternal genes have an interest not simply in the offspring's growth, but in motivating parental investment in it by females. The *Mest* gene in mice and humans is paternally active. Adult female mice who lack the gene are growth-retarded and deficient in maternal behaviour. They fail to retrieve pups, to free them from birth membranes and the placenta, and to nurse them. As the researchers argue: 'The involvement of a paternally-expressed gene in nurturing behaviour suggests that the evolutionary pressures leading to genomic imprinting in mammals might have selected for genetic functions involved in the control of energy transfers between provider and offspring, not only in utero (by regulation of embryonic growth and placental function), but also postnatally' (Lefebvre et al. 1998).

Imprinted genes control brain development in mice

Recently, it has been possible to show that imprinted genes play a critical role in brain development, and not just the hypothalamus. Mice can be produced that are either *androgenetic chimeras* (ag, containing a diploid set of paternal genes) or *parthenogenetic chimeras* (pg, containing a diploid set of maternal genes). In the case of mice, ag and pg chimeras seldom survive past the eleventh day of development. However, the problem can be overcome by creating chimeric mice that are mixtures of maternal or paternal and normal cells. In other words, some of the cells in the embryo have both a father and mother, but others have just a mother or just a father (pg or ag respectively). The resulting embryos are then implanted in receptive female mice and grown to maturity. The artificially introduced single-parent ag or pg cells can be stained so that they can be identified under a microscope. Other experiments have found that in chimeras ag cells are strongly represented in skeletal muscle but make little contribution to the brain. By contrast, pg chimeras show the opposite pattern: cells with genes exclusively from the mother contribute to brain development much more than to muscle and body growth. Indeed, pg chimeras are notably growth-retarded, while ag chimeras grow so large that they usually have to be delivered by Caesarian section. In other words, brain growth is enhanced by maternally expressed genes, while body growth is enhanced by paternally expressed genes (Keverne et al. 1996b).

Pg chimera cells (those with a mother but no father) are found in large numbers in the neocortex and forebrain but very few are found in the lower, limbic brain – especially the hypothalamus. This is true both of mature, fully grown pg chimeras and even more so of pg chimera foetuses, where there is a complete absence of pg cells from the hypothalamus. In both cases, pg chimera cells are found to be particularly clustered in the frontal lobes of the cortex. Ag chimera cells, by contrast, are the exact opposite: these are found in the hypothalamus and limbic brain, but not in the neocortex. The few that are found in the forebrain tissue of embryos don't proliferate and are subsequently eliminated. However, no such difference is found in the brain stem, which appears to be equally the work of maternal and paternal genes (Allen et al. 1995) (figure 6.4).

Pg chimeras also have significantly larger brains for their body size, despite the fact that pg chimeras are notably growth-retarded overall. As I pointed out earlier in this chapter, naturally occurring human equivalents mirror these findings. Those with twice as many paternal as maternal genes have small heads but well-developed bodies with large placentas, whereas those with twice as many maternal as paternal genes are the opposite: they have large heads, growth-retarded bodies and small placentas. As the researchers who made this discovery put it, 'functional differences between parental genomes could provide a

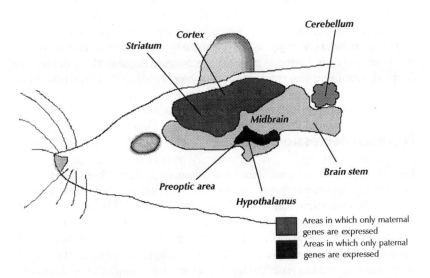

Figure 6.4   Imprinted genes as expressed in the mouse brain

mechanism for the exquisite control of the proliferation and differen-tiation of neuronal patterning that is perhaps unique to the develop-ment of the mammalian forebrain.' They also suggest that 'genomic imprinting may be responsible for a change in strategy controlling brain development in mammals. In particular, genomic imprinting may have facilitated a rapid non-linear expansion of the brain, especially the cortex, during development over evolutionary time' (Keverne et al. 1996b).

The hypothalamus also regulates the production of pituitary growth hormones, which, along with adrenal, thyroid and sex hormones, ei-ther directly or indirectly control growth. The pituitary is sometimes called 'the master endocrine gland' of the body, but is itself under the control of the hypothalamus, both neurologically and chemically. Neurologically, the posterior pituitary is just a part of the hypothalamus that protrudes from the brain and is not a gland in its own right (Thomson 1985). From this point of view, you could see the hypothalamus as performing a role in the body analogous to that of *Igf2* in the genome. Like *Igf2*, the hypothalamus is concerned with growth and, again like it, mammalian mothers appear to place im-prints on the genes that build it, just as they do the *Igf2* gene. Presum-ably this is because imprinting limbic brain genes limits the growth that would result if the genes for building the limbic brain from both parents were expressed. Cells in the embryonic hypothalamus are criti-cal for later development. The sizes of populations of cells in hypothalamic regions in the foetus could provide a prediction of the subsequent neurohormonal activity during later life (Deacon 1990). In other words, imprinted genes that control the growth of nerve cells in the development of the foetal brain could indirectly determine body size.[2]

Postnatal depression

Between 50 and 70 per cent of women experience feelings of mild depression accompanied by periods of weeping within a few days of delivery, sometimes called 'third day blues' (Pitt 1973). As the authors of a detailed study of 39 mothers who had just given birth noted, the period of depression 'occurs *after* delivery at a time when one would expect women to feel joyous'. The chief symptom found in two-thirds of this group was crying lasting for at least five minutes and 'usually . . . described as sporadic, short-lived, and inexplicable to the patient, with no obvious precipitating factor'. Five women cried continuously for over two hours. The study found that 'Some women are inordinately vulnerable and sensitive to minor rebuffs.' They also report that 'Exaggerated empathy may occur, such as weeping over news stories in the daily paper,' and list mild fatigue, irritability, restlessness, sleep disturbances, undue concern about the baby, and 'a mild confusional state' among other symptoms. Three-quarters of the new mothers 'expressed some degree of ambivalence' about giving birth. 'Without exception the mothers maintained reality testing, were puzzled at their response, and commented that this concern and behaviour was uncharacteristic of them' (Yalom et al. 1968).

But this is not so in the case of a small minority of new mothers. One or two out of every thousand develop a serious psychosis within six months of delivery, but usually within the first 2–3 weeks. Symptoms include severe depression, hallucinations, confusion and insomnia (Hamilton 1962; Brockington et al. 1978).

> Such depression is apparently especially likely when the mother is young, single, at odds with the father, or otherwise lacking in social support, and when the infant is suffering from poor health. These circumstances are very similar to the infanticide circumstances described in the ethnographic literature. Women suffering from extreme postpartum depression are sometimes characterized by clinicians as delusional, but the typical content of the 'delusions' seems not at all fantastic: concern about their inability to care for the baby, fear of not having enough love for the baby, and guilt aroused by infanticidal thoughts. (Daly and Wilson 1995)

There is evidence that normal baby blues occurs at the same time as heightened levels of cortisol in the mother's blood, while the less usual 'high' that some mothers experience immediately after giving birth is associated with a reduced level of the hormone (Taylor et al. 1994). Human breast milk contains opiates (casomorphins) that are released by digestion. Research suggests that the opiates in question may be prematurely released in the breasts of mothers who suffer from severe postnatal depression (Lindström et al. 1984; Nyberg et al. 1988). If we interpret this in accordance with the rule that maternal genes moderate demands on the mother's resources and with the suggestion made in the quotation immediately above, we might see both the soporific effect produced in the baby by these substances and the depression they cause in the mother as serving the interests of her genes rather than the father's. But this would only be true if we see postnatal depression as a mechanism that might induce mothers to terminate newborn babies whose cost had exceeded their value to the mother's reproductive success.

'Baby-blues' need not be seen as pathological

The reason why even mild postnatal depression has seemed to be a form of mental illness in the past may have been that it was seen in the wrong context. If you look at the mother and baby as a single whole, it certainly looks pathological. For example, according to John Bowlby, a human mother presented with her newborn infant should perceive its helplessness and its need for her care, and during the hours and days that follow be overwhelmed by feelings of love, attachment and responsibility (Stevens and Price 1996: 8). But if you see the mother as a product of genes which have a vested interest in her reproductive future that may on occasions demand termination of investment in a baby at birth, things begin to look very different. What appears to be an illness in the mother could be no more pathological as far as her genes are concerned than hypertension, diabetes and morning sickness in pregnancy are now believed to be.

Conflict between mother and baby does not necessarily end with the birth. On the contrary, birth presents a new occasion for conflict because for the first time the mother has total command of the baby: she is physically independent of it in a way that she has not been since about the seventh week of pregnancy, when, as we saw earlier, the foetus normally takes control by escalating its own production of pregnancy-protecting hormones. Birth releases the mother from this hormonal hold and allows her to regain the initiative. The human newborn is totally helpless and – at least in the primal conditions that have constituted the whole of human evolutionary history up to recent centuries – can't survive without the dedicated care of a lactating female. After birth, the mother can terminate the newborn baby's life without the threat to herself that a spontaneous – or, even more so, induced – abortion late in pregnancy would have implied. Such abortions carry a major risk of haemorrhage and death for the mother and probably explain why the vast majority of spontaneous abortions occur in the first three months of pregnancy. However, birth frees the mother from this constraint and presents her with an opportunity to abandon a baby without severe physical risk to herself.

Birth provides the mother's genes with an opportunity to test the quality of the baby. Genes in the mother that direct parental investment would be shooting themselves in the foot if they encouraged her to waste resources on infants who had no chance of passing them on in their turn. By comparison, other genes that were more discriminating and insisted that a baby prove its value before they allowed the mother to invest in it would be favoured. Studies suggest that soon after the delivery the new mother typically makes

> an *assessment*, in the immediate postpartum period, of the quality of the child and the quality of the present circumstances. . . . the new mother is not invariably eager to raise her baby, and it would be curious if she were. The emotional flatness or 'indifference' that is experienced by some new mothers – and is often alarming to hospital staff – seems to reflect such an assessment phase. (Daly and Wilson 1988: 71–2)

A study of over a thousand depressed mothers found that 'loss of interest' in the baby affected 61.5 per cent, as compared to only 2 per cent of a non-depressed control group, and was second only to 'sad or depressed mood' (Campbell and Cohn 1991). Another study found that depressed mothers had more negative or detached feelings about the baby than non-depressed women and had considered abortion more often. The same study found that alienation from the baby was not associated with depression before the birth but was significantly associated with depression after the delivery (Kumar and Robson 1984). A recent summary of these findings concludes that depressed mothers are ambivalent about their pregnancies and have difficulty emotionally investing in, and interacting with, their infants, consistent with a loss of interest and reduced investment in them. The same study adds that there is clear evidence that problems with the infant are significantly associated with postpartum depression. It concludes that there is overwhelming evidence that a perceived lack of support and problems with the pregnancy, delivery or infant are strongly associated with postpartum depression, irrespective of how you assess it (Hagen 1996).

So total is the reliance of the baby on the mother in the first few days after its birth that the mother doesn't even have to do anything positive to terminate it. She most certainly doesn't need to become conscious of any conflict about whether she should accept the baby and then try to resolve it one way or the other. All she need do is to fail to feed or protect it, and she need not even make up her mind about that. In primal conditions, just a few days of diffidence on her part would probably be enough to fatally compromise a baby who actually was sickly, malformed, or otherwise unfit. And the longer the mother remained uncommitted, the more likely would it be that a failing baby would die in any event.

Although no one could actually carry out an experiment on newborn babies to see how long they could survive neglect, the Mexico City earthquake of 1985 effectively did this when it buried an obstetric clinic. Babies born just before the earthquake struck were retrieved alive from the rubble up to seven days after the disaster and long after their mothers were dead. Human babies are characterized by considerable reserves of fat at birth, amounting to between 11 and 28 per cent of their body mass and as much as three to four weeks of their energy requirements. This could well be a parallel adaptation in them to normal postnatal depression in their mothers.

Prader-Willi children become obese in the first or second year because of an excessive deposition of fat at the expense of normal growth. One possibility is that the maternal genes known to underlie the syndrome may cause children to put on weight because fatter children make fewer demands on their mothers for food in times of scarcity (Haig 1993). Such times would probably have come fairly regularly in the primal hunter-gatherer way of life that accounts for the vast majority of human evolutionary history. This would simply have been because primal hunting-and-gathering was a chancy, hand-to-mouth existence, without much scope for storing food. However, the same principle might apply to the notable fat reserves of human newborns. These too could serve the mother's genetic self-interest if their effect is to fuel the survival of a baby during a period of postnatal depression designed to test its potential as a long-term investment for the mother's resources.

But of course, all this is speculative. Until we know exactly what causes normal postnatal depression, we shall not be able to say whether it really once had any adaptive value or not. Ideally, we would have to be able to trace both the depression in the mother and the fat accumulation in the newborn to maternal genes, and at present this is not possible. However, Prader-Willi syndrome sets an intriguing precedent and implies that such findings are far from impossible.

Weaning conflicts

One of the best examples of parent–offspring conflict is provided by *weaning conflicts*, that is, conflicts relating to the termination of a period of investment in the offspring. In mammals, females show an extreme form of sex role specialization by means of which they – and only they, never the male – provide the young with a specially produced food resource in the form of milk. At first, the young are totally dependent on it and can take nothing else, but later milk is a supplement to the diet, so that offspring can be weaned. This is the point at which conflict can occur, especially because persistent nipple stimulation inhibits the sexual cycles of female mammals. The consequence is that the mammalian mother faces a very real conflict between the interest of her existing offspring to consume more milk (with a presumed benefit to their ultimate reproductive success), and the alternative reproductive success open to her in the form of new offspring. However, the fact that she cannot expect to conceive these as long as her existing offspring are suckling results in an inevitable conflict, since almost always existing offspring will rate the benefit to themselves of more of their mother's milk above the benefit of the birth of further siblings. Nowhere is this conflict more extreme and unmistakable than in the case of human beings. Here weaning conflicts can be seen as an extension of the conflicts we have already seen in pregnancy.

At birth the placenta is simply thrown away, and the newborn baby is disarmed of its most potent intra-uterine weapon. The baby's paternal genes lose their opportunity to intervene directly in the mother's biochemistry. No longer can the paternal genes of the foetus and placenta express products that pass straight into the mother's bloodstream and compete to control her vital processes. Now the conflict between the genes of the mother and the paternal genes of the child is played out on a wider stage and involves new strategies. What had been a purely biochemical and physiological interaction now becomes a psychological one.

Following birth, a new organ comes into its own that might superficially seem to take over from the placenta and continue its function: the breast. Nutrients that formerly passed directly from the mother's to the foetus's blood across the placenta now pass from mother to baby in the form of breast-milk. In the past, breast-feeding was seen as a simple, unproblematic continuation of the role originally fulfilled by the placenta. There seemed no possibility that conflict or confrontation could exist between mother and baby over this fundamentally 'natural' process. Like the placenta, the breast simply nourished the growing child.

Clearly, there are both costs to the mother and benefits to the baby in breast-feeding, explaining why 'human weaning conflict can be intense, and is especially evident for that minority of modern women who breast-feed their babies to an age of advanced language capability. A three-year-old can be not only loud but impressively eloquent in offering reasons why Mommy should continue nursing' (Williams 1996: 107). But the very fact that breast-fed toddlers are such a tiny minority in modern societies leaves little doubt about which party to the conflict has got the upper hand, despite the manifest benefits to the baby's health of prolonged breast-feeding. This illustrates the fact that, contrary to traditional views which saw the mother and baby as a harmonious unit, there is a fundamental conflict between them where breast-feeding is concerned because most of the benefits are the baby's and most of the costs are the mother's.

In this respect there is a fundamental difference between the breast and the placenta. The breast, unlike the placenta, is part of the mother, not part of the baby. The mother can control it directly, simply by offering or withholding it – something made very much easier by clothing, which allows a mother to deny the breast to a baby even when she is carrying it. Again, breast-milk is the product of the mother's body, and the baby has no influence over it whatsoever. It has been suggested that the outcome of the struggle between maternal and paternal genes within the child could be influenced by factors in the mother's milk. Human milk contains Valium-like substances (benzodiazepines) whose soporific, calming effect make it more likely the baby will sleep quietly after a feed, rather than make more demands on the mother. Precedents for the maternal and paternal genes in question can be found in Prader-Willi and Angelman syndromes, which, as we have seen, produce very different outcomes depending on whose genes – the mother's or the father's – predominate. Additional paternal genes in Angelman syndrome make for a more demanding, more active and more frequently suckling baby, while a preponderance of maternal ones in Prader-Willi have the opposite effect (Haig 1993).

Weaning conflict may explain the Freudian 'oral phase'

The critical role of the breast in early infancy may explain why psychoanalysts have reported that it seems to be such an important object in early childhood. But a breast demands a mouth to suck it, and it is significant that Sigmund Freud should have described the first stage of psychological development as the *oral phase*.

Although Freud could hardly be accused of underestimating the importance of the oral period, he was unaware of the fact that in primal hunter-gatherer and modern Third World conditions the birth of a sibling within the first four or five years of an existing child's life is the single greatest threat to that child's continued existence. This is another consequence of the fact that newborn infants are so dependent on their mothers and demand so much from them. In primal conditions, where breast-feeding is obligatory, it is usually very difficult for a mother to maintain two closely spaced babies at once. In modern Africa, the colloquial term for the balloon belly and emaciated form

Box 6.3

Why breast is best

Breast-milk is critical for brain growth. One essential fatty acid (docosahexaenoic acid) makes up about 10% of grey matter in the brain and more of the retina. Its concentration in the brains of formula-fed ten-week-old babies is less than a tenth of what it is in breast-fed ones. Indeed, it has even been suggested that the recently discovered tendency for the mother's brain to undergo slight shrinking in the last three months of pregnancy may be a result of the foetus's demands on it for nutrients critical to its own brain growth. Premature babies fed breast-milk have IQs averaging eights points higher than those fed on formula that lacks the critical fatty acids, as well as having better visual and brain development. Studies that exclude the effects of possible confounding variables (such as social class, family size, birth order, etc.) have detected a significantly greater degree of intellectual impairment in bottle-fed compared with breast-fed children. Others have reported significant differences between test scores of breast-fed versus bottle-fed infants. Finally, two separate studies have shown that breast-feeding is significantly less common in the case of schizophrenics than it is in the rest of the population.

Breast-milk is also critical to the baby's immune system. Doctors have long known that infants who are breast-fed contract fewer infections than do those who are fed on formula. Until fairly recently, most physicians presumed that breast-fed children fared better simply because milk supplied directly from the breast is free of bacteria. Formula, which must often be mixed with water and placed in bottles, can become contaminated easily. Yet even infants who receive sterilized formula suffer from more meningitis and infection of the gut, ear, respiratory tract and urinary tract than do breast-fed youngsters.

Human breast-milk contains a long list of active biochemical agents that directly aid, arm, and mature the newborn's immune system, increasing its resistance to infection. Foremost among these are antibodies produced by the mother's immune system in response to challenges in her immediate environment that are also likely to threaten her baby. By producing these and passing them on in breast-milk the mother not only protects herself but defends her baby too.

However, the mother's immune system discriminates only against disease-causing bacteria so that the antibodies she transfers in breast-milk encourage the growth of beneficial bacteria in the baby's gut that both aid digestion and provide further protection against disease. White blood cells that fight infection directly and activate other defence mechanisms against disease are abundant in human milk and in the colostrum that precedes it in the first phase of breast feeding. Among these cells are

- macrophages which directly attack and destroy microbes in the baby's gut;
- T-lymphocytes which kill infected cells and mobilize other parts of the immune response;
- B_{12} binding protein which reduces the amount of vitamin B_{12} that bacteria can use to grow;
- fatty acids which coat the membranes of certain viruses and help to destroy them;
- fibronectin which helps to repair tissue damaged by infection;
- gamma-interferon which enhances antimicrobial activity of immune cells;
- lactoferrin which denies iron to many bacteria that need it;
- mucins and oligosaccharides which adhere to bacteria and viruses, preventing them from attaching to the baby's gut;
- many hormones and growth factors which mature and stimulate the baby's digestive tract.

For these reasons both UNICEF and the World Health Organization advise breast-feeding to 'two years and beyond', but as the author of a recent account points out, 'a child's immune system does not reach full maturity until age five or so' (Newman 1995).

that results from gross underfeeding of an infant is 'the disease of the displaced child' (Thapa et al. 1988).

However, in primal conditions, persistent sucking of the mother's nipples by an existing baby inhibits the re-establishment of her sexual cycles for up to three years after giving birth. Nerve impulses from the nipples caused by the baby sucking are received by the hypothalamus of the mother. There they set in train a complex series of reflexes resulting, among other things, in the release of oxytocin by the pituitary, which in turn causes milk ejection from the breast. Other reflexes mediated by the hypothalamus inhibit oestrogen production from the ovaries, reducing the likelihood of ovulation (Short 1987).

In a study in Africa, 39 Dogon women aged 20–34 years were found to have spent only 15 per cent of the time menstruating, 29 per cent of it pregnant and 56 per cent not having sexual cycles whilst breast-feeding (Strassmann 1996). Given that it may take several cycles for a woman to become pregnant again, the natural birth interval in hunter-gatherer conditions has been found to be approximately four years (Birdsell 1979; Howell 1979). Findings such as these have led to the suggestion that a four-year pattern of birth spacing was typical of our primal hunger-gatherer ancestors (Lancaster and Lancaster 1983). In such conditions, persistent sucking would benefit an existing child by delaying the birth of potentially life-threatening rivals to a very significant extent – quite apart from the importance of breast milk for the development of the brain and the immune system (both of which take up to five years to become mature) (see box 6.3, 'Why breast is best').

Sucking in early childhood appeared to be compulsive to Freud because it occurs independent of hunger, and certainly seems more like a reflex that is periodically triggered than a straightforward expression of the need for food or drink. Common observation shows that even satiated babies will obsessively suck fingers, toes, dummies, or whatever else comes to hand – or, rather, mouth. When we take into account the fact that a need to compulsively suck the mother's nipples may literally save the life of a child in primal conditions, it isn't difficult to understand why this behaviour has become instinctive, or to imagine the role that natural selection may have played in forming it. In primal conditions, babies who sucked compulsively and postponed the birth of siblings whose existence might otherwise have fatally compromised their own would have passed on more of their genes to future generations than would those who didn't suck so enthusiastically and thereby probably acquiesced in their own destruction. And equally clearly, paternal genes had an even bigger vested interest in an existing child in whom they found themselves than in a successor in whom they might – or just as well might not – have been present because it had a different father. Maternal genes, however, would always be present in both an existing child and a younger child born from the same mother, and so would have somewhat less self-interest in the existing child's survival and more in the newborn's. Indeed, as David Haig points out, genes expressed in mothers will favour shorter inter-birth intervals than will genes expressed in offspring (Haig 1999).

Psychological conflict between parent and child

In conflicts with its parents, the child is at a disadvantage. It cannot physically dominate its parents in the way they can dominate it. Nor has it the benefit of their experience of life or fully developed, adult skills. Yet, for all that, the infant does have weapons of its own in its battles with its parents. Because of its physical inferiority in size and maturity, these will tend to be psychological rather than physical and social, but they will be real nevertheless.

One example of this is crying. At first sight, you might think that crying is simply a means of communication by which an infant signals its needs and distress to an adult. But, as Robert Trivers pointed out in his original, landmark paper on parent–offspring conflict, once evolved, infants can use the crying signal out of context, or can amplify it to get more attention or care than the parent might think appropriate. In this way a signal originally evolved to indicate real hunger, for example, could be used to try to elicit just a little more feeding, even when the baby was largely satiated. Since it is precisely in these marginal areas of parental investment that conflict is most likely to occur, infants have an incentive to exploit distress signals like crying to secure any additional investment which they might favour, but the parent might not (Trivers 1981: 28).

Another psychological tactic open to the offspring is regression. What this means is behaving or appearing younger than one really is. Because the need for parental care tends to be greater the younger an offspring is, the quantity that adults are selected to provide will tend to reflect the offspring's age and developmental status, as they judge it. However, an offspring intent on a little more investment might solicit it successfully if it could mislead its parents about its actual developmental progress, and appear to be less advanced than it really is, thereby indicating to the parents the need for somewhat greater investment. Once again, we find much evidence of this in the case of human beings, among whom regression has long been a familiar finding to psychologists, especially in children (Trivers 1981).

Is the Oedipus complex a further case in point?

Smiling, like crying, is an innate, emotional response, and has been observed even in premature babies and in those born deaf and blind. By four months most babies will smile back, even if the stimulus is just two dots representing eyes on a face-sized oval card. Smiling is something that Angelman children (the 'happy puppets' with extra paternal genes) do to excess. A smile indicates a positive emotional response to another person, and such responses can profit even a very young baby. A mother is much more likely to respond positively to a baby who responds positively to her than she is to one who is totally unresponsive and inert. Long before the infant can speak, a smile can do excellent service as a positive response which says, 'Thank you', 'I remember you', 'I like you', or even 'I love you.' Indeed, you could envisage an arms race between increasing exploitation of smiling and other positive emotional responses by infants, and corresponding increasingly cynical responses to it by mothers analogous to the situation with crying mentioned just now. The final result might be selection for strongly positive emotional responses to the mother that were deeply and sincerely felt by the child.

This may in part be the genetic basis of what Freud called the *Oedipus complex*. It is also, if correct, the explanation of why in the light of experience he modified his original view that such a thing was only found in the case of little boys to insist that little girls initially showed much the same reactions to their mothers, and that in early infancy both sexes had an Oedipus complex centred on the mother. In short, the Oedipus complex in both sexes may partly be a question of children showing passionate love and devotion to the mother as a means of exploiting her. As such, the Oedipus complex would be the successor of the placenta in this respect: a psychological structure that evolved to extract resources from the mother, not by directly tapping into her blood supply or dosing her with hormones, but by working on her emotions and seducing her with the almost irresistible power of passionate, genuine and deeply felt love (Badcock 1994).

This interpretation of the Oedipus complex has a precedent in nature. American coots are grey-black as adults, but as newborn chicks they have bright orange crowns of feathers around a bald patch on their heads (hence the saying, 'bald as a coot'). Coot chicks do not call for attention from their parents because of the danger of being overheard by predators. Instead they display their head ornaments and use these to compete for their parents' attention. Experimental manipulation of chicks showed that parents preferred chicks with the gaudiest plumage when given a choice, and that the preferred chicks grew more rapidly and survived better (Lyon et al. 1994). This shows that displays by offspring can affect the parents' response to them in ways that do dramatically improve their chances of surviving and reproducing in their turn. Substitute Oedipal behaviour in young children of both sexes for the gaudy plumage in coots and the parallel becomes apparent.

Preferential parental investment in males might also explain penis envy in little girls. If boys are likely to be favoured – for example, by way of the Trivers–Willard effect described earlier (see above, pp. 179–87), little girls vulnerable to such discrimination should assess their and their siblings' sex objectively, and be motivated to compete for what they may not be getting. Given that the primary sex difference is the best indicator in childhood (because secondary sex differences only emerge at puberty), feelings of envy could easily become associated in little girls with observations of the penis in their brothers. And it would certainly explain a second reproach that Freud reports women make in this connection: 'It is that her mother did not give her enough milk, did not suckle her long enough . . . that she did not feed her sufficiently' (Freud 1961c: 234).[3]

Genetic conflict and Freudian psychodynamics

We saw earlier in this chapter that imprinted genes are now believed to play radically different roles in the brain, and that there is evidence that the cortex is built exclusively by maternally active genes, while the limbic system is the product of paternally active ones. Here an important consideration is that paternal genes have to rely on themselves alone to build and program the limbic brain so that it motivates behaviour that benefits them, because the person of the father himself can't necessarily be relied on to be present to influence the child in the way that the mother usually can. As we have seen, the mammalian father makes no necessary contribution to the growth of the offspring in the way that the mother does during pregnancy and lactation. Although a mammalian father may be present to help nurture his offspring, as many human fathers indeed are, the point is that such a presence is not biologically obligatory in the way in which the mother's is. Essentially, this is yet another expression of the fundamental principle: mother's baby – father's? maybe!

In his absence, all that a father's genes could rely on is their own, 50 per cent presence in an offspring and their innate ability to affect its growth, development and behaviour. Instinct costs less than learned behaviour, in the currency of genetic information (Williams 1966: 83), and as we have seen, fathers characteristically pay less of the cost of their offspring than do mothers. From these considerations we might deduce that the pleasure principle is likely to be more serviceable to paternal genes than to maternal ones because it epitomizes genetic, rather than environmental, influence on behaviour, just as Darwin, Spencer and Freud maintained. Whatever evolutionary psychologists may (or may not) say about it, you could argue that the pleasure/pain principle is not only authentically Darwinian but, unlike most modules and mechanisms that they have proposed, can now be traced to particular genes, and located in specific structures in the brain (see above, pp. 125–9).

In this respect, it is perhaps not coincidental that one of the symptoms of Prader-Willi syndrome is a high pain threshold, which is what you would expect if the pleasure/pain mechanism were compromised in these cases in a way that tended to serve maternal, rather than paternal, genetic self-interest thanks to an over-representation of maternal genes (Franke et al. 1995). Angelman, by contrast, is sometimes known as 'happy puppet syndrome' because affected children are both poorly co-ordinated and prone to frequent paroxysms of laughter (Angelman 1965). Given that the genetic basis of Angelman is an addition of paternal or a deletion of maternal genes that are implicated in hypothalamic functions like pleasure and pain, the outcome is again as you might expect: a reduced threshold for experiencing pleasure rather than the increased pain threshold seen in Prader-Willi children (see above, pp. 204–6, and box 6.2).

Is the id the agent of paternal genes, and the ego that of maternal ones?

According to Freud, there was a particular psychological agency which was under the domination of the pleasure principle and which he eventually called the *id*. Significantly in view of the fact that conflict between imprinted genes hinges on parental investment during development, Freud found that the id was present from birth, always remained infantile in quality, was fixated on the mother, and was primarily concerned with the gratification of basic biological needs (Freud 1961b).

Although Freud himself resolutely refused to localize purely psychological agencies such as the id in brain anatomy, his further discovery that the id was wholly concerned with the immediate self-gratification of instinctual appetites and basic biological drives beautifully fits the finding that paternal genes exclusively build the hypothalamus and are predominantly expressed in other limbic brain structures, such as the amygdala. We have already seen that it is the limbic brain in general and the hypothalamus in particular that are concerned with the basic reward system governing fundamental drives, appetites and impulses (see above, pp. 125–8). Consequently, it seems only natural to suggest that if we are justified in speaking of a distinct 'emotive' brain at all, then we might also be justified in suggesting that Freud's id looks very like the epigenetic agent we might expect to find in such a brain (see above, pp. 69–71). As MacLean pointed out many years ago, the limbic or 'visceral brain would have many of the attributes of the unconscious id' (MacLean 1949).

Another compelling reason for seeing the id as a psychological agent of the paternal genome of the individual is that its antagonist – what Freud called the *ego* – looks very much like what we would expect to find in the maternally constructed cortical brain. For Freud, the ego was a mental agency chiefly distinguished from the id by being subject to what he called the reality principle, rather than the pleasure principle which reigns in the id. As a result he originally called it the *reality ego* to distinguish it from the *pleasure ego*, which later became the id. The reality principle was intimately connected to perception and to consciousness via attention, which was 'a special function ... instituted ... periodically to search the external world, in order that its data might be familiar already if an urgent internal need should arise' (Freud 1958a: 220).

Whereas the id is linked to the automatic nervous system that produces reflex responses like fight-or-flight arousal, and instinctual reactions like erection in relation to sex or salivation in connection with hunger, the ego is characterized by its command of voluntary movement, thought and intention. Unlike the id, which is dominated by the internal needs of the organism and motivated by the pleasure principle to gratify them, the ego is both open to the environment and able to respond to it. To this extent, the id proposes but the ego disposes. It is this characteristic of the ego in particular which makes it very much the mental agent of the maternal genome. Indeed, Freud – notwithstanding his routine reluctance to localize purely mental agencies within the brain (Freud 1957c: 174–5) – hints at a link between the cerebral cortex and the ego when in one of his last works he comments that the ego develops out of the id 'like a cortical layer, through the influence of the external world' (Freud 1964: 96). (See box 6.4, 'A new view of the superego' and box 6.5, 'Freud's dream theory')

The evolution of ambivalence

The fundamental genetic and interpersonal conflicts reviewed in this chapter may have one further aspect of important significance for evolutionary psychology. They may underlie the thing that perhaps more than anything else makes us psychologically distinctive as a species: our vulnerability to mental conflicts of all kinds. These range from mild ambivalence and trivial conflicts of preference through neurosis to completely disabling mental illnesses like schizophrenia. As we have seen in this chapter, severe postnatal depression is another example, but the more normal baby blues may be a much more typical one. At whatever intensity it may be experienced, the new mother often feels painful, conflicting currents of feeling about her baby that she can neither understand nor completely master.

Box 6.4

A new view of the superego

Freud found that a subdivision of the ego – the *superego* – developed in later childhood, specialized in censoring the ego and especially the id, and was strongly influenced by the father. However, perhaps because there is little evidence that fathers are in fact important agents of socialization by comparison with mothers, Freud attributed the foundation of the superego's sense of guilt to evolved, heritable factors.

Nevertheless, the new findings about genetic conflict suggest that, if the ego could be seen as an epigenetic agent of the mother's genes, the superego might be that of the overlapping genetic self-interest of both maternal and paternal genes in the individual if the same father is shared with other children in the family. In this circumstance, relatedness of paternal and maternal genes in each child is the same, and so there is less conflict of interest between maternal and paternal genomes within the individual (see above, pp. 189–92).

Although there is much evidence that the presence of the father has a strong positive effect on the social adaptation and behaviour of his children, the effect has long been presumed to be purely psychological (Lamb 1981). However, if the enhanced degree of agreement between paternal and maternal genomes within each child is in fact the basis of this positive effect, common paternity might rely more on the sense of smell than anything else. Numerous studies have shown that infants, children and other family members can correctly identify one another by odour alone (Segal 1995). Although none of these cases concerned children assessing the paternity of themselves and their siblings, these findings suggest that you most certainly could not rule out the possibility that there might be some kind of genetic basis for family odour, particularly in view of the fact that genetically related individuals have skin glands which function in a like manner and contribute identifiably related odour signatures (Stoddart 1990). Paternal genes are now known to construct the *rhinencephalon* ('smell-brain') that discriminates odour, and this may be an added reason why: paternal genes are much more critically concerned with relatedness within the family than maternal ones simply because paternity is notoriously uncertain, and unrelated paternal genes in different children of the same mother have absolutely no incentive to co-operate.

Freud's finding that the superego develops only in later childhood might be based on the fact that births in primal societies tend to be spaced about four years apart and that it is almost always older, existing children who are expected to make sacrifices for younger ones, rather than vice versa (see above, pp. 214–17). This might explain why the superego is an agency of the personality that only becomes effective in later childhood, and hardly exists before the age of four. The conditional nature of co-operation on the part of paternal genes might also explain why it is found to be so variable in its nature, and why the presence of a father in the family is critical. Given that the majority of brain growth and development has taken place by the age of five to six, and can't be undone, the default setting for paternal genes may be to assume that they are unrelated to any other children in the family. However, if informed by the limbic system that shared paternity does exist within the family, development of a psychological agency excelling in inhibition, repression and social sensitivity may be initiated to encourage greater co-operation and altruism.

Box 6.5

Freud's dream theory

A paper published in the world's leading interdisciplinary science journal, *Nature*, by Crick and Mitchison (1983) is often cited as an important contribution to the modern scientific literature on dreaming. According to these authors, 'Although we dream for one or two hours every night, we do not remember most of our dreams. Earlier thinkers, such as Freud, did not know this.'

However, you only have to read 35 pages of *The Interpretation of Dreams*, before you find Freud remarking that 'Dreams are phenomena that occur in healthy people – perhaps in everyone, perhaps every night.' Two entire sections (I D, VII A) are devoted to 'Why dreams are forgotten after waking' and 'The forgetting of dreams'. In particular Freud remarks that 'The forgetting of dreams . . . remains inexplicable unless the power of the psychic censorship is taken into account.'

As Anthony Stevens and John Price have pointed out, 'Crick and Mitchison's hypothesis received so much attention that one might have thought that it was something startlingly new, but one would have been misguided. A very similar idea was proposed as long ago as the 1880s by Robert.' As they also point out, it was discussed by Freud in *The Interpretation of Dreams* (Stevens and Price 1996: 210). Evidently, neither Crick and Mitchison nor any of *Nature's* reviewers or editors had any real knowledge of what Freud and other writers like Robert actually said about dreams, and clearly none of them had read Freud's principal work on the subject – or even bothered to look at its table of contents!

Crick and Mitchison implicitly adopt the adaptationist approach of evolutionary psychology to dreaming to the extent that they try to find some useful function for it. However, dreaming, like many of the symptoms of pregnancy (see above, pp. 198–204), does not have to have a useful adaptive function just because it evolved. On the contrary, it would be easy to understand dreaming as an expression of genetic conflict, based ultimately on the differing roles that maternal and paternal genes play in constructing different parts of the brain.

Freud found that the dream was the outcome of a conflict between instinctual wishes originating in the id and the desire of the ego to go on sleeping and not be roused to seek gratification for them. Recent brain-imaging studies confirm that, as the Freudian theory would predict, dreaming is motivated by the paternally constructed limbic system, but that the motor cortex remains inhibited. The infantile wishes to do with basic drives and appetites that Freud found motivated nearly all dreams in both adults and children might be seen simply as limbic brain expressions, disturbing the sleep of the cortical brain much as a baby in bed with its mother might periodically interrupt her sleep to demand feeding. Like the mother, the maternally constructed cortical brain would do all it could to quiet the child and send it back to sleep.

This insight would also readily explain why anxiety dreams are so common, despite the fact that, as Freud himself conceded, they seem to contradict his wish fulfilment theory of dreams. It may simply be that, as part of the paternally constructed limbic system, the amygdala and other parts of the lower brain concerned with anxiety responses are equally likely to disturb the sleep of the maternally made neocortex with false alarms. If dreaming is an adaptation of any kind, it may be one to a fundamental genetic conflict built into the brain long before birth, psychologically institutionalized in what Freud called the ego and the id, and fought out repeatedly every night of our lives in dreams and nightmares.

Although such feelings can hardly appear 'adaptive', 'functional' or 'well designed' if you consider the individual as an integrated whole – still less the mother and baby as a single unit – they need not look this way from the point of view of the gene. As we saw earlier in this chapter, conflict can definitely occur at the genetic level, such as that between *Igf2* and *Igf2r*. We have also seen that such conflicts can escalate to astonishing intensity and generate veritable arms races between a pregnant mother and her foetus. Postnatal depression raises a possibility that genetic conflicts may be fought out not merely at the level of the individual gene, nor even only between mother and foetus, but within the mind itself, and with purely psychological weapons.

This was certainly the view of the late William Hamilton (see above, pp. 79–84), who provides a fitting conclusion to this chapter in the following extract from an autobiographical essay:

Seemingly inescapable conflict within diploid organisms came to me both as a new agonizing challenge and at the same time a release from a personal problem I had had all my life. In life, what was it I really wanted? My own conscious and seemingly indivisible self was turning out far from what I had imagined and I need not be so ashamed of my self pity! I was an ambassador ordered abroad by some fragile coalition, a bearer of conflicting orders from the uneasy masters of a divided empire. Still baffled about the very nature of the policies I was supposed to support, I was being asked to act, and to act at once – to analyse, report on, influence the world about me. Given the realization of an eternal disquiet within, couldn't I feel better about my own inability to be consistent in what I was doing, about my indecision in matters ranging from daily trivialities up to the very nature of right and wrong? In another metaphor, I was coming to see that I simply am the two or the many quarrelling kids who are pretending to false unity for a few minutes just so that their father will withdraw his threats and take them to the beach. As I write these words, even so as to be able to write them, I am pretending to a unity that, deep inside myself, I now know does not exist. I am fundamentally mixed, male with female, parent with offspring, warring segments of chromosomes that interlocked in strife millions of years before. (Hamilton 1996: 133–5)

Suggestions for further reading

Badcock, C. R. (1998) *PsychoDarwinism: The New Synthesis of Darwin and Freud.*

Crawford, C. and D. Krebs (eds) (1988) *Handbook of Evolutionary Psychology: Ideas, Issues and Applications.*

Haig, D. (1999) Genetic Conflicts of Pregnancy and Childhood. In *Evolution in Health and Disease*, ed. S. C. Stearns.

Mock, D. W. and G. A. Parker (1997) *The Evolution of Sibling Rivalry.*

Reik, W. and A. Surani (1997) *Genomic Imprinting.*

Trivers, R. and A. Burt (1999) Kinship and genomic imprinting. In *Genomic Imprinting*, ed. R. Ohlsson.

7

Nature, Nurture, Language and Culture

In this final chapter we come to what is by far the most fraught and controversial aspect of evolutionary psychology: the nature/nurture question. I have left consideration of this until the very last because I wanted my readers to have as full an understanding as possible of the many subsidiary issues on which the nature/nurture controversy rests. These include the role of natural selection and of genes in evolution, development and behaviour (chapters 1–2 above), the evolution and psychology of co-operation (chapter 3), mind and consciousness (chapter 4), parental investment (chapter 5), and parent–offspring and genetic conflict (chapter 6). In my experience, much confusion and many misunderstandings surrounding the nature/nurture controversy originate in a failure to understand the basic biological and evolutionary factors on which the debate hinges. It is my hope that, after so much space devoted to explaining them here, my readers will now be ready to apply them to the controversy without running too great a risk of error or misinterpretation.

Normally, books on evolutionary psychology open with the nature/nurture question, rather than close with it. For some writers, it is a misunderstanding that only needs to be put in the right terms to be got out of the way, and once this has been done, it can be ignored. For others, it is a continuing controversy that intrudes into just about every issue in evolutionary psychology, so that once opened, it can hardly be closed. Another reason why I have barely mentioned nature/nurture until now is that I do not think that it is simply a misconception that can be dismissed at the beginning, or that it is a debate that can profitably be raised in connection with just about every aspect of evolutionary psychology. Instead, I shall take this opportunity to suggest a completely new way of looking at the issue of nature and nurture cumulatively based on the preceding chapters and notably on the remarkable new findings about genetic conflict and brain development set out in the preceding chapter.

Evolutionary psychology and the SSSM

The nature/nurture dichotomy has been important because it has provided two opposed positions around which the biological and social sciences have largely polarized. Today most of the social sciences take the view that human nature and behaviour are the product of social influences rather than natural ones. The nurture view dominates social studies and provides them not merely with a point of view about human development, but with an article of faith that defines them as social rather than natural sciences. Many evolutionary psychologists like to contrast their approach with that of what they call the *standard social science model* or SSSM for short (Tooby and Cosmides 1992). By comparison with evolutionary psychology, the SSSM can be characterized in terms of three fundamental tendencies.

1   Holism   According to the SSSM, society is a whole greater than the sum of its parts. **Émile Durkheim** (1857–1917), a founding father of social science, claimed that a 'collective consciousness' exists which creates and controls individual consciousness through socialization and social pressure, so that even such an individual act as suicide has social rather than individual causes (Durkheim 1951). According to Durkheim, religion is in reality the worship of society itself, and the moral and spiritual force of the sacred is a symbolic expression of the irresistible power of the collective consciousness over the individuals who make it up (Durkheim 1976). In the SSSM in general, holism means that society as a whole or the social classes or groups that make it up are the most important units for understanding. The result is a top-down, rather than bottom-up approach to explanation.

The problem with the holistic approach to any system, social or otherwise, is that it makes analysis difficult or impossible, because it suggests that the whole cannot be analysed in terms of its parts. Durkheim – who ironically claimed to have founded sociology on a scientific, factual basis (Durkheim 1982) – admitted that because of its holistic nature, society was inexplicable since it was above and beyond reason. According to him, the ultimate categories of society arise out of collective emotion which 'is naturally refractory to analysis, or at least, lends itself uneasily to it, because it is too complex. Above all, when it has a collective origin it defies critical and rational explanation' (Durkheim and Mauss 1963: 86).

2 Cultural creationism Franz Boas (1858–1942), the founding father of cultural anthropology, claimed that 'not only our knowledge, but also our emotions, are the result of the form of our social life.' The mind, he declared, is 'determined largely by the social surroundings of the individual' because 'The social stimulus is infinitely more potent than the biological mechanism' (Freeman 1996b). Boas and his followers asserted that 'all human behaviour is the result of social conditioning,' adding that 'the power with which society holds us . . . does not give us a chance to step out of its limits' (Freeman 1983: 40, 46).

According to **Alfred Kroeber** (1876–1960), Boas's foremost student, culture is 'a thing so utterly woven into us' that it is 'utterly uncontrollable by our wills'. He added that human beings are 'exempt from the operation of the laws of biological evolution' (Kroeber 1917). The doctrines of Boas, Kroeber, Durkheim and others amounted to a social equivalent of religious creationism where human behaviour and psychology were concerned. Kroeber, for example, claimed that culture was 'beginningless' in much the same way that creationists believe God to have existed eternally before the temporal world which he created out of nothing. Like God for biblical creationists, society is seen as the uncaused cause of human nature, the timeless origin of history, the inexplicable explanation of everything social. According to the SSSM, the social sciences are quite different from the natural ones, in part because human beings are not like other organisms, but are defined as such by their cultures, classes or societies. This means that although biology, evolution and genetics may be able to say something about the human body, they are of little or no relevance to the human mind or behaviour – and none whatsoever to human society. The latter are allegedly the unique province of the social sciences. (But see Box 7.1, 'Non-human culture?')

Cultural creationism tends to portray human beings as hapless victims of social circumstances, passive subjects of cultural conditioning, or impotent casualties of historical forces. Taken to extremes, it makes individual moral accountability impossible because it implies that, whatever anyone does, society or some other social entity, rather than the individual, is always ultimately responsible. If culture really were the omnipotent determining factor that many social scientists have claimed, any individual initiative would be futile because only the cultural whole could determine anything. (See box 7.2, 'Margaret Mead and Samoa'.)

Box 7.1

Non-human culture?

The anthropologist Alfred Kroeber (1876–1960) thought that you could only talk of an animal other than a human having culture if the following criteria were fulfilled:

- invention of a new behaviour or modification of an existing one;
- transmission of this innovation to others;
- stylization or consistency in what is transmitted;
- persistence of the learnt behaviour long after the demonstration of it;
- spreading of the learnt behaviour to other social units;
- endurance of the learnt behaviour over generations.

At the time he was writing (1928), Kroeber believed that these criteria had not been met in any case by a non-human species. However, a recent survey of the modern literature on animal culture concludes that 'culture is no longer the exclusive domain of anthropology' (McGrew 1998). It goes on to claim that various populations of Japanese macaques, both captive and wild, have shown a variety of behavioural patterns that fulfil Kroeber's criteria for culture.

For example, in 1953 a young female macaque spontaneously washed a muddy potato in a stream on the island of Koshima. This food-processing technique first spread horizontally to her peers, and then vertically to older kin. In less than ten years it became the norm for the group, and over generations it was seen in 46 of 57 monkeys in the colony. In 1956 the same individual discovered how to separate wheat left on the beach by experimenters from the sand on which it lay. She did this by throwing handfuls of sandy wheat on to the sea, where the wheat floated and was reclaimed while the sand grains sank. This process took almost 20 years to become the norm, and in 30 was used by over 90% of the group. In Honshu, a different group of Japanese macaques adopted bathing in hot springs as a means of keeping warm in subzero temperatures.

In the case of chimpanzees, all of Kroeber's criteria are now known to have been met many times over. A systematic synthesis of information from the seven most long-term studies accumulated 151 years of combined observations and found that 39 different behaviour patters, including tool use, grooming and courting behaviour were customary or habitual in some communities but absent in others. In some cases, two or more tools are used together to solve the same problem. The same raw material may have many uses: a leaf may be used as a drinking vessel, napkin, fishing probe, or medication. Again, some populations have unique cultural practices: only the subspecies *Pan troglodytes verus* uses stone hammers and anvils to crack nuts (Whiten et al. 1999). Indeed, on the basis of material culture, a recent survey concludes that it is hard to differentiate between chimpanzees and the earliest known populations of *Homo*, or even from the simplest living human foragers (McGrew 1998).

Box 7.2

Margaret Mead and Samoa

Credulity for the claims of cultural conditioning was greatly encouraged by the work of Margaret Mead (1901–1978). Mead's book *Coming of Age in Samoa* (1928) was hailed as proving cultural determinism 'to the very hilt', and called 'an outstanding achievement' and 'an absolutely first rate piece of descriptive anthropology' by influential anthropologists of the time. Mead described her account of Samoa as 'a precious permanent possession . . . forever true because no truer picture could be made . . . true to the state of human behavior as it was in the mid 1920s; true to our hopes and fears for the future of the world'.

According to Mead, the Samoans were 'one of the most amiable, least contentious, and most peaceful peoples in the world' thanks to a relaxed, unauthoritarian regime of child-rearing. Others had called them 'perhaps the most ferocious people to be met with in the South Seas' (Freeman 1983: 158). In the mid-1960s cases of serious assault in Western Samoa were proportionately 67% higher than in the United States, 494% higher than in Australia, and 847% higher than in New Zealand, while the rate for common assault was five times higher than that of the United States. Physical punishment of children by parents and elder siblings was common in the 1960s and resulted in the death of one 12-year-old following a punishment beating by her elder brother (Freeman 1983: 157–73).

Despite Mead's assertion that in Samoa 'love between the sexes is a light and pleasant dance,' that male sexuality 'is never defined as aggressiveness that must be curbed', police statistics showed that Samoa had one of the highest rates of rape in the world during the 1960s – twice as high as that of the United States and 20 times higher than England. At the time Mead was there, rape was the third most common offence after assault and larceny.

A cult of virginity institutionalized in the culture was one of the reasons for the astonishingly high rate of rape. A man who successfully deflowered a girl by whatever means could insist that she must marry him because, having lost her virginity, no one else would marry her. Using rape in this way, men of inferior social status could force marriages on girls from families of better standing. According to Mead, 'the idea of forceful rape or of any sexual act to which both participants do not give themselves freely is completely foreign to the Samoan mind.' Yet in 1922 a Samoan woman recounted how 'when the man came to me as I was sleeping he held me down and put his fingers into my private parts . . . then I sat up and wept, and as it was no use for me to remain with my own family, went to his family.'

Mead's belief that Samoa was a sexually permissive culture where girls had 'as many years of casual love-making as possible' before marriage has been shown to be a myth. Nor was adultery 'not regarded as very serious', as Mead pretended. Before the arrival of Europeans adultery was punishable by death, and it was still sanctioned by fines and imprisonment in Mead's time. Far from exhibiting a different pattern thanks to the allegedly permissive regime of child-rearing, crime statistics for Samoa show that the pattern of adolescent crime was exactly the same as it is everywhere else – one where most crime is committed by young males, peaks sharply at about age 18, and then declines rapidly until about age 40, when it flattens out and tails off (Freeman 1983: 226–68).

One of Mead's principal female informants has since made a sworn confession that she and a friend playfully lied to her, not realizing that Mead was an anthropologist and would be so foolish as to believe what they had told her. According to Derek Freeman: 'It is now apparent that for decade after decade in university and college lecture rooms throughout the Western world students were misinformed about an issue of fundamental importance by professors who, by placing credence on Mead's conclusion of 1928, had themselves been cognitively deluded' (Freeman 1996a).

3   **Biophobia**   This has been defined as 'a tendency to avoid considering biological causes of human behaviour'. According to the sociologist, Lee Ellis, it has four principal causes:

● a definition of the 'social' as having exclusively social causes;
● a lack of training in, and knowledge of, biology among social scientists;
● an exclusive focus on human beings;
● political and moral prejudices against anything biological (Ellis 1996).

At the very least, the SSSM has been strident in its claims to be able to explain social phenomena in terms of purely social causes, so you could see its biophobia as another inevitable consequence of an exclusive concentration on the social defined in a way that limits it to human societies. Nevertheless, many social behaviours manifestly do have individual, psychological and biological causes, and many also have clear parallels in animal behaviour. Ignorance of biology is no excuse for failing to see that human beings are not the only species on the planet that has complex social behaviour. And whatever the moral and political objections to anything might be, it is still important to understand it as clearly and completely as possible.

Effectively, the SSSM cuts the social sciences off from all the other sciences, and puts human beings in a special category, distinct from all other species. Although this might be very flattering to human self-esteem, there are good reasons for thinking that we ought to be less elitist in this respect and realize that we share the planet with many others who are not so different from ourselves. Again, separation of the social sciences from the other sciences makes it easier to evade the criticism and comment that the findings of other sciences might properly suggest. At the very least, this compromises the unity of the sciences, and builds barriers between human social behaviour and that of other species. Finally, the position of psychology becomes very controversial, because if the natural sciences explain the body and the social sciences society, where does the human mind – which clearly bridges the two – fit in, and who can explain it?

Is the SSSM a caricature of social science?

Defenders of the SSSM would probably rightly claim that some of its critics have tended to caricature it, and that in reality there is no such thing as a standard social science model. Again, they would probably want to point out that much of the language of pioneers such as Durkheim, Boas and Kroeber could be explained by the fact that these writers were struggling to establish the social sciences in a world which at the time was often hostile to them and was crudely literal in its beliefs about the role of biology. This may have led to exaggerations on occasions, but did not prevent many of these writers also expressing more balanced views at other times. Despite his claims for cultural creationism quoted above, Boas for example also admitted that

> There is no doubt in my mind that there is a definite association between the biological make-up of the individual and the physiological and psychological function of his body. The claim that only social and other environmental conditions determine the reaction of the individual disregards the most elementary observations. (Quoted by Orans 1999)

Again, surveys of the private views of present-day social scientists on issues like crime and delinquency, academic and career achievement, sex and race differences, show that they do in fact attribute much more relevance to biological factors than the picture of the SSSM drawn by evolutionary psychologists might suggest. Indeed, the list of sociologists who have included biological concepts in their research and theorizing since the early 1970s is surprisingly long – and growing all the time (Ellis 1996).

Nor are all social scientists content to perpetuate the holistic, cultural-creationist and biophobic prejudices of their subject. Recently the sociologists Joseph Lopreato and Timothy Crippen stated in *Crisis in Sociology* (1999) that 'Sociology will never get anywhere but far-ther out of the scientific course as long as it adheres to the banality that the fundamental cause of behavior resides exclusively in the im-mediate influence of culture and social structure.' They point out that 'Despite the extraordinarily intense focus on ethnic prejudice and conflict in American sociology, no one in sociology even imagined that, as part of the turmoil in Eastern Europe, the Balkan volcano would explode and the republics of the old Yugoslavia proceed to erupt in genocidal hostilities.' Lopreato and Crippen candidly comment that 'at present sociology offers a shallow and distorted view of human nature that prevents it from understanding the real world and thus from the likelihood of demonstrating its utility to society.' 'Science', conclude Lopreato and Crippen,

> is the art of 'regressing' the why – inquiring into the more enduring causes of phenomena. The environmental conditions that trigger ethnic clashes vary considerably from time to time and place to place. They too are an important part of scientific explanation. But to transcend the level of mere historical description, they must be anchored to more con-stant tools of explanation. These refer to the evolutionary forces that confronted our distant ancestors.

In the view of Lopreato and Crippen, the next 25 years will show that 'the survival of sociology depends very much on whether the profes-sion can cope with the extraordinary revolution now taking place in evolutionary biology.' They conclude that 'little in sociology makes lasting sense except in the light of modern evolutionary theory' (Lopreato and Crippen 1999: 34, 37, 43, 275–6, 83).

Memes

Another aspect of the nature/nurture controversy is the widely held view that animal behaviour is mainly the result of nature, but that human behaviour is largely the product of culture. It goes with a belief that genetic determinism in nature is paralleled by a corresponding cultural determinism brought about by nurture. Indeed, a new term has been specially coined for this purpose by Richard Dawkins as a parallel to 'gene'. Dawkins is the author of *The Selfish Gene*, a popu-lar book which forcefully argues that genes are the ultimate replicators in biology and that organisms can be seen as their transient embodiments. Its provocative title expresses the view that as far as the

Box 7.3

Information viruses

A *virus* is a piece of genetic information that promotes its own replication by means of the copying mechanisms and raw materials of the cells that it infects. However, such parasitic cloning is not limited to the world of DNA, but happens in human information systems too. The following example, known as the St Jude chain letter, was in existence in various versions for most of the twentieth century, and is still replicating. It is reproduced here with original spelling from a copy published in *Nature*:

> With Love All Things are Possible. This paper has been sent to you for Luck. The original is in New England. It has been sent around the world. The Luck has been sent to you. You will receive good luck within 4 days of receiving this letter pending in turn you send it on. This is no joke. You will receive good luck in the mail. Send no money. Send copies to people you think need good luck. Do not send money cause faith has no price. Do not keep this letter. It must leave your hands within 96 hrs. An A.R.P. officer Joe Elliot received $40,000,000. George Welch lost his wife 5 days after this letter. He failed to circulate the letter. However before her death he receive $7,750,000. Please send copies and see what happens after 4 days. The chain comes from Venezula and was written by Saul Anthony Degnas, a missionary from S.America. Since that copy must tour the world. You must make 20 copies and send them to friends and associates after a few days you will get a surprise. This is love even if you are not superstitious. Do Note the following: Contonare Dias received this letter in 1903. He asked his Sec'y. to make copies and send them out. A few days later he won a lottery of 20 million dollars. Carl Dobbit, and office employee received the letter + forgot it had to leave his hands within 96 hrs. He lost his job. After finding the letter again he made copies and mailed 20 copies. A few days later he got a better job. Dolan Fairchild received the letter and not believing he threw it away. 9 days later he died. In 1987 the letter was received by a young woman in Calif. It was faded and hardly readable. She promised her self she would retype the letter and send it on but, she put it aside to do later. She was plagued with various problems, including expensive car problems. This letter did not leave her hands in 96 hrs. She finally typed the letter as promised and got a new car. Remember send no money. Do not ignor this – it works. St. Jude

If recipients made 20 copies each as the letter commands, by the end of eight replication cycles there would be a total of 20^8, or 2.56×10^{10} copies – enough for approximately four copies for every person in the world! Other chain letters currently in circulation involve the exchange of women's underwear, postcards of naked Asian girls, and protests on the disappearance of a young woman. One particularly virulent case requesting get-well wishes and/or business cards for a young cancer patient produced more than 70 million copies (Goodenough and Dawkins 1994).

Nowadays numerous examples flourish on the internet. Most email users have received ostensible warnings of computer viruses contained in messages like the following:

> If you receive an E-mail titled JOIN THE CREW or PENPALS, DO NOT OPEN IT!. It will erase EVERYTHING on your hard drive. Send this letter out to as many people as you can. This is a new virus and not many people know about it. This information was received this morning by IBM, please share it with anyone that might access the internet. PENPAL appears to be a freindly letter asking if you are interested in a penpal, but by the time you read the letter it is TOO LATE!! The Trojan Horse virus will already have infected the boot sector of your Hard Drive, destroying all the data present. It is a self replicating virus, once the message is read it will AUTOMATICALLY forward itself to anyone whose E-mail address is present in your box. This virus will destroy your hard drive and holds the potential to destroy the hard drive of anyone whose mail is in your box and whose mail is in their box and so on and so on. So delete any message titled PENPAL or JOIN THE CREW.

These warnings have always been hoaxes, because simply opening an email wouldn't have resulted in a viral infection (opening an attached file might have been a different matter). Nevertheless, the alarm they cause is usually sufficient to get them copied by recipients who think that they are countering a virus, when in reality they are promoting one, albeit more like the St Jude chain letter than a true computer virus.

individual gene is concerned, evolutionary success is just a question of getting itself copied by the organism in which it temporarily finds itself. Genes that do this have been naturally selected; those that don't, haven't – evolution is as simple as that (see above, pp. 54–5).

Dawkins goes on to claim that human culture has introduced a new kind of replicator: the *meme*. According to the *Oxford English Dictionary* a meme is an element of a culture that may be considered to be passed on by non-genetic means, especially imitation. Just as genes are genetically encoded information, so memes are mentally encoded information. Anything from a tune to the complete works of Plato qualifies. (Indeed, the term *meme* has, by the criteria of the meme theory, itself become a successful meme!) Like the gene, all that matters is that the meme should get itself copied, and remembering and whistling are as good as printing and reading. Just as bodies are the biodegradable packaging of an organism's genes, so brains are the living storage medium for memes:

Once the genes have provided their survival machines with brains which are capable of rapid imitation, the memes will automatically take over. We do not even have to posit a genetic advantage in imitation, though that would certainly help. All that is necessary is that the brain should be capable of imitation; memes will then evolve which exploit the capability to the full.

Dawkins concludes, 'We are built as gene machines and cultured as meme machines' (Dawkins 1978: 214). (See box 7.3, 'Information viruses'.)

How different is the meme theory from the SSSM?

According to a book by Daniel Dennett enthusiastically endorsed by Dawkins,

A human mind is itself an artifact created when memes restructure a human brain to make it a better habitat for memes. The avenues of entry and departure are modified to suit local conditions, and strengthened by various artificial devices that enhance fidelity and prolixity of replication: native Chinese minds differ dramatically from native French minds, and literate minds differ from illiterate minds.

But if memes are socially rather than biologically determined, as they indeed appear to be, it is hard to see how this is any different from Boas's words quoted earlier to the effect that the mind is 'determined largely by the social surroundings of the individual'. This impression is reinforced when Dennett claims that 'Whereas animals are rigidly controlled by their biology, human behaviour is determined by culture, an autonomous system of symbols and values.' He concludes that 'The invasion of human brains by culture, in the form of memes, has created human minds' (Dennett 1995: 361–9).

In *The Meme Machine*, the most recent addition to the meme theory literature, Susan Blackmore asks us to '*Imagine a world full of brains, and far more memes than can possibly find homes. Which memes are likely to find a safe home and get passed on again?*' (1999: 41, emphasis in the original). Her answer is, a meme 'that not only grabs the attention but tends to make its host keep on mentally rehearsing it'. Although Blackmore adds that this may also be a meme that relates 'to the core needs for sex and food', she also stresses that successful memes may be 'ones that provide especially good tools for creating more memes, or which fit neatly into already installed memeplexes like political ideology or belief in astrology'. She likens the brain to an empty piece of earth in which many different species of plants compete for occupation: she calls this 'the weed theory' of memes.

Blackmore goes on to claim that 'The enormous human brain has been created by memes,' rather than simply genes. 'The reason we talk so much is not to benefit our genes, but to spread our memes.' Grammatical language, says Blackmore, 'is not the direct result of any biological necessity, but of the way the memes changed the environment of genetic selection by increasing their own fidelity, fecundity and longevity'. In her view, genes drive the evolution of memes by conventional Darwinian means, but memes also drive genes in a non-biological manner. However, where psychology is concerned, memes are dominant: 'Memes provide the driving force behind what we do, and the tools with which we do it. Just as the design of our bodies can be understood only in terms of natural selection, so the design of our minds can be understood only in terms of memetic selection.' Indeed, in her view the self is 'the ultimate memeplex', created by memes to aid their replication: 'That is, I suggest, why we all live our lives as a lie, and sometimes a desperately unhappy and confused lie. The memes have made us do it – because a "self" aids their replication' (Blackmore 1999: 104, 234).

Blackmore concludes that 'sociobiologists' – with whom she includes evolutionary psychologists – 'have missed a crucial point. . . . By contrast, sociologists have long realized the power of social forces.' Going on to quote Karl Marx to the effect that 'social existence determines consciousness', she believes that only the meme theory can integrate the social and biological accounts of human behaviour, providing a missing evolutionary basis for the former and a second, co-evolving replicator to complement the latter: the meme (Blackmore 1999: 235). Clearly, the meme theory and the SSSM are not necessarily as different as all that, at least if you are prepared to believe in memes and to accept the largely passive role that human beings are claimed to play in their propagation (Whitmeyer 1998).

Conditioning

Both the SSSM and the meme theory make far-reaching but seldom articulated assumptions about human psychology. For example, the meme theory assumes that the human mind is readily and eagerly imitative, and the SSSM presumes that thinking can be easily influenced by social representations. Nevertheless, such assumptions are rarely discussed in the light of what is actually known about the extent to which behaviour can be influenced by such external influences. As we shall see now, even if the problem is restricted to laboratory animals and to simple, scientific tests of conditioning, the outcome is more complicated and more interesting than might once have been supposed.

Behaviourism was the dominant school of academic psychology during the middle part of the twentieth century (see above, pp. 111–13). Behaviourists made extreme claims for the power of nurture in the form of their belief that behaviour could be directly *conditioned* by the appropriate programmes of stimulation and reinforcement. **Ivan Pavlov** (1849–1936) showed that whereas no unconditioned dog would salivate at the sound of a dinner bell, conditioned dogs did, thanks to having a bell sounded every time they ate, until eventually just the bell sufficed to bring on expectant salivation even in the absence of food. Behaviourism represented nurture because conditioned behaviour was learned rather than innate. It was natural for dogs to salivate when the stimulus was food, but they had to be conditioned to salivate at the sound of a bell. And of course, it need not have been a bell. Pavlov discovered the phenomenon of conditioning when he noticed that the dogs began to salivate when they saw the white coat of the lab assistant who had come to feed them.

His successor, **John B. Watson** (1878–1958) went on to assert that all behaviour is learned, and that psychology no longer had any need of the term 'instinct' because 'Everything we have been in the habit of calling an "instinct" today is largely the result of training.' Even breathing or the beating of the heart were seen as becoming conditioned shortly after birth' (J. Gould and Gould 1994: 48). Watson boasted that with behaviourist conditioning he could mould a child to any desired psychological specification:

> we no longer believe in inherited capacities, talent, temperament, mental constitution, and characteristics. Give me a dozen healthy infants, well-formed, and my own specified world to bring them up in and I'll guarantee to take any one at random and train him to become any type of specialist I might select – doctor, lawyer, merchant-chief and yes, even beggar-man and thief, regardless of the talents, penchants, tendencies, abilities, vocations, and race of his ancestors. (J. Watson 1970: 104)

B. F. Skinner (1904–1990) claimed that 'All behavior is constructed by a continual process of differential reinforcement from undifferentiated behavior, just as a sculptor shapes his figure from a lump of clay'

(J. Gould and Gould 1994: 52). Here the 'sculptor' is a metaphor, but in reality behaviourism appeared to give enormous influence to persons who could mould the behaviour of others, such as parents, teachers and, above all, behaviourist psychologists. Here was a doctrine that extolled the power of nurture over nature to an extreme degree and which reduced the mind to little more than a blank slate on which conditioning could inscribe anything it chose.

Behaviourism failed to take account of evolved, innate factors

Behaviourism made much of experiment in its self-conscious attempt to appear scientific, but not everyone managed to reproduce its findings. For example, students of Skinner's who tried to apply his methods commercially confessed that 'After 14 years of continuous conditioning and observation of thousands of animals, it is our reluctant conclusion that the behavior of any species cannot be adequately understood, predicted, or controlled without knowledge of its instinctive patterns, evolutionary history and ecological niche' (J. Gould and Gould 1994: 58).

Experiments carried out by John Garcia and colleagues showed that

- rats can quickly be conditioned to associate the size of a food item with an electric shock, and so avoid the item;
- however, rats can't be conditioned to associate a shock with the taste of food, even if the shock is administered immediately on eating it;
- nevertheless, when food is paired with imperceptible X-ray exposure that causes illness one hour later, rats quickly learn to associate the taste of the food with the illness but can't learn to associate the size of a food item with it.

What is fascinating about these experiments is that they show that both cues associated with the reward of food – its taste and its size – could be learnt by the rats and that both punishments – the electric shock and falling ill one hour later – could be associated with a cue. But what they also show is that while the taste of the food could easily be associated with falling ill later, the size of the food could not. And while the size of the food could readily be associated with an electric shock, its taste could not. The rats therefore showed an innate, instinctive bias about what they could and could not be conditioned to learn (Garcia 1981).

Behaviourism cannot explain why this is so, but evolution easily can. If rats can be conditioned to associate the taste of food with falling ill even when the lapse of time between eating and being ill is as long as 12 hours, as Garcia found it sometimes could be, it is not difficult to see that this may be because rats have an instinctual tendency to assume that the taste of food and its ability to cause illness are naturally linked. Illness from eating bad or poisoned food would certainly have taken a toll on rats in their natural habitat, and recourse to poisons by humans in attempts to control rat infestations must also have had an effect. It is by no means far-fetched to assume that rats who happened to have a tendency to link the taste of such items to the illness they caused and so avoid them would have left more descendants than those who had no such bias and could not learn to make the association. Almost certainly, this explains why rats are notoriously shy of baits and usually avoid unfamiliar foods.

Similarly, it is not difficult to see that rats may have an evolved bias to assume that the size of a food item might be related to an instantaneous insult like a shock if in nature items of a certain size turned out to be insects with stings or fruits with barbs. But rats would have been most unlikely to encounter poisoned or bad food that was principally distinguished by its size, or instantaneous insults associated only with the taste of a food item. Clearly, some pre-existing associations exist within the rat's brain that behaviourism can't explain.

Indeed, there are many other examples of the way in which innate, instinctive factors interfere with classical behaviourist conditioning in laboratory animals:

- Rats, if given the choice, will opt to receive an electric shock that is heralded by a warning signal rather than one that is not, even though the expected shock is three times stronger and lasts nine times longer than the unannounced shock. This suggests that having a warning is innately preferred by rats to not having one, and that you can't condition them to treat a shock without prior warning in the same way as they treat one with it.
- Pigeons can't be conditioned to associate odour or sound with food, but will readily associate its appearance, as they do in nature. Yet pigeons can be conditioned to associate sound with shocks, much as they would in nature if the shock were the attack of a predator or hunter. Similarly, pigeons readily learn to associate sounds but not colours with danger, and colours but not sounds with food.
- Quails can't be conditioned to associate sounds or smells with dangerous foods, but readily learn to avoid them by sight.

- Honey bees can be trained to associate various cues such as the perfume, colour and shape of flowers with a nectar reward, but they learn the most reliable cue – perfume – quickest, and the least reliable – shape – much more slowly. However, even though they use polarization of light as a habitual means of navigating to flowers, bees cannot be conditioned to associate it with a food reward at a particular flower because flowers never naturally provide cues in the form of polarized light. Nor can they learn non-floral perfumes as easily as they can floral ones. Again, bees are good at learning which way a hive faces, but they will not learn in which direction a flower faces.

Even when classical behaviourist conditioning has seemed to go according to plan, closer inspection has usually shown that the behaviour being nurtured was much nearer to nature than might appear:

- Pecking is a natural food-finding activity for pigeons, so it is not surprising that they can be easily conditioned to peck at objects to get a food reward. But experiment showed that if pigeons are shown an illuminated key just before the food is delivered they will quickly learn the association with it, but also insist on pecking the key, even if no peck is necessary. Attempts to condition the pigeon *not* to peck the key by making pecking it prevent the food reward have no effect. Once established, the pecking habit persists, even if the pigeon subsequently starves to death as a result! And even when pecking keys to obtain food rewards, pigeons peck in innately different ways that are appropriate to whether the reward is liquid or solid.

Behaviourism overlooked the fact that the very capacity to condition an animal by reward and/or punishment, for example by food or electric shock, is itself dependent on an evolved, innate mechanism. Before any conditioning of a Pavlovian kind could take place, the animal would first of all have to have both the ability to sense and distinguish pleasurable, rewarding sensations from painful, punishing ones, and the capacity to learn associations accordingly (in other words, it would need a pre-existing pleasure/pain principle, just as Darwin and Spencer foresaw, and as Freud found was also true of human beings: see above pp. 125–8). This explains why animals in laboratories are starved to 80 per cent of their normal body weight to be highly motivated to find food and why other experiments rely on the universal desire of animals to avoid punishment (J. Gould and Gould 1994).

Both the meme theory and the SSSM require the human mind to be a general purpose learning device: something that can be programmed by culture or memes in more or less any way. Behaviourism is relevant to both because it showed that even laboratory animals cannot be regarded as blank slates, conditionable at the whim of the behaviourist. On the contrary, behaviourism's failures suggest that if there are strict limits to the conditioning of animals, there are likely to be even stricter ones where human beings are concerned.

The nurture assumption

Of course, apologists for the SSSM or meme theory might claim that human learning and the conditioning of laboratory animals are two quite different things, and that memetic or cultural conditioning are somewhat different. Nevertheless, according to Judith Rich Harris (1999a, 1999b), the usual view of cultural transmission – that the culture is passed down from the parents to the child – is inadequate and misleading. An example is language in the US. The children of immigrants who speak English with a heavy accent end up speaking English with no foreign accent at all if they grow up in a neighbourhood of native-born Americans. They don't end up with something in between what they learned from their parents and what they learned from their peers: they acquire the language of their peers.

Harris thinks that other aspects of a culture are transmitted in the same way as language. In developed societies the parents start the process at home, so that children come out of the house already knowing something. But whether they keep what they learned at home will depend on what they find when they get outside. And in her view they don't have to learn *anything* at home. There are many societies where the parents hardly talk to their babies at all, and the babies don't learn the language until they graduate from their mothers' arms into the local play group. They learn both the language and how to behave from the older children in such groups.

Nevertheless, Harris does not deny that the home is unimportant. She concedes that to a large extent parents can determine how their children will behave at home. But she insists that they can't determine how their children will behave when they are *not* at home. She points out that children today are being raised very differently from the way their grandparents were raised: they are getting more praise and kisses, fewer smacks and scoldings. But she also points out that there is no evidence that children today are any less aggressive than they were two or three generations ago, are nicer, or happier. On the contrary, rates of violence, of depression and of suicide have gone up, not down. She asks why culture as a whole has not become more benevolent if parenting styles have become more compassionate?

Parents don't have to be socializers: it could be peers

According to Harris's theory, children find out pretty early on that behaviours that were acceptable at home, such as displays of emotion, are not acceptable outside. The consequences of behaving correctly or incorrectly are also different inside the home and outside. At home, children can cry or wet their pants or say something foolish, and nothing terrible is likely to happen, whereas if they do these things at school they might be laughed at or picked on or given an unflattering label that could stick to them for years.

Harris claims that by the time they are two, children have acquired mental categories for grown-ups and children, men and women, girls and boys. They know which ones they belong to, and they are already showing a preference for their own social category. Children are attracted to other children, even at an age when they are wary of strange adults. When they have a choice, most little girls prefer to play with girls, most little boys prefer boys. By kindergarten age, girls and boys split up into sex-segregated groups whenever they have the chance and whenever there isn't an adult insisting that they play together. In the playground boys act tough: they hide their weaknesses and vie with each other for dominance. Girls don't have to hide their weaknesses; instead they use them as tokens of good faith. Timid girls often remain timid, but timid boys tend to become less timid as they get older – a change that is usually attributed to socialization by the parents. Our culture frowns on timid boys, the story goes, so parents teach their sons not to be timid. But Harris believes that it is not the parents but the peer group that is responsible for this (Harris 1999a, 1999b).

Language

As we have just seen, one area where nurture, conditioning and culture appear to reign supreme is language. Here, surely, is something that is wholly the product of learning and the social environment. Indeed, language appears to be a *paradigm* in this respect, and certainly has been regarded as such. Someone learning English, for example, would only need to know the pattern or paradigm of one regular noun like *apple* to know that the plural is normally formed by adding 's': *apples*. The historian of science Thomas Kuhn also used the term 'paradigm' to designate strategic concepts, key experiments or fundamental methods that came to characterize a science. In both cases the root of the idea is that a paradigm is an example or epitome that serves as a model or precedent to be followed in other cases (Kuhn 1970).

Language has been a paradigm of the nurture side of the nature/ nurture dispute because words are apparently arbitrary inventions. An apple need not be called an apple because the French call it *une pomme*. And what is true of the word for an apple is true of any other word: it could always have been something else. All that is required is that all the speakers of a language should agree that that is what the word is. This is what we mean when we say words are arbitrary. Some have gone even further and have claimed that the essential difference between things that are cultural as opposed to natural is that culture is arbitrary, but nature necessary. This seems to explain why children need to be taught culture but why what is natural seems universal and to emerge without teaching. Socialization is a process of learning arbitrary, cultural conventions, like the one that says that an apple in French is *une pomme*.

From here it seems but a short step to claim that the whole of culture is a kind of language, with myths, rituals and religion, styles of dress and conventions of behaviour, food, drink and cooking, politics, economics and even heredity being different symbolic 'languages', each as arbitrary as the other. One of the most extreme versions of this idea reduced women to the status of mere 'messages' exchanged between groups of men! Thus kinship was a 'language' and heredity a cultural artefact, for all its apparent basis in genetics (Lévi-Strauss 1969).

Looked at from this point of view, the whole of an individual's culture was a 'mother tongue', and the individual's mind a blank sheet on which Mother Nurture wrote whatever she wished. In this way language became a crucial case of nurture because it seemed to be something that no one could deny was arbitrary rather than necessary, learned rather than innate, and symbolic rather than literal. As such, it became a paradigm for the social sciences and appears to have defined them as fundamentally distinct from biology. What appeared to work so well for language was assumed to work also for most other aspects of culture.

According to B. F. Skinner, even the most fundamental statement of your own existence, such as the famous claim of the French philosopher René Descartes (1596–1650), *I think, therefore I am*, proves to be illusory: 'Descartes could not begin, as he thought he could, by saying, "*Cogito ergo sum.*" He had to begin as a baby – a baby whose subsequent verbal environment eventually generated in him . . . certain responses of which "*cogito*" was an example' (Skinner 1969: 241). This is summed up in the Sapir-Whorf hypothesis, which holds that people's thoughts are determined by the categories made available by their language – or, in other words, conditioned by culture and learning (Sapir 1921). (See box 7.4, 'Does language affect colour perception?'.)

In the past, behaviourists like Skinner claimed that the rules for combining words correctly were produced by simple conditioning. It was alleged that parents and other members of the speech community socialized children into grammatical speech by providing examples and then rewarding them if they got it right and correcting them if they got it wrong. But simple observation shows that this is not by any means always true. Parents and other socializers often do not correct children. Often they set the wrong examples for them. Nor do they necessarily reward children every time they say something correctly.

The weakness of behaviourism was that it assumed that conditioning could do it all, and that any stimulus could condition any response. The whole point about speaking grammatically is that any word can't be followed by any other and that many of the words speakers use they will never previously have encountered in exactly the same sentence. This means that, beyond very simple, short, stereotyped sentences, there is no way that speakers could be conditioned in advance for every possible word combination they will use. Clearly, what they do have to learn is a set of rules. If you restrict learning to concrete behaviour, rewarded or punished as the case may be, you simply can't explain how general rules could be learnt unless you are ready to accept that something may be going on inside the brain of those doing the learning to make sense of their experience.

Specific language impairment reveals the genetic basis of language

Today there is accumulating evidence that some highly specific aspects of linguistic competence are strongly and selectively affected by heritable factors. One classic test that illustrates the way that children learn language is the *wug test*. Children are shown a picture of an imaginary animal and told that it is a *wug* or a *zat*, or some other such made-up

Box 7.4

Does language affect colour perception?

According to the Sapir-Whorf theory, we construct our understanding of the world through the language we speak. Because there are big differences in both the number and the meaning of terms designating colours in human languages, colour terminology is a critical test of the relative contributions of nature and nurture to perception. Some evolutionary psychologists claim to have proved that, contrary to the Sapir-Whorf theory, colour perception is universal and not affected by cultural factors, even if the terms used to describe it are. A study of the stone-age Dani tribe of Irian Jaya appeared to establish that although they only had two terms to describe colour, Dani memory for colour seemed little different from that of English speakers.

However, a recent attempt to replicate the findings among the Berinmo, a previously unstudied tribe of hunter-gatherers living in Papua New Guinea, casts doubt on this finding. Subjects were asked to name 160 different colours in a standard array, and used five basic indigenous colour terms to do so. Both the range and the boundaries of these terms showed good agreement between subjects. But when the Dani experiment was repeated with the Berinmo, statistical analysis showed that the best fit between naming and memory was consistent with the Sapir-Whorf hypothesis.

The differences between English and Berinmo allowed a further critical test. Berinmo doesn't make a distinction between blue and green, but does have a colour boundary between colours called *nol* and *wor* that doesn't exist in English. Subjects were asked to remember a colour over an interval of 30 seconds and then select one of two similar alternatives. Sometimes the incorrect choice was from the same colour category, and sometimes from a different one. English subjects were good at discriminating blue from green, but poor at discriminating *nol* from *wor*. Melanesians were the opposite: poor at blue/green, but good at *nol/wor*, just as the Sapir-Whorf theory would predict.

If categories always fall on natural breaks in perceptual space, as the universalistic theory claims, it should be easy to learn another language's colour categories. Berinmo speakers were asked to learn the English blue/green distinction, and English speakers to learn the Berinmo *nol/wor* one, along with an arbitrary, control distinction between two shades of green not found in either language. Berinmo speakers found learning the arbitrary distinction just as hard as the blue/green one, and English speakers found the *nol/wor* distinction as difficult as the arbitrary one. The study concluded that tasks in which subjects divide stimuli varying in hue, brightness and saturation into two colour categories are performed better if the division corresponds to a linguistic rather than a supposed universal distinction, and that the results from the experiments were consistent with there being a considerable degree of linguistic influence on colour categorization (Davidoff et al. 1999).

name. Then they are shown a picture of two and asked to complete the sentence, 'Now there are two . . . ?' Since children have never encountered a *wug* or a *zat* before, they could not have been conditioned directly to provide the correct plural. In order to do so they must apply a paradigm derived from other words that they do know and go on to generate the new plural: *wugs, zats,* or whatever.

In another test, someone with the disorder known as specific language impairment (SLI) might be shown the following sentence and be asked what was wrong with it: *The boy ate three cookie.* Almost always they can see that something is wrong somewhere, but when asked to put it right will give answers like *The boy ate four cookie.*

The ability to apply rules like the one breached in this example is exploited to comic effect in the following joke:

Child: Do you have some soap?
Shop assistant: Do you want it scented?
Child: No thank you, I'll take it with me.

Some members of one particular family with SLI would not be able to pass the *wug* test, put the cookie sentence right, or get this joke. Children of this family produce unevenly grammatical English, such as *On Saturday I wash myself and watched TV and went to bed.* The previous week the child in question had been taught that the past tense of 'watch' is *watched,* and had clearly remembered it. She also knew the irregular past tense *went.* But she was unable to render 'wash' as *washed* despite getting *watched* right (Maynard Smith and Szathmáry 1995, citing data from Myrna Gopnik).

There is no evidence that the affected members of this family have a general cognitive deficit or low IQ. Their grammatical difficulties seem to be limited to being unable to apply simple linguistic paradigms to infer that if one *apple* becomes two *apples,* one *wug* should correspondingly become two *wugs.* This explains why these children can deal with irregular verbs better than regular ones. Irregular verbs have to be learnt individually – *go/went, see/saw,* etc. – but regular ones can be generated easily, so long as you can apply them as paradigms. Apparently some members of this family can't do that.

The incidence of the disorder is also interesting. Overall, SLI affects 16 out of 30 members spanning three generations, all descended from one couple of whom only the mother was afflicted. Of her five children, four had it – three daughters and a son – while one son was unaffected. None of the unaffected son's children were themselves affected. Of the families of the four afflicted children, two boys in one

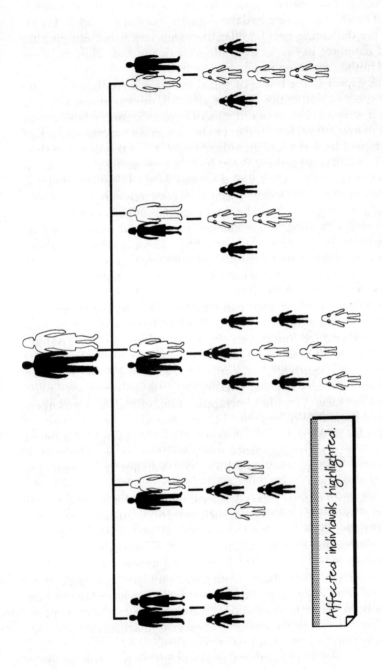

Figure 7.1 The inheritance of a specific language disorder

Affected individuals highlighted.

family had it, but not two girls. One boy and two girls of another family of an affected parent had the disorder, but not two other daughters. In the remaining two families, two sons had it but not another son and daughter in one case, while four out of nine children were afflicted in the remaining family (see figure 7.1).

If some aspect of the home or social situation were the cause, you would expect to find entire families affected, or only one sex or age group if it were a question of differences in socialization related to age or sex. Environmental factors can't explain why on average about half the children of both sexes of an afflicted parent had this deficit in their linguistic competence but the other half were perfectly normal. Consider, however, the possibility of a genetic factor being the explanation. The pattern of inheritance seen here is exactly what you would expect of a single gene. This is because each parent passes on half their genes to each offspring, so the chances of any child receiving a particular gene from one parent are fifty-fifty. This explains why about half of all the children of an affected parent were themselves affected. They were the unlucky half that inherited the gene in question (Maynard Smith and Szathmáry 1995: 300–3).

This pattern of inheritance can't be that of a recessive gene because affected individuals appear to need to have only one of their parents to be affected to stand an approximately even chance of having the disorder themselves. Again, every sufferer themselves had a parent who was a sufferer, something that does not have to happen in the case of a recessive gene. Finally, the gene can't be a sex-linked recessive like Queen Victoria's haemophilia because males are as likely to get it as females – ruling out both the X and Y chromosomes as likely sites for it. All in all, it looks very much like a single, dominant gene that is located on an autosome – one of the other 22 chromosomes (see above, pp. 45–9, and box 7.5, 'Williams and Down syndromes').

Does this mean that we have found a single gene 'for language' – or, at least, one important aspect of it, such as learning and applying paradigms? Hardly. What this evidence shows is that a single gene can have effects that disrupt this particular aspect of language competence. It does not necessarily mean that the gene in question is normally 'for' forming regular verbs or plurals from paradigms. Just as a single spanner thrown into some very complex works could have far-reaching implications for what the works could consequently do – or more probably *not* do – so this particular gene appears to disable language ability in a way that shows up as I have described.

The gene in question has other effects too, and in no sense can genes

Box 7.5

Williams and Down syndromes

The chief evidence against linguistic ability being just a part of wider cognitive function and for it being specifically heritable comes from Williams syndrome. This disorder is associated with a gene that is involved in calcium regulation and has complex effects on the brain, heart, skull and nervous system during development. Affected children have a characteristic impish appearance, suffer from heart problems and are mentally retarded, with average IQs around 50 that make them comparable to sufferers from Down syndrome (which is caused by an extra copy of chromosome 21).

However, what distinguishes Williams syndrome from Down syndrome is the remarkably uneven way in which the disorder affects performance in mental tasks. Although they are unable to live independent lives, and find simple tasks like tying shoelaces almost impossible to master, Williams sufferers are sociable and talkative. They are often musically gifted and have an unusual – and sometimes painful – sensitivity to noise. In tasks demanding visual and spatial skills, such as drawing an object or copying a figure, Down adolescents matched for age and IQ with Williams children come out much better. Yet the opposite is the case where recognition of strange faces in different orientations and lighting conditions is concerned – indeed, here Williams children are as good or better than most normal adults.

But the most marked contrast with Down sufferers is in tests of language competence. In this respect Williams subjects almost always score much better than the Down ones, and even exceed the average for normal children. For example, asked to name as many animals as they can think of in 60 seconds, a Down subject produced the following list: *goats, rabbits, bunnies, horsey, french fries, goats, monkeys, horsey, ice cream*. A comparable Williams response was *brontosaurus, tyrannadon, brontosaurus rex, dinosaurs, elephant, dog, cat, lion, baby hippopotamus, ibex, whale, bull, yak, zebra, puppy, kitten, tiger, koala, dragon*.

Responses like this give a flavour of the linguistic sophistication of Williams sufferers, despite their cognitive limitations in certain other respects. Asked to correct the faulty sentence *I hope you to eat all your supper*, a typical Williams response was *I hope that you eat all your supper*, while a matched Down subject simply replied, *chicken*. The speech skills imparted by Williams syndrome despite the specific cognitive impairments that go with it are vividly illustrated by the following comment by an 18-year-old sufferer with a measured IQ of 49: *You are looking at a professional book writer. My books will be filled with drama, action and excitement. And everyone will want to read them. I am going to write books, page after page, stack after stack. I'm going to start on Monday* (Bellugi et al. 1992).

Taken as a whole, these findings suggest that language competence is not just an expression of some broader cognitive skill that could equally well show itself in other ways – or indeed that the mind is a clean slate on which socialization or conditioning can write anything. They argue that the ability to learn words and apply grammatical rules to them is in part a product of genes and not simply the outcome of learning. Williams syndrome sufferers seem to have these linguistic abilities intact or even somewhat enhanced, despite their serious cognitive limitations in most other respects.

be seen as computer codes that control behaviours directly, such as forming plurals or regular past tenses. That involves direct manipulation of speech output. Genes don't work like this, and usually make their critical contribution during development. Here, if anywhere, 'genes for language development' could definitely exist. They would presumably work by controlling the development of parts of the brain involved in speech synthesis, and here a single gene could indeed have far-reaching effects (see above, pp. 61–3). Dyslexia, for example, has been associated with the short arm of chromosome 6, and some sufferers from SLI have been shown to have larger right hemispheres of the brain than left during foetal development. The significance of this is that, as we have already seen, 95 per cent of people have language on the left side of the brain – the one that is underdeveloped in these cases (see above, pp. 137–48).

What SLI establishes is not that there is a single gene controlling any one aspect of language, but that a single gene can disable a specific aspect of language competence, while apparently leaving the rest largely intact. This is important, because if genes exist that contribute to the development of specific language abilities, you would have to be able to show that linguistic competence is distinct from more general cognitive ability, such as that measured by IQ tests. This is precisely what SLI suggests, because members of the affected families showed few abnormalities in other cognitive skills, and one of the sufferers was better than average at maths. Another was a computer engineer who managed to get every answer in a written test of verbal ability correct. However, it took him a considerable time to do it and demanded tremendous concentration. So sufferers from specific language disorders can overcome their impediments, but they do so at a considerable cost. As one sufferer remarked to Myrna Gopnik (who carried out much of this research), 'Don't you find it tiring to talk?' She replied yes, but only when she had to speak in French – or, in other words, when she had to apply paradigms consciously, rather than speak with the unconscious fluency that comes to a normal speaker with their native language (Myrna Gopnik, personal communication).

Again, the fact that children with this disorder have such difficulty learning to apply paradigms for regular verbs but can more easily learn irregular forms shows that, whatever the mind is, it is not a clean slate on which anything can be written as behaviourists, sociologists and meme theorists have claimed. In the case of SLI, the slate seems to be highly resistant to having some things written on it, but not at all resistant to others. And the fact that a single gene has been implicated in this strongly argues against the view that the mind is a blank and formless medium unaffected by heredity. Furthermore, studies of brain-damaged patients show that some have damage to areas of the brain that affect the very same ability compromised in SLI: the ability to form regular – but not irregular – verbs. Others have injuries to a different part of the brain in a way that leaves regular verbs largely intact, but impairs irregular ones. These findings reinforce the supposition that the regular and irregular past tenses are supported by different neural systems, which can become dissociated by damage to the brain (Marslen-Wilson and Tyler 1997).[1]

Turner's syndrome

It has long been known that boys are substantially more vulnerable than girls to a variety of developmental disorders affecting speech, language and reading ability, as well as more severe conditions to do with social behaviour, such as autism, which is much more prevalent in males than females (see above, pp. 113–15).

Common observation suggests that women usually have greater social sensitivity than men, and are often more responsive to others. In the case of primates in general, females more than males provide social stability and group cohesion, are more affiliative, and sustain the continuity of the group over successive generations. Females are the primary caregivers, with social rank of daughters, but not sons, being related to that of their mothers. Males, on the other hand, show greater mobility from the natal group, are more exploratory, and their hierarchies are more overt, with high levels of sexual promiscuity and aggression (Keverne et al. 1996a).

Although such sex differences are often routinely regarded as culturally conditioned in the human case, there is now evidence that they are at least in part genetic, and may have an evolutionary basis. For example, according to a recent survey, 'the single interpretation that

Box 7.6

Sex roles: nurture 1 – nature 9

Does nature or nurture determine adult sex role and gender identity? According to some, 'Women and men are products of social relations, if we change the social relations, we change the categories "woman" and "man" ... we would argue that, to put it at its bluntest, social relations determine sex differences rather than biological sex producing social divisions between the sexes' (Brown and Jordanova 1981).

A study in the Dominican Republic found 18 cases of boys who, thanks to a rare genetic disorder, were born appearing to be girls. All of them had been unambiguously assigned a female sex and socialized as girls by parents who had no idea that their 'daughters' might be sons. This occurred in a traditional, rural, unsophisticated Latin American society with clear and distinct differences in male and female sex role behaviour. Because of their genetic peculiarity, physical masculinization was delayed until puberty, but then proceeded more or less as normal. At the time of their sex change, several of the subjects were already engaged to be married to men. All had girls' names, dressed as girls and regarded themselves as girls until the sex change.

Here was a case in which sex of nurturing was contrary to genetic sex: one in which males by nature had been nurtured to think that they were female. A clearer or more crucial test of the relative importance of nature or nurture in determining sex role could hardly be imagined. Parents effectively had told their children that they were girls in circumstances where their genes – but not their physical appearance – indicated that they were boys. To all intents and purposes, their female sex role socialization was complete and apparently effective. If the claims of cultural determinists are to be believed, these natural males, nurtured as females, should have matured as women, at least psychologically and socially. Although nature may have prevented them from playing a female biological role, the irresistible power of social conditioning should have seen to it that they played a female role socially and that psychologically they continued to regard themselves as female.

In the event, the study reported that following puberty all the subjects developed male genitals along with the other secondary sexual characteristics of adolescent males. The ages at which subjects first experienced morning erections, nocturnal emissions, masturbation and sexual intercourse were not appreciably different between those raised as girls who changed to a male gender identity and a control group raised as boys from the beginning.

Sixteen out of 18 subjects unambiguously raised as girls (89%) changed to a male sex role at puberty, despite parental consternation, their own initial shock, and considerable social pressure to the contrary. One of the remaining two continued to dress as a woman, had sexual relations with women but not men, and had masculine mannerisms. The other persisted in the female role and lived with a man for a year until he left her. She was described by the study as having masculine build and mannerisms but wore false breasts and at the time of the study desired a sex change operation to make her a more normal woman. Of the 18, she was the only one who persisted in all respects with the female sex role which she had been assigned at birth. Fifteen of the 16 (94%) who made the full sex role change were living with, or had lived with, women at the time of the study. The remaining subject lived alone.

Strikingly similar findings emerged from the Simbari Anga tribe of Eastern Papua New Guinea, where the disorder is also found but in which adolescent boys play a 'feminine' sexual role in ritual oral sex with older men (Imperato-McGinley et al. 1979, 1991).

best describes the research findings across a wide range of studies is that women have greater inhibitory abilities than men on most tasks involving sexual, social, emotional and behavioural content.' The authors speculate that 'because of women's greater involvement in childbearing (coupled with the prolonged childhood of their offspring), it would have been to their selective advantage to inhibit behaviours that would conflict with the best interests of their children' (Bjorklund and Kipp 1996: 163–88). These findings are confirmed by a recent discovery which suggests that differences between the sexes in this respect may be to some extent accounted for by a gene on the X chromosome. (For evidence that sex roles are predominantly under genetic rather than cultural control, see box 7.6, 'Sex roles: nurture 1 – nature 9'.)

Normally, women have two X chromosomes – one from each parent, just like any other chromosome. However, *Turner's syndrome* is caused by the entire or partial absence of a second sex chromosome as a complement to an existing X. This means that some affected individuals might have been male or female, depending on whether the X chromosome they have came from their mother or father. If it came from the mother (X^m for 'maternal X chromosome'), the missing sex chromosome from the father might have made them a normal male or female, depending on whether it was another X or a Y. If the X they have came from the father (X^p for 'paternal X'), they could be regarded as females without a second X chromosome from their mother (see above, pp. 47–9 and figure 7.2).

Ninety-five per cent of all embryos deficient in this way are aborted, but about two to three in 5,000 births is a case of Turner's syndrome (although often not diagnosed as such at the time). Those individuals

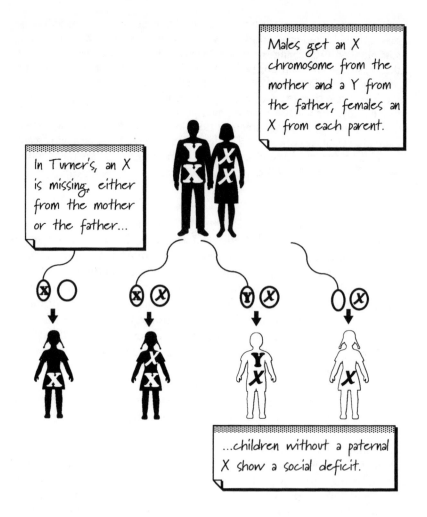

Figure 7.2   Turner's syndrome

affected grow up to be unusually short; they appear to be female, but fail to mature sexually at adolescence. Although sufferers from Turner's syndrome usually have normal intelligence and are often attractive in appearance, some tend to be socially insensitive, easily upset, impulsive and difficult to control. Indeed, their degree of social maladjustment can be greater than that seen in achondroplasia (hereditary

Box 7.7

Social adjustment in Turner's syndrome

In a questionnaire completed by the families of Turner's syndrome subjects, the following questions were found to correlate most strongly with the differential inheritance of a maternal as compared to a paternal X chromosome. Two separate unpublished twin studies found evidence that the social cognition competence trait measured by this questionnaire is strongly heritable (Skuse 1999).

All the questions concern social adjustment and sensitivity to other people. The families were asked to what extent the following statements described their daughter:

- lacking an awareness of other people's feelings;
- does not realize when others are upset or angry;
- is oblivious to the effect of her behaviour on other members of the family;
- behaviour often disrupts normal family life;
- very demanding of other people's time;
- difficult to reason with when upset;
- does not seem to understand social skills: e.g. interrupts conversation;
- does not pick up body language;
- unaware of unacceptable social behaviour;
- unknowingly offends people with behaviour;
- does not respond to commands;
- has difficulty following commands unless carefully worded (Skuse et al. 1997).

dwarfism), which suggests that it is not entirely due to appearance, or to social discrimination.

Closer analysis has revealed that the reason why social maladjustment is found in some cases of Turner's and not in others is that there are two different forms of the syndrome, depending on which parent the single X chromosome came from (X^p or X^m). A recent study found that X^p Turner's patients (with a paternal X, or those who would have been normal females had they received an X from their mothers) scored markedly better on measures of social sensitivity and responsiveness than X^m patients (those whose X chromosome came from their mother, and who might have been male or female depending on which sex chromosome they would have got from their father). X^m subjects were particularly deficient in a test that demands the inhibition of an inappropriate response in favour of a more appropriate one. On the same test, X^p subjects tended to have similar scores to normal women with two X chromosomes (see box 7.7, 'Social adjustment in Turner's syndrome').

Unlike women, men have only a single X chromosome from their mother, paired with a single Y chromosome from their father. For this reason men should resemble the X^m Turner's syndrome patients (those who might have been normal males or females, depending on which sex chromosome they would have got from their father), rather than X^p patients (who would have been normal females in any event because the sex chromosome they are lacking would have had to have been an X from the mother). The study found that Turner's syndrome patients with a paternal X like normal females did indeed score better on the inhibition test than did males. Again like males, X^m Turner's syndrome sufferers might be expected to be more vulnerable to disorders of language and social adjustment than normal females or X^p Turner's syndrome patients, and this was also confirmed by the study. Indeed, almost 4 per cent of the X^m Turner's syndrome women patients included in the sample were found to be suffering from autism, which normally affects less than one in 10,000 females but from three to ten times more males (see above, pp. 113–15).

Further experiments on eight subjects who were lacking only part of the paternal X chromosome suggested that the cause of their deficits in social responsiveness was a single gene that is expressed when it is part of the X chromosome inherited from the father but is silent when it is part of that from the mother (in other words, an imprinted gene: see above, pp. 192–6). This would explain why Turner's syndrome patients with only a paternal X do so much better in measures of social behaviour than do those with just the copy of the X chromosome that they inherited from their mothers.

It would also explain why X^m Turner's syndrome patients resemble males – who also have a maternal X – in respect of deficits in social sensitivity more than they do females, who have a paternal X (see figure 7.2 above) (Skuse et al. 1997). As David Skuse (who led the team that discovered the X chromosome gene implicated in Turner's syndrome) points out, if you were a male hominid 'it could have been an advantage to be socially undeveloped up to adolescence. You wouldn't find many women prepared to face the guns at Gallipoli, but there were plenty of men prepared to do it. Maybe if you are going out to kill people, less empathy is an advantage' (Hawkes 1997). Given that homicidal conflict is an almost exclusively male activity in all known societies (Daly and Wilson 1988), and that in cases like the Yanomamö a man's reproductive success is directly related to the number of homicides he has committed (see above, pp. 165–6), Skuse

Box 7.8

Darwin's intellectual pedigree

The figure illustrates part of Charles Darwin's family tree. Brilliant and scientifically gifted men are highlighted to show the way in which their intellectual talents may have been transmitted through the female line. There is now evidence that Charles Darwin received Joshua Wedgewood's X chromosome and therefore his intelligence through his mother Susanna. Similarly, Erasmus Darwin's brilliance reappeared in Francis Galton via his mother, Frances, rather than his father. (Mary Howard was also related to the Galtons.) Until recently, exactly the same facts were interpreted to suggest that the intellectual eminence of these men was transmitted through the Y chromosome: Darwin, having received Erasmus Darwin's Y chromosome via his own gifted father, and Francis Galton having received it from his grandfather. (Summarized and redrawn from Resta 1995.)

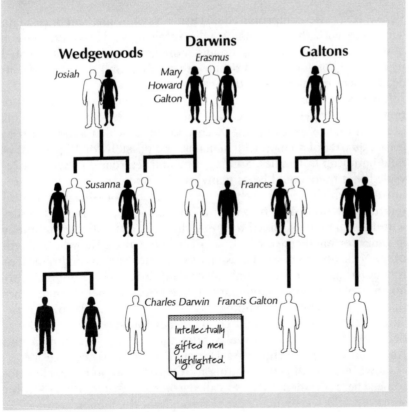

clearly has a point. At the very least, because the male psyche is biased towards risk-taking (see above, p. 14), the number of situations in which men demonstrate consistently superior inhibitory abilities to women can be expected to be few (Bjorklund and Kipp 1996).

More recent brain-imaging studies have revealed that there are indeed regular differences in brain structure between X^m and X^p Turner's syndrome patients. Those with a maternal X have reductions in the amount of grey matter in a part of the brain believed to be involved in recall of verbal memory, and do correspondingly worse on measures of such recall as compared with X^p patients. However, X^p subjects do less well on tests of spatial recall than do X^m individuals, and have brain peculiarities in areas concerned primarily with the processing of motor skills (Skuse 1998).

IQ has a maternal dimension

Verbal IQ is also compromised in Turner's syndrome, and once again it is those with the maternal X who suffer most. However, there is now compelling evidence that many more genes than the one isolated by the study of Turner's syndrome are involved and that these do indeed benefit members of both sexes.

It has been known for a hundred years that mental handicap is more prevalent in males by an excess of the order of 25–50 per cent. This excess is due to genes on the X chromosome, which account for at least a quarter of all handicap in males, and possibly for 10 per cent of mild handicap in females. Studies of mental retardation have now revealed that there could be as many as 150-odd genes on the X chromosome which are directly or indirectly responsible for mental retardation. According to a recent summary, genes found in families with mental deficits linked to the X chromosome indicate mutations in genes for intelligence which are distributed along the whole length of the X chromosome, and presumably code for various anatomical or functional parts of the neural substratum of IQ. There are presently no known genes, either dominant or recessive, on other chromosomes that could explain these findings (G. Turner 1996a, 1996b). For example, a study of 4,383 children in Orkney found that verbal IQ was definitely X-linked in normal school-age children (Goodman and Anderton 1997). (See box 7.8, 'Darwin's intellectual pedigree'.)

However, not all genes relating to IQ are found on the X chromosome. There is evidence that so-called *general cognitive ability* – g, for short – is affected by many genes throughout the human genome. As such, *g* is measured by standard IQ tests, and has been claimed to be one of the most highly heritable behavioural traits. For example, a recent report of a 20–year longitudinal adoption study showed that adopted children become increasingly like their biological parents from childhood through adolescence and to the same degree as children in non-adoptive families (Chorney et al. 1998).

More recently still, Robert Plomin and colleagues studied 51 children aged 6 to 15 years with mean IQ scores of 136, and compared them with a control group of similar size and age but with a mean IQ of 103 (100 is the average IQ for the population as a whole). Plomin and his fellow researchers then searched chromosome 6 for DNA markers that might correlate with IQ. They had no particular target gene in mind, and had only chosen this chromosome because they had been advised that this would be the first to be fully sequenced by the human genome project. The gene they found was the human form of *IGF2R*. The study's authors are quick to point out that 'this association accounts for only a small portion of genetic influence on *g*; it is not the gene for *g* but may be one of many genes responsible for the high heritability of *g*.' Moreover, they add that *IGF2R* 'does not even have this small effect on each individual': the association with *IGF2R* 'refers only to an average effect in the population'. But whatever qualifications need to be made about it, the fact remains that this is a landmark discovery in being the first to find a specific gene linked to high IQ anywhere in the human genome (Chorney et al. 1998).

As the authors of this paper also point out, the fact that *IGF2R* has been found to be statistically associated with high IQ in their sample does not mean that the gene is in fact contributing to *g*. What they have found may simply be a genetic marker that is close to other genes that do directly contribute to measures of IQ. To this extent, the finding may be coincidental. Nevertheless, we have already seen that *Igf2r* is a paradigmatic maternally active gene (at least in mice), and that it works by producing a sink for a paternally active insulin-like growth factor (see above, pp. 196–8). Furthermore, there is recent evidence that insulin may play a role in spurring neuronal growth that contributes to learning and memory in the brain (Wickelgren 1998). This raises the question of how an *Igf2*-antagonist in mice (and presumably also in ancestral mammals) came to evolve into a gene that is linked to high IQ in some human beings. Until we know the details of how *IGF2R* works in humans we shall not be able to answer this question, but a possible explanation will serve both to bring this book to a conclusion, and to suggest a completely new way of looking at the nature/nurture controversy – not to mention IQ.[2]

Nature, Nurture, Language and Culture

The nature of nurture

The nature/nurture controversy is often seen as pitting genes against culture. However, to the extent that the cultural, nurture factor represents other people (such as socializers who may be parents or peers), the conflict is not so much between genes and culture as between genes in the individual and genes in other people. As Robert Trivers has pointed out,

> it is clearly a mistake to view socialization in humans (or in any sexually reproducing species) as only, or even primarily, a process of 'enculturation' by which parents teach offspring their culture. . . . one is not permitted to assume that parents who attempt to impart such virtues as responsibility, decency, honesty, trustworthiness, generosity, and self-denial are merely providing the offspring with useful information on the appropriate behaviour in the local culture; for all such virtues are likely to affect the amount of altruistic and egoistic behavior impinging on the parent's kin, and parent and offspring are expected to view such behavior differently. . . . socialization is a process by which parents attempt to mold each offspring in order to increase their own inclusive fitness, whereas each offspring is selected to resist some of the molding and to attempt to mold the behavior of its parents (and siblings) in order to increase its own inclusive fitness. Conflict during socialization need not be viewed solely as conflict between the culture of the parent and the biology of the child, it can also be viewed as conflict between the biology of the parent and the biology of the child. Since teaching (as opposed to molding) is expected to be recognized by offspring as being in their own self-interest, parents would be expected to overemphasize their role as teachers in order to minimize resistance in their young. According to this view, then, the prevailing concept of socialization is to some extent a view that one would expect adults to entertain and disseminate. (Trivers 1981)

The recent discovery of genomic imprinting and its apparent role in building the mammalian brain suggests a further fascinating development of this line of thinking. From this point of view of the nature/nurture issue, parental genes are ranged on different sides of the conflict: as we have already seen, paternal genes alone appear to build the emotional, limbic brain, while maternal genes alone construct the cerebral cortex. To the extent that the limbic system is implicated in the control of drives, appetites and basic emotional responses such as fear, pleasure and pain, you could see it as predominantly identified with the nature side of the nature/nurture conflict. Equally, you could iden-

Box 7.9

Genetic conflict, brain evolution, learning and culture

The recent discovery that maternal and paternal genes have antagonistic interests and play different roles in building discrete parts of the brain suggests a
completely new approach to brain evolution, learning and culture (see above,
pp. 204–8). This is the possibility that the exponential growth of the human
brain in recent evolutionary history might be the outcome of an evolutionary
arms race between maternal and paternal genes for control of growth, development and behaviour. The massive proliferation of the cerebral cortex might
be explained as an attempt by maternal genes to build an ever larger neurological buffer to counter escalating demands from the paternally controlled limbic
system which requires much less in the way of additional neuronal circuitry. To
this extent, the cortex could be seen as a cognitive jammer primarily designed
to drown out the instincts of the limbic system in the self-interest of the mother's genes.

Such a theory would immediately and aptly explain the maternal energy hypothesis: the finding that mammals have the largest brains their mothers can
afford. It would also explain why it is human mothers rather than anyone else
who pay most of the costs of human brain development thanks to the enormous resource demands and the obstetric complications that the human neocortex inflicts on them (see above, pp. 33–6). Again, this would explain why all
adaptationist theories of human brain evolution have failed; according to this
point of view, if the human brain is adapted for anything, it is adapted primarily
for psychological expression of the genetic conflict that results from the fact
that the individual is a temporary coalition of maternal and paternal, male and
female genes (see above, pp. 189–98). Finally, Freudian psychology would find
an immediate and unexpected evolutionary foundation in the suggestion that
the ego and the id could be seen as epigenetic agents of the maternal and
paternal genomes of the individual respectively (see above, pp. 212–22).

Once one side in an evolutionary arms race has the ability to learn – and, still
more, to pass on its expertise to the next generation – it has an enormous
advantage if the other side is reliant simply on mutation (Dawkins and Krebs
1979). In the case of the two parts of the brain, it is clear that both have evolved
the ability to learn, but only one of them – the cortical brain – has acquired the
capacity to pass on its learning in the form of instruction via language and
gesture. This is because speech and voluntary movement are controlled from
the maternally constructed cortex, rather than from the paternally built limbic
brain.

What the cortical brain learns is what is most distinctive of human beings:
our conscious, verbally expressible knowledge or culture. Up to now, culture
was often seen as something antithetical to – or at least quite different from –
nature, and has been widely regarded as having taken over from biological

evolution as the driving force of human progress. But now we can begin to see an astonishing new possibility. This is that, far from being exempt from nature or emancipated from evolution, culture may be another product of genetic conflict and of the evolutionary arms race that this has set up between the different parts of the brain that conflicting genes build. Far from culture going beyond nature or evolving beyond biological evolution, it may be that culture is the product of an evolutionary escalation in learning abilities that gave the human neocortex an ability to acquire knowledge by instruction, and to teach it to new generations.

At the very least, the fact that both parts of the brain may have acquired a strongly developed capacity for learning as part of an evolutionary arms race readily and immediately explains how human beings could have evolved an ability to learn in general and to excess, rather than simply to learn specific skills or behaviours that might have been selected (such as how to throw stones accurately or avoid predators). If an ability to learn irrespective of what was learnt was an enormous advantage to one side in the evolutionary arms race between the two parts of the brain, the brain would have been pre-adapted to all the modern uses to which its impressive learning abilities can now be put.

Indeed, if the memory system of the cortex were more superficial and fallible than that of the limbic brain, as it indeed appears to be, it might also be much less discriminating about what you could teach it, and as a result would be able to learn more or less anything. Such knowledge might be more difficult to learn in certain respects and much more easily forgotten than what is learnt by the limbic brain, but there would be much more of it, and what it lacked in emotive force it might make up for in cognitive complexity. Certainly, purely cognitive features such as plausibility, logical coherence and internal consistency would be important to this type of learning, and could be expected to be vastly enhanced in attempts to make it compelling. Here may lie the evolutionary origins of logic, philosophy, science and all forms of knowledge that exploit rational argument to make their point – evolutionary psychology included (Badcock, in press).

tify the cerebral cortex with most of what we take to be cultural and nurtured: conscious self-control; everything that is learnt by instruction and precept; language; and social awareness (see above, pp. 204–8).

According to this approach, the nature/nurture controversy would not be so much *about* genes and culture as a product of a deeper genetic conflict: one between maternal and paternal genes that build different brain systems, motivate different types of behaviour, and conflict over fundamental issues like egoism and altruism, heredity and environment, instinct and intellect.

The maternal genome of the individual will be biased in favour of *altruism* because maternal genes will always be shared with other offspring of the same mother to a 50 per cent probability, even if paternal genes are not so shared. As we saw in this chapter, female primates tend to be more pro-social than males, and as we saw in an earlier chapter, relatedness is critical to altruism (see above, pp. 79–88).

Maternally active genes will have a prejudice in favour of *environment* over heredity because the mammalian mother *is* the offspring's environment before birth and usually remains the most powerful and pervasive influence on it for a considerable time afterwards, thanks to breast-feeding and a universal tendency for the mother to be the primary caregiver. Paternal genes, however, may have to rely on themselves alone if the father is not present, or is much less of an important influence on the child, especially in early childhood (see above, pp. 220–2).

Lastly, the maternal genes of the individual will favour *intellect* over instinct for much the same reasons: instinct can be biologically programmed by paternal genes, but the mother's genes can rely on her nurturing role and pervasive environmental influence to educate and mould the psychology of her children by instruction, precept and example.

Again, intellect can often control, suppress and inhibit more basic instinctual responses in ways that serve the interests of the maternal genome. In an earlier chapter we saw that, according to the evidence from readiness potentials, action is unconsciously initiated well before consciousness becomes aware of having made up its mind to do something. However, the same studies showed that conscious awareness does appear to be able to inhibit an action just before it is executed (see above, p. 136). Indeed, according to a recent summary of the experimental findings relating to the role of inhibition in human cognition,

> much of what is special about human cognition and social control of behavior seems to involve significant inhibitory components above and beyond that displayed by our close genetic relatives. We show greater voluntary control of emotions, particularly sexual behavior, than any other species; we are able to delay gratification (sometimes for years) in the quest of a goal; we can deceive others or hide our true feelings, often to our political (or simply physical) advantage. Each of these behaviours, while perhaps not unique to humans, reaches its zenith in *Homo sapiens* and contributes to our success as a species. Each also involves inhibition. Thus, humans' apparently increased emotional control relative to other primates is not likely [to be] due to a reduction in the role of the limbic system in human behavior; we remain highly emotional

animals. A more likely cause is inhibition from the prefrontal cortex. (Bjorklund and Harnishfeger 1995)

Finally, we have seen earlier in this chapter that there is now considerable evidence of a maternal bias in genes linked to IQ, language ability and social behaviour – all of these functions being primarily supported, of course, by the maternally made neocortex of which the prefrontal cortex is just the most prominent part. (See box 7.9, 'Genetic conflict, brain evolution, learning and culture'.)

The new insights can remedy the failings of both the SSSM and evolutionary psychology

The nature/nurture debate is often dismissed as little more than a foolish misunderstanding or a case of confused categories. However, if the reasoning suggested here is correct, we can now see that, far from being a superficial issue, the nature/nurture controversy has profound evolutionary and biological roots. If it is true that the nurture view represents a bias of the maternal genome built into the brain in the form of the cerebral cortex and that the nature side of the controversy does indeed express the prejudice of paternally active genes that build the limbic system, then this conflict is one that is rooted in the genome and has a history stretching back to the origin of the mammals and their imprinted genome 200-odd million years ago.

This way of looking at the controversy suggests that, whatever some evolutionary psychologists may say, the SSSM contains much truth and is securely founded on a genetic reality: the evolutionary self-interest of maternal genes. Consequently, the claims of studies based on the assumptions of the nurture position can't necessarily be rejected out of hand as worthless or without a biological basis. On the contrary, the new insights into genetic conflict suggest that, albeit unknowingly, the SSSM indeed has a secure biological basis, and one, furthermore, which could remedy all three of the principal criticisms that evolutionists make against it.

Although pioneers of sociology like Durkheim might have been completely unable to provide a reductive, scientific basis for their claims about society, enough has been said in this book to suggest that today the situation may be quite different. The chapter on the evolution and psychology of co-operation showed clearly that group behaviour can have both a bottom-up as well as a top-down explanation: group conformity can pay individuals as individuals and does not necessarily have to be imposed on them against their will or self-interest from above (see above, pp. 76–8).

Again, the recent insights into Turner's syndrome described earlier in this chapter show that genes for aspects of social behaviour definitely exist – and indeed have demonstrable effects on brain development and manifest behaviour. The chapter on sex and mating gave several examples of how fundamental biological realities like parental investment and variance of reproductive success affect many different aspects of behaviour in all human societies. And although the chapter on mind and emotion showed that cultural determinists were wrong about the expression of basic emotions and that Darwin was right, it also ended by showing how the very topography of consciousness has been shaped by human social interaction, and could hardly have evolved without it (at least if Trivers and others are to be believed: see above, pp. 132–48).

No longer need sociologists be trapped in the vicious circularities of society-creates-society cultural creationism or make excuses that society is too complex or inherently inexplicable to be explained in simpler terms. Instead, the new insights from evolution and genetics could provide a sound scientific foundation to complement and complete the traditional holistic approach of the social sciences. No more need the social sciences be distinguished by their biophobia and fear of anything evolutionary or genetic. On the contrary, with a secure foundation in evolution and genetics, sociology could rediscover its historic claims to be a science and might once again start being taken seriously by those outside its ever narrowing confines.

If something like this were to come about in the social sciences, evolutionary psychology would find its proper place as the discipline that mediated between genes and evolution on the one side and society and culture on the other via its peculiar competence: the psychology of the evolved mind. As I have emphasized throughout this book, evolutionary psychology is essentially the study of the way in which natural and sexual selection have shaped brains to act as the epigenetic agents of the genes that build them (see above, pp. 69–71). However, to date, evolutionary psychology has thought about the problem principally in terms of the whole organism, and has seldom considered the possibility of conflict between different parts of the individual's genome. Nevertheless, if the approach suggested in the last two chapters of this book is in any way correct, it suggests a new possibility. This is that there is not just one brain with one evolved psychology, but at least two, and that different brain systems motivate different behaviour to benefit different sets of genes. And as I have just been arguing, the nature side of the nature/nurture controversy appears to correspond to one of these, and the nurture side to the other. Clearly, if evolutionary psychology is to succeed as an enterprise it must be the psychology of both, and should not allow itself to be biased in favour of one or the other. As such, it could transcend and resolve the nature/nurture debate in the way I have just suggested and make itself a complete science of the mind.

However, in order to do that it would have to overcome its one-sided emphasis on the cortex and cognition that I mentioned earlier, and ought to reassess its attitude to brain evolution in particular and mental adaptations in general (see above, pp. 123–5 and 24–36). Indeed, if the argument of the last chapter is taken seriously, evolutionary psychology ought to return to its true historical roots in Darwin *and* Freud and re-emerge as a complete science of the mind, cognitive *and* emotional, conscious *and* unconscious, evolved *and* cultured. Whether it can meet this challenge remains to be seen, but time will tell.

Essentially, the issue is the one with which we began: although we may be the only organisms in the known universe to have begun to comprehend their own evolution, it remains an open question to what extent we will ever really be able to understand it. Like it or not, evolutionary psychology will be the test of our success or failure.

Suggestions for further reading

Blackmore, S. (1999)   *The Meme Machine.*
Freeman, D. (1983)   *Margaret Mead and Samoa: The Making and Unmaking of an Anthropological Myth.*
Gould, J. and C. Gould (1994)   *The Animal Mind.*
Harris, J. R. (1999b)   *The Nurture Assumption: Why Children Turn Out the Way They Do.*
Plomin, R. et al. (1997)   *Behavioral Genetics.*

Glossary of Technical Terms

abreaction The expression of a repressed mental content along with the allied emotions, memories and associations.

adaptation A feature of an organism that results from natural selection and is assumed to promote its possessor's survival and/or reproductive success.

allele A particular copy of a gene, especially one of the two copies of each gene found in organisms that receive complete copies of their genome from each parent.

altruism Any behaviour whereby one organism promotes the reproductive success of another at its own expense.

ambivalence The simultaneous existence of contradictory feelings, ideas or wishes about the same object.

amygdala A component of the limbic system primarily concerned with fear reactions, but also involved in memory and face recognition.

androgenetic (ag) chimera A chimera composed predominantly of paternal cells.

anisogamy The typical difference in size between gametes or sex cells.

anorexia A psychological syndrome featuring aversion to eating, almost always in young women.

anosognosia A disorder in which a patient suffering a physical deficit (typically a left-side paralysis) denies all knowledge of it.

anti-mentalism The belief that the mind and mental states can't be the subjects of scientific scrutiny.

antithesis Darwin's second principle of the expression of the emotions which proposes that some expressions take the form they do by way of being negations, denials or reversals of other expressions.

artificial selection As opposed to natural selection, this means the differential survival and reproductive success of organisms as the result of human intervention.

autosome Any chromosome that is not a sex chromosome.

behaviourism A school of psychology that emphasized conditioning and believed that only an organism's behaviour could be the subject of scientific study.

biophobia A prejudice against anything biological.

blindsight   Unconscious visual perception.

bridewealth   A payment made by a man for a wife, usually to the bride's family.

catharsis   The relief of psychological symptoms through abreaction.

cerebral commissurotomy   The partial or complete severance of the links between the two halves of the cerebral cortex.

chimera   An organism composed of cells from different organisms in a way that would never normally occur in nature.

chromosome   An extended piece of DNA encoding many genes and coiled up as one unit in the nucleus of a cell.

clone   A genetically identical copy of an organism.

cryptic oestrus   Concealment of any sign of impending ovulation in a sexually cycling female.

degree of relatedness (r)   The proportion of identical genes which two related individuals share by common descent.

diploid   An adjective indicating that two complete sets of genes are present, for example, one inherited from each parent.

DNA   An acronym for deoxyribonucleic acid, the organic polymer in which genetic information is encoded in nearly all known organisms.

dominant allele   An allele is dominant if it is preferentially expressed in relation to a corresponding recessive one on the paired chromosome.

dowry   A payment which the bride or her family makes to her husband on marriage.

ego   A term used by Freud to describe the partly conscious, largely unconscious agency of the personality charged with responsibility for voluntary thought and action.

environment of evolutionary adaptedness   The conditions in which an adaptation originally evolved.

enzyme   A biochemical catalyst, or substance that controls or facilitates chemical reactions without necessarily being changed itself.

epigenesis   A mode of development in which organisms are generated from sets of instructions rather than being preformed.

epigenetic agent   The organism seen as an agent of its genes.

epigenetics   The study of the way in which genes are translated into organisms and their behaviour.

eusociality   A reproductive division of labour in which some organisms are sterile and others not.

evolution   According to Darwin, a process of gradual change resulting from some organisms leaving more descendants than others as a consequence of natural selection.

evolutionary stable strategy (ESS)   A strategy which, if adopted by all members of a population, can't be invaded by any other strategy.

exogamy   A social norm requiring individuals to marry outside their natal group.

female   Where sex cells vary in size, the female always has the larger.

female choice   A tendency for females to prefer some males as reproductive partners to others.

fitness   In strict Darwinian terms, the ultimate reproductive success of an organism in some indefinite, future generation.

g   A measure of general cognitive ability.

gamete   A sex cell, such as an egg or sperm.

gene   A sequence of DNA coding for one particular protein.

genetic code   Triplets of DNA bases that spell out specific amino acids or act as punctuation marks for transcription.

genome, genotype   The total complement of genetic information in an organism.

genomic imprinting   The expression or silencing of alleles dependent on which parent bequeathed them.

germ line   The lineage of cells through which genes are passed from one generation to another.

group selection   The idea that natural selection can act on entire groups of organisms.

haplo-diploid   A genetic system in which some individuals are haploid and some are diploid, for example the social insects, where males are haploid and females diploid.

haploid   An adjective indicating that only one complete set of genes is present.

holism   The belief that the whole is greater than the sum of its parts.

hypergyny   Marriage of a woman into a group of superior status.

hypothalamus   Part of the limbic system concerned with drives, appetite, metabolism, temperature control, and basic emotional reactions.

id   Freud's term for the unconscious part of the personality constituted by repressed elements and primal drives.

inclusive fitness   The sum total of the reproductive success of identical genes carried in related organisms by common descent.

kin altruism   Any behaviour by means of which related individuals promote one another's reproductive success.

Lamarckism   The evolutionary theories of Jean-Baptiste Lamarck, but nowadays especially the belief in the inheritance of acquired characteristics.

leakage clues   The tendency of those practising a deception to reveal the truth inadvertently through voice, gesture or body language.

limbic system   Also referred to as the 'emotional brain', it is the lower, unconscious part of the brain concerned with 'gut reactions', drives and motivation.

major histocompatibility complex (MHC)   Part of the genome which plays a key role in the immunological response to pathogens.

male   Where sexes can be distinguished, the male is always characterized by the smaller, more mobile sex cell.

maternally active   An allele that is expressed when inherited from the mother, but not when inherited from the father.

meiosis   The halving of the number of chromosomes that occurs when diploid organisms produce haploid sex cells.

meme   A cultural entity corresponding to the gene that replicates itself in human minds and cultural practices.

menarche   The point at which menstruation in particular, and sexual cycling in general, begin to occur in a woman.

mental module   A functional organization of the mind that has been evolved for one specific adaptive purpose.

mentalism   The belief that the mind and mental states are valid subjects of scientific scrutiny.

mitochondria   Specialized subunits of the cell involved in metabolism.

monogamy A mating system in which one male is normally mated to one female, either for a season or for longer.

mutation Any change in a gene that is heritable.

natural selection The influence which purely natural factors have on the differential survival and reproductive success of organisms.

neocortex The outer, convoluted covering of the brain that supports perception, motor control, thought, conscious memory, and the more characteristically human functions of the mind such as language and consciousness.

neurotransmitter A chemical that facilitates communications between nerve cells.

nice strategy In prisoner's dilemma a strategy is nice if it begins with a co-operation.

oestrus A point in the sexual cycle of a female when ovulation occurs.

pangenesis Darwin's theory of inheritance which proposed that 'gemmules' circulated throughout the body carrying features of the organism (including some acquired ones) to the sex cells so that they could be passed on to the next generation.

paradigm An example, epitome or model that can be used to generate new instances of something.

parental investment Any benefit to the reproductive success of an offspring at a cost to the remainder of the parent's reproductive success.

parthenogenetic (pg) chimera An organism composed predominantly of maternal cells.

paternally active An allele that is expressed when inherited from the father, but not when inherited from the mother.

phenotype The totality of an organism's body and behaviour.

pleasure principle According to Freud, the prime motivation of the unconscious concerned with gratifying the organism's needs irrespective of reality or others.

polyandry A mating system in which one female is mated to a number of males.

polygamy A mating system in which a number of females are mated to a number of males.

polygyny A mating system in which one male is mated to a number of females.

preconscious Anything that could be voluntarily recalled to consciousness.

preformationism The belief that everything in the adult organism is already contained in the fertilized egg or embryo.

prisoner's dilemma A situation in which the pay-off for co-operating with or defecting against another individual is determined by the other individual's co-operation or defection in such a way that co-operating when the other defects is always the worst outcome, defecting when the other co-operates is always the best, and mutual co-operation is more rewarding than mutual defection.

prosopagnosia The inability to recognize well-known faces such as those of family, friends or famous people.

pseudogene A sequence of DNA that is not translated into protein.

readiness potentials Electrophysiological responses in the brain that signal cerebral initiation of a voluntary act.

reality principle According to Freud, the ego's awareness of reality which conflicts with the workings of the pleasure principle in the id.

recessive allele An allele which is not expressed if paired with a dominant one on the corresponding chromosome.

reciprocity   The equalization of benefit in a two–party interaction.

regression   Action or appearance which makes an organism seem younger than it really is.

repression   The active exclusion of thoughts, wishes and feelings from consciousness.

reproductive success   The total number of an organism's descendants.

reverse-engineering   The process of inferring an adaptation's function from its design.

rhinencephalon   The lower brain, or limbic system, and especially the part of it concerned with the sense of smell.

ribosome   A subunit of the cell responsible for transcribing the genetic code into proteins.

robust strategy   In prisoner's dilemma a strategy is robust if it can't easily be exploited by other strategies.

Sapir-Whorf hypothesis   The belief that language constrains thought and meaning.

selfish DNA   DNA that gets itself copied into future generations, but does not code for protein and is therefore of no use to the organism.

sex ratio   The relative numbers of males and females in a population.

sexual bimaturism   The tendency for the sexes typically to mature at different ages.

sexual dimorphism   A regular difference in appearance between the sexes which is typical of the sex in question.

sexual selection   Selection for traits which bear closely on sex, mating or reproductive success.

Social Darwinism   The political movement associated with Spencer's erroneous understanding of evolution as a progressive mechanism.

somatic cells   Those cells of the organism which are distinct from the germ line and so do not pass genes on to subsequent generations.

standard social science model (SSSM)   The view of human nature and psychology characteristic of mid and later twentieth-century social science and typified by an emphasis on social causes, holism and a neglect of biological factors.

superego   According to Freud, a part of the ego constituted by a sense of guilt and internalization of, and identification with, parental figures, values and aspirations.

theory of mind   The ability to intuit that other people have minds and to interpret, predict and react to their behaviour accordingly.

topographic   The differentiation of consciousness into various levels and parts, such as conscious and unconscious.

unconscious   That which is inaccessible to conscious, voluntary recall.

variance of reproductive success   Deviations from average reproductive success in a population, typically greater in males.

variation   Any heritable differences in a population.

X^m   The maternal X chromosome.

X^p   The paternal X chromosome.

Notes

Chapter 1   Selection and Adaptation

1   We shall look at mutation again in chapter 2, where it will be set in the context of something that Darwin got completely wrong but was critical to his theory: inheritance (see below, pp. 38–44).

2   The extent to which natural selection is the only or even the principal mechanism of evolution has always been controversial, and remains so today. As we shall see in chapter 5 below, Darwin also invoked sexual selection, but a discussion of this is best left until the whole issue of sex is dealt with (see below, pp. 149–88).

3   As we shall see in chapter 3, p. 88 below, our modern concept of fitness – inclusive fitness – makes Social Darwinist misunderstandings of the concept all the more obvious, but we must postpone further consideration of the issue until then.

4   More about clutch sizes can be found in chapter 3 below: see p. 74.

5   The most rigorous way of reverse-engineering an adaptation would be to specify what gene or genes were responsible for it because genes are the ultimate units of heredity and all adaptations must be heritable. But as we shall see in the next chapter, reverse-engineering genes is impossible, both in principle and in practice (see below, pp. 55–71).

6   A later chapter will examine the attitude of evolutionary psychology to Darwin's views on the evolution of the emotions: see chapter 4 below, pp. 115–25.

7   Reasons why mothers should have an evolutionary self-interest in brain development will be suggested later: see box 7.9, 'Genetic conflict, brain evolution, learning and culture', p. 263. For a more complete attempt to answer this question see Badcock (in press).

Chapter 2   Genetics and Epigenetics

1   In the last two or three decades, further exceptions to Mendel's laws – although only where the expression rather than the inheritance of genes is con-

cerned – have been found. These are so important and so critical to evolutionary psychology that much of an entire chapter will be devoted to them: see below, chapter 6, pp. 192–6.

2 Admittedly, so-called *homeobox genes* do map in their order on the chromosome the order of segmentation of the embryo during development. However, this is a very weak form of mapping, and in no way corresponds to the strict one-to-one equivalence you find between blueprints and the articles made from them.

3 Because genes are not blueprints, they can't be reverse-engineered in the sense that you could take an adaptation and work backwards to the genes that code for it. This means that the reverse-engineering approach of evolutionary psychology discussed in the previous chapter is ultimately a futile pursuit, and can only produce speculations about adaptations, never their physical embodiment in genes (see above, pp. 16–22).

4 In what follows, human genes are italicized and upper case, mouse genes are italicized lower case.

Chapter 3   The Evolution and Psychology of Co-operation

1 In discussing the meaning of 'fitness' in the first chapter, I pointed out a number of common misunderstandings and fallacies to which it can lead. One virtue of inclusive fitness is that it is much less likely to encourage misunderstanding because it is self-evidently a technical term, and rests on a quantitative measure. Hamilton's insight means that we should rephrase Spencer's notorious slogan as 'survival of the inclusively fittest' (see above, pp. 6–9).

2 Further suggestions by Trivers relating to the evolution of human psychology in the context of reciprocity will be taken up in the next chapter, pp. 132–48 below. As we shall see there, Trivers's insights have some important implications for the evolutionary psychology of consciousness.

Chapter 4   Mind, Emotion and Consciousness

1 More will be said about behaviourism and in particular about conditioning in the concluding chapter (see below, pp. 238–43).

2 But see pp. 23–4 above for a more recent view, at least where gesturing accompanying speech is concerned.

3 We saw in the second chapter that evolutionary psychologists in the main ignore the 'triune brain' theory, which LeDoux's research into the neurological basis of emotion has tended to corroborate (see above, pp. 24–7).

4 It is also perhaps worth adding that although Lumsden and Wilson deserve credit for giving due prominence to the concept of epigenetic rules, they notably fail to mention the pleasure/pain principle as the obvious example in animal behaviour, despite the precedent set by both Darwin and Spencer (Lumsden and Wilson 1981: 131).

Chapter 6   Growth, Development and Conflict

1   If so, this might provide a genetic explanation for the finding that the presence of a father appears to be critical for the social development of children in a family (Lamb 1981). See box 6.4, p. 223 below.

2   Further consideration is given to the role of imprinted genes in human psychology and brain development in the concluding chapter, pp. 253–60, and 262–8 below.

3   Nevertheless, there is probably more to the Oedipus complex than this. In later childhood when it is focused on the parent of the opposite sex in both girls and boys, the male Oedipus complex at least may be an instance of *sexual imprinting*. Male ducks who are placed as eggs in the nests of another duck species or male sheep or goats who are reared by mothers of the other species usually attempt mating with females of the adoptive species when they mature. This has been interpreted as a naturally selected mechanism to ensure that males (who can be notoriously unselective about whom or what they mate with) choose mates of their own species rather than another by taking their own mothers as models of sexual objects. As a recent report remarks, 'This indirectly supports Freud's concept of the Oedipus complex' (Kendrick et al. 1998), and another adds that 'in both mammals and birds imprinting is typically much stronger between mothers and sons than between mothers and daughters' (Owens et al. 1999). This may explain why Freud found the Oedipus complex to be a much more pronounced factor in men than in women.

Chapter 7   Nature, Nurture, Language and Culture

1   Not everyone accepts this view of SLI. For a recent account of the controversy that puts it in the context of evolutionary psychology see Ridley 1999: 91–102.

2   At the very least, it suggests that my comment earlier about the cortical brain being to the limbic system somewhat as *Igf2* is to *Igf2r* is not completely speculative, but does in fact relate to *IGF2R* in humans – at least in so far as it may be implicated in a prime cortical function: IQ (see above, pp. 204–8).

References

Adams, H. E., L. W. Wright and B. A. Lohr (1996) Is homophobia associated with homosexual arousal? *Journal of Abnormal Psychology* 105(3): 440–5.

Aiello, L. C. and P. Wheeler (1995) The expensive-tissue hypothesis: the brain and the digestive system in human and primate evolution. *Current Anthropology* 36(2): 199–221.

Alexander, R. D. and K. M. Noonan (1979) Concealment of ovulation, parental care, and human evolution. In *Evolutionary Biology and Human Social Behaviour*, ed. N. Chagnon and W. Irons, North Scituate, Mass.: Duxbury.

Allen, N. D. et al. (1995) Distribution of parthenogenetic cells in the mouse brain and their influence on brain development and behavior. *Proceedings of the National Academy of Sciences, USA* 92(11/95): 10782–6.

Allman, J. and L. Brothers (1994) Faces, fear and the amygdala. *Nature* 372: 613–14.

Andelman, S. J. (1987) Evolution of concealed ovulation in vervet monkeys. *American Naturalist* 129: 785–99.

Anderson, J. L. and C. B. Crawford (1992) Modelling costs and benefits of adolescent weight control as a mechanism for reproductive suppression. *Human Nature* 3(4): 299–334.

Angelman, H. (1965) 'Puppet' children: a report on three cases. *Developmental Medicine and Child Neurology* 7: 681–8.

Armelagos, G. (1997) Disease, Darwin, and medicine in the third epidemiological transition. *Evolutionary Anthropology* 5(6): 212–20.

Augee, M. and B. Gooden (1993) *Echidnas of Australia and New Guinea*. Kensington: New South Wales University Press.

Axelrod, R. (1984) *The Evolution of Cooperation*. New York: Basic Books.

Badcock, C. R. (1994) *PsychoDarwinism: The New Synthesis of Darwin and Freud*. London: HarperCollins.

Badcock, C. R. (1998) PsychoDarwinism: the new synthesis of Darwin and Freud. In *Handbook of Evolutionary Psychology: Ideas, Issues and Applications*, ed. C. Crawford and D. Krebs, Hillsdale, N.J.: Lawrence Erlbaum.

Badcock, C. R. (in press) *The Maternal Brain and the Battle of the Sexes in the*

Mind. Munich: Carl Hanser.

Baker, R. and M. Bellis (1995) *Human Sperm Competition: Copulation, Mastur-bation and Infidelity*. London: Chapman and Hall.

Barash, D. (1979) *Sociobiology: The Whisperings Within*. London: Souvenir Press.

Barker, D. J. P. (1996) The unbearable lightness at birth. *Science and Public Affairs* (Spring): 33–7.

Barker, D. J. P. (1998) *Mothers, Babies and Health in Later Life*. Edinburgh: Churchill Livingstone.

Barker, D. J. P. (1999) The fetal origins of coronary heart disease and stroke: evolutionary implications. In *Evolution in Health and Disease*, ed. S. C. Stearns, Oxford: Oxford University Press.

Barkow, J., L. Cosmides and J. Tooby (eds) (1992) *The Adapted Mind: Evolutionary Psychology and the Generation of Culture*. Oxford: Oxford University Press.

Barlow, D. (1995) Gametic imprinting in mammals. *Science* 270 (8 Dec.): 1610–13.

Baron-Cohen, S. (1989) Are autistic children 'behaviourists'? An examination of their mental-physical and appearance–reality distinctions. *Journal of Autism and Developmental Disorders* 19(4): 579–600.

Baron-Cohen, S. (1995) *Mindblindness: An Essay on Autism and Theory of Mind*. Cambridge, Mass.: MIT Press.

Baron-Cohen, S. and P. Howlin (1993) The theory of mind deficit in autism: some questions for teaching and diagnosis. In *Understanding Other Minds*, ed. S. Baron-Cohen, H. Tager-Flusberg and D. J. Cohen, Oxford: Oxford University Press.

Bechara, A., H. Damasio, D. Tranel and A. R. Damasio (1997) Deciding advantageously before knowing the advantageous strategy. *Science* 275: 1293–5.

Beckers, R., O. Holland and J. Deneubourg (1994) From local actions to global tasks: stigmergy and collective robotics. In vol. 4 of *Artificial Life*, ed. R. Brooks and P. Maes, Cambridge, Mass.: MIT Press.

Bellugi, U. et al. (1992) Language, cognition, and brain organization in a neurodevelopmental disorder. In *Developmental Behavioral Neuroscience: The Minnesota Symposia on Child Psychology*, ed. M. Gunnar and C. Nelson, Hillsdale, N. J.: Lawrence Erlbaum.

Bereczkei, T. and R. I. M. Dunbar (1997) Female-biased reproductive strategies in a Hungarian Gypsy population. *Proceedings of the Royal Society of London B* 264: 17–22.

Berg, P. and M. Singer (1992) *Dealing with Genes: The Language of Heredity*. Mill Valley, Calif.: University Science Books.

Bernds, W. and D. Barash (1979) Early termination of parental investment in mammals, including humans. In *Evolutionary Biology and Human Social Behavior*, ed. N. Chagnon and W. Irons, North Scituate, Mass.: Duxbury.

Betzig, L. (1986) *Despotism and Differential Reproduction: A Darwinian View of History*. New York: Aldine de Gruyter.

Betzig, L. (ed.) (1997) *Human Nature: A Critical Reader*. New York: Oxford University Press.

Binmore, K. (1998) *Game Theory and the Social Contract*, vol. 2: *Just Playing*. Cambridge, Mass.: MIT Press.

Birdsell, J. B. (1979) Ecological influences on Australian Aboriginal social organization. In *Primate Ecology and Human Origins: Ecological Influences on Social Organization*, ed. I. S. Bernstein and E. O. Smith, New York: Garland.

Bittles, A., W. Mason, J. Greene and N. Rao (1991) Reproductive behavior and health in consanguineous marriages. *Science* 252: 789–94.

Bjorklund, D. F. and K. K. Harnishfeger (1995) The evolution of inhibition mechanisms and their role in human cognition and behavior. In *Interference and Inhibition in Cognition*, ed. F. N. Dempster and C. J. Brainerd, New York: Academic Press.

Bjorklund, D. F. and K. Kipp (1996) Parental investment theory and gender differences in the evolution of inhibition mechanisms. *Psychological Bulletin* 120(2): 163–88.

Blackmore, S. (1999) *The Meme Machine*. Oxford: Oxford University Press.

Blum, K., J. C. Cull, E. R. Braverman and D. E. Comings (1996) Reward deficiency syndrome. *American Scientist* 84: 132–45.

Blumenfeld, Z. et al. (1992) Spontaneous fetal reduction in multiple gestations assessed by transvaginal ultrasound. *British Journal of Obstetrics and Gynaecology* 99: 333–7.

Bogen, J. E. (1990) Partial hemispheric independence with the neocommissures intact. In *Brain Circuits and Functions of the Mind*, ed. C. Trevarthen, Cambridge: Cambridge University Press.

Boone, J. L. I. (1988) Parental investment, social subordination, and population processes among the fifteenth and sixteenth century Portuguese nobility. In *Human Reproductive Behavior*, ed. L. Betzig, M. Borgerhoff Mulder and P. Turke, Cambridge: Cambridge University Press.

Booth, A. and J. Dabbs (1993) Testosterone and men's marriages. *Social Forces* 72: 463–77.

Bowlby, J. (1982) *Attachment*. London: Hogarth Press and the Institute of Psychoanalysis.

Boyce, N. (1999) High and lows: can we switch mood on or off? *New Scientist* (London), 22 May, p. 11.

Breuer, J. and S. Freud (1955) Studies on hysteria. In vol. 2 of *The Standard Edition of the Complete Psychological Works of Sigmund Freud*, ed. J. Strachey, A. Freud, A. Strachey and A. Tyson, London: Hogarth Press and the Institute of Psychoanalysis.

Brockington, I. F., E. M. Schofield and P. Donnely (1978) A clinical study of puerperal psychosis. In *Mental Illness in Pregnancy and the Puerperium*, ed. M. Sandler, Oxford: Oxford University Press.

Brown, J. L. and A. Eklund (1994) Kin recognition and the major histocompatibility complex: an integrative review. *American Naturalist* 143: 435–61.

Brown, J. R. et al. (1996) A defect in nurturing in mice lacking the immediate early gene *fosB*. *Cell* 86: 297–309.

Brown, P. and L. Jordanova (1981) *Oppressive Dichotomies: The Nature/Nurture Debate*. Cambridge Women's Studies Group. London: Virago.

Burke, T. E. A. (1989) Parental care and mating behaviour of polyandrous dunnocks. *Nature* 338: 249–51.

Burley, N. (1979) The evolution of concealed ovulation. *American Naturalist* 114: 835–58.

Buss, D. M. (1994) *The Evolution of Desire: Strategies of Human Mating*. New York: Basic Books.

Buss, D. M. (1995) Evolutionary psychology: a new paradigm for psychological science. *Psychological Inquiry* 6(1): 1–30.

Buss, D. M. (1997) Sex differences in human mate preferences: evolutionary hypotheses tested in 37 cultures. In *Human Nature: A Critical Reader*, ed. L. Betzig, Oxford: Oxford University Press.

Buss, D. M. (1999) *Evolutionary Psychology: The New Science of the Mind*. Boston: Allyn and Bacon.

Campbell, S. B. and J. F. Cohn (1991) Prevalence and correlates of postpartum depression in first-time mothers. *Journal of Abnormal Psychology* 100(4): 594–9.

Carter, C. S. and L. G. Lowell (1993) Monogamy and the prairie vole. *Scientific American* 268(6): 70–6.

Chagnon, N. (1988) Life histories, blood revenge and warfare in a tribal population. *Science* 239: 985–90.

Chorney, M. J. et al. (1998) A quantitative trait locus associated with cognitive ability in children. *Psychological Science* 9(3): 1–7.

Clutton-Brock, T. H., F. E. Guinness and S. D. Albion (1982) *Red Deer: Behavior and Ecology of Two Sexes*. Chicago: Chicago University Press.

Coen, E. (1999) *The Art of Genes: How Organisms Make Themselves*. Oxford: Oxford University Press.

Cohen, P. (1998) Hand signals. *New Scientist* (London), 21 Nov., p. 25.

Cosmides, L. and J. Tooby (1987) From evolution to behavior: evolutionary psychology as the missing link. In *The Latest on the Best: Essays on Evolution and Optimality*, ed. J. Dupré, Cambridge, Mass.: MIT Press.

Cosmides, L. and J. Tooby (1992) Cognitive adaptations for social exchange. In *The Adapted Mind: Evolutionary Psychology and the Generation of Culture*, ed. J. H. Barkow, L. Cosmides and J. Tooby, New York: Oxford University Press.

Crawford, C. and D. L. Krebs (eds) (1998) *Handbook of Evolutionary Psychology: Ideas, Issues, and Applications*. Hillsdale, N.J.: Lawrence Erlbaum.

Crick, F. and G. Mitchison (1983) The function of dream sleep. *Nature* 304: 111–14.

Cronk, L. (1993) Parental favoritism toward daughters. *American Scientist* 81: 272–9.

Crook, J. H. and S. J. Crook (1988) Tibetan polyandry. In *Human Reproductive Behavior*, ed. L. Betzig, M. Borgerhoff Mulder and P. Turke, Cambridge: Cambridge University Press.

Cummins, J. (1999) Evolutionary forces behind human infertility. *Nature* 397: 557–8.

Dahaene, S. et al. (1998) Imaging unconscious semantic priming. *Nature* 395: 597–600.

Daly, M. and M. Wilson (1988) *Homicide*. New York: Aldine de Gruyter.

Daly, M. and M. Wilson (1995) Discriminative parental solicitude and the relevance of evolutionary models to the analysis of motivational systems. In *The Cognitive Neurosciences*, ed. M. Gazzaniga, Cambridge, Mass.; MIT Press.

Daly, M., M. Wilson and S. L. Weghorst (1982) Male sexual jealousy. *Ethology and Sociobiology* 3: 11–27.

Damasio, A. R. (1994) *Descartes' Error*. London: Macmillan.

Damasio, A. R. (1997) Thinking and feeling. Review of *The Emotional Brain* by Joseph LeDoux. *Scientific American* 276(6): 117–18.

Darwin, C. (1871) *The Descent of Man, and Selection in Relation to Sex*. London: John Murray.

Darwin, C. (1877) A biographical sketch of an infant. *Mind: A Quarterly Review of Psychology and Philosophy* 2: 285–94.

Darwin, C. (1886) *The Various Contrivances by which Orchids are Fertilized by Insects*. New York: Appleton.

Darwin, C. (1909) *The Foundations of The Origin of Species: Two Essays Written in 1842 and 1844 by Charles Darwin*, ed. F. Darwin. Cambridge, Cambridge University Press.

Darwin, C. (1958) *The Autobiography of Charles Darwin, 1809–1882*, ed. Nora Barlow. London: Collins.

Darwin, C. (1968) *The Origin of Species* (1859). London: Penguin.

Darwin, C. (1983–4) *The Correspondence of Charles Darwin*, ed. F. H. Burkhardt and S. Smith. Cambridge: Cambridge University Press.

Darwin, C. (1988) *Variation of Animals and Plants under Domestication*. London: William Pickering.

Darwin, C. (1998) *The Expression of the Emotions in Man and Animals* (1872). London: HarperCollins.

Davidoff, J., I. Davies and D. Roberson (1999) Colour categories in a stone-age tribe. *Nature* 398: 203–4.

Davies, P. S., J. H. Fetzer and T. R. Roster (1995) Logical reasoning and domain specificity: a critique of the social exchange theory of reasoning. *Biology and Philosophy* 10: 1–37.

Davis, A. (1998) Age differences in dating and marriage: reproductive strategies or social preferences? *Current Anthropology* 39(3): 374–80.

Dawkins, R. (1978) *The Selfish Gene*. Oxford: Oxford University Press.

Dawkins, R. (1986) *The Blind Watchmaker*. Harlow: Longman.

Dawkins, R. (1989) *The Selfish Gene*, revised and expanded edn. Oxford: Oxford University Press.

Dawkins, R. and J. R. Krebs (1979) Arms races between and within species. *Proceedings of the Royal Society of London B* 205: 489–511.

Deacon, T. (1990) Fallacies of progression in theories of brain-size evolution. *International Journal of Primatology* 11(3): 193–236.

Deacon, T. (1997) *The Symbolic Species: The Co-evolution of Language and the Human Brain*. Harmondsworth: Allen Lane.

Dennett, D. C. (1995) *Darwin's Dangerous Idea: Evolution and the Meanings of Life*. London: Allen Lane.

Diamond, J. (1997) *Why is Sex Fun? The Evolution of Human Sexuality*. London: Weidenfeld and Nicolson.

Dickemann, M. (1979) Female infanticide, reproductive strategies, and social stratification: a preliminary model. In *Evolutionary Biology and Human Social Behavior*, ed. N. Chagnon and W. Irons, North Scituate, Mass.: Duxbury.

Dixson, A. F. (1987) Observations on the evolution of the genitalia and copulatory behaviour in male primates. *Journal of the Zoological Society of London*

213: 423–43.

Dixson, A. F. (1999) *Primate Sexuality: Comparative Studies of the Prosimians, Monkeys, Apes, and Human Beings.* Oxford: Oxford University Press.

Domínguez, C. (1995) Genetic conflicts of interest in plants. *Trends in Ecology and Evolution* 10 (10 October): 412–16.

Driscoll, D. J. (1994) Genomic imprinting in humans. In *Molecular Medicine*, ed. T. Friedman, New York: Academic Press, vol. 4.

Dunbar, R. (1993) Coevolution of neocortical size, group size and language in humans. *Behavioral and Brain Sciences* 16: 681–735.

Dunbar, R. (1996) *Grooming, Gossip and the Evolution of Language.* London: Faber.

Durkheim, É. (1951) *Suicide.* New York: Random House.

Durkheim, É. (1976) *The Elementary Forms of the Religious Life.* London: Allen and Unwin.

Durkheim, É. (1982) *The Rules of Sociological Method and Selected Texts on Sociology and its Method.* London: Macmillan.

Durkheim, É. and M. Mauss (1963) *Primitive Classification.* London: Cohen and West.

Ekman, P. (1985) *Telling Lies: Clues to Deceit in the Marketplace, Politics, and Marriage.* New York: W. W. Norton.

Ekman, P. (1998) Introduction and Afterword to the Third Edition of Darwin's *Expression of the Emotions in Man and Animals.* In C. Darwin, *The Expression of the Emotions in Man and Animals*, London: HarperCollins.

Ellis, B. J. and D. Symons (1997) Sex differences in sexual fantasy: an evolutionary psychological approach. In *Human Nature: A Critical Reader*, ed. L. Betzig, Oxford: Oxford University Press.

Ellis, L. (1996) A discipline in peril: sociology's future hinges on curing its biophobia. *American Sociologist* 27: 21–41.

Falk, D. (1992) *Evolution of the Brain and Cognition in Hominids.* New York: American Museum of Natural History.

Falls, J. G., D. J. Pulford, A. W. Wylie and R. L. Jirtle (1999) Genomic imprinting: implications for human disease. *American Journal of Pathology* 154: 635–47.

Fearon, D. T. (1997) Seeking wisdom in innate immunity. *Nature* 388: 323–4.

Fischer, R. A. (1992) *To Dwell among Friends: Personal Networks in Town and City.* Chicago: University of Chicago Press.

Fisher, H. (1991) Monogamy, adultery, and divorce in cross-species perspective. In *Man and Beast Revisited*, ed. M. H. Robinson and L. Tiger, Washington DC: Smithsonian Institution Press.

Fisher, H. (1992) *The Anatomy of Love.* New York: W. W. Norton.

Fisher, R. A. (1930) *The Genetical Theory of Natural Selection.* Oxford: Clarendon Press.

Flinn, M. and B. England (1995) Childhood stress and family environment. *Current Anthropology* 36: 854–66.

Forsyth, D. W. (1997) Proposals regarding the neurobiology of oedipality. *Psychoanalysis and Contemporary Thought*, no. 2: 163–206.

Franke, U., J. A. Kerns and J. Giacolone (1995) The SNRPN gene Prader-Willi syndrome. In *Genomic Imprinting: Causes and Consequences*, ed. R. Ohlsson,

K. Hall and M. Ritzen, Cambridge: Cambridge University Press.

Freeman, D. (1983) *Margaret Mead and Samoa: The Making and Unmaking of an Anthropological Myth.* Cambridge, Mass.: Harvard University Press.

Freeman, D. (1996a) False paradise. *The Australian,* 3 Apr.

Freeman, D. (1996b) The debate, at heart, is about evolution. In *The Certainty of Doubt: Tributes to Peter Munz,* ed. M. Fairburn and W. Oliver, Wellington: Victoria University Press.

Freud, S. (1953) Fragment of an analysis of a case of hysteria. In vol. 7 of *The Standard Edition of the Complete Psychological Works of Sigmund Freud,* ed. J. Strachey, A. Freud, A. Strachey and A. Tyson, London: Hogarth Press and the Institute of Psychoanalysis.

Freud, S. (1955) The Moses of Michelangelo. In vol. 13 of *The Standard Edition of the Complete Psychological Works of Sigmund Freud,* ed. J. Strachey, A. Freud, A. Strachey and A. Tyson, London: Hogarth Press and the Institute of Psychoanalysis.

Freud, S. (1957a) On narcissism: an introduction. In vol. 14 of *The Standard Edition of the Complete Psychological Works of Sigmund Freud,* ed. J. Strachey, A. Freud, A. Strachey and A. Tyson, London: Hogarth Press and the Institute of Psychoanalysis.

Freud, S. (1957b) Repression. In vol. 14 of *The Standard Edition of the Complete Psychological Works of Sigmund Freud,* ed. J. Strachey, A. Freud, A. Strachey and A. Tyson, London: Hogarth Press and the Institute of Psychoanalysis.

Freud, S. (1957c) The unconscious. In vol. 14 of *The Standard Edition of the Complete Psychological Works of Sigmund Freud,* ed. J. Strachey, A. Freud, A. Strachey and A. Tyson, London: Hogarth Press and the Institute of Psychoanalysis.

Freud, S. (1958a) Formulations on the two principles of mental functioning. In vol. 12 of *The Standard Edition of the Complete Psychological Works of Sigmund Freud,* ed. J. Strachey, A. Freud, A. Strachey and A. Tyson, London: Hogarth Press and the Institute of Psychoanalysis.

Freud, S. (1958b) A note on the unconscious in psychoanalysis. In vol. 12 of *The Standard Edition of the Complete Psychological Works of Sigmund Freud,* ed. J. Strachey, A. Freud, A. Strachey and A. Tyson, London: Hogarth Press and the Institute of Psychoanalysis.

Freud, S. (1959) An autobiographical study. In vol. 20 of *The Standard Edition of the Complete Psychological Works of Sigmund Freud,* ed. J. Strachey, A. Freud, A. Strachey and A. Tyson, London: Hogarth Press and the Institute of Psychoanalysis.

Freud, S. (1961a) Civilization and its discontents. In vol. 21 of *The Standard Edition of the Complete Psychological Works of Sigmund Freud,* ed. J. Strachey, A. Freud, A. Strachey and A. Tyson, London: Hogarth Press and the Institute of Psychoanalysis.

Freud, S. (1961b) The ego and the id. In vol. 19 of *The Standard Edition of the Complete Psychological Works of Sigmund Freud,* ed. J. Strachey, A. Freud, A. Strachey and A. Tyson, London: Hogarth Press and the Institute of Psychoanalysis.

Freud, S. (1961c) Female sexuality. In vol. 21 of *The Standard Edition of the Complete Psychological Works of Sigmund Freud,* ed. J. Strachey, A. Freud, A.

Strachey and A. Tyson, London: Hogarth Press and the Institute of Psychoanalysis.

Freud, S. (1964) Moses and monotheism. In vol. 23 of *The Standard Edition of the Complete Psychological Works of Sigmund Freud*, ed. J. Strachey, A. Freud, A. Strachey and A. Tyson, London: Hogarth Press and the Institute of Psychoanalysis.

Fried, I., C. L. Wilson, K. A. MacDonald and E. J. Behnke (1998) Electric current stimulates laughter. *Nature* 391: 650.

Frisch, R. (1988) Fatness and fertility. *Scientific American* 258(3): 70–7.

Galin, D. (1974) Implications for psychiatry of left and right cerebral specialization: a neurophysiological context for unconscious processes. *Archives of General Psychiatry* 31: 572–83.

Galin, D., R. Diamond and D. Braff (1977) Lateralization of conversion symptoms: more frequent on the left. *American Journal of Psychiatry* 134: 578–80.

Garcia, J. (1981) Tilting at the paper mills of academe. *American Psychologist* 36(2): 149–58.

Gaulin, S. and C. Robbins (1991) Trivers-Willard effect in contemporary North American society. *American Journal of Physical Anthropology* 85: 61–9.

Gazzaniga, M. S. (1994) *Nature's Mind*. London: Penguin.

Gazzaniga, M. S. (1998) *The Mind's Past*. Berkeley: University of California Press.

Geist, V. (1971) *Mountain Sheep: A Study in Behavior and Ecology*. Chicago: University of Chicago Press.

Gloor, P. (1986) Role of the human limbic system in perception, memory, and affect: lessons from temporal lobe epilepsy. In *The Limbic System: Functional Organization and Clinical Disorders*, ed. B. K. Doane and K. E. Livingston, New York: Raven Press.

Gomendio, M., A. H. Harcourt and E. R. S. Roldán (1999) Sperm competition in mammals. In *Sperm Competition and Sexual Selection*, ed. T. R. Birkhead and A. P. Møller, San Diego: Academic Press.

Goodenough, O. and R. Dawkins (1994) The 'St Jude' mind virus. *Nature* 371: 22–3.

Goodman, J. D. T. and R. B. Anderton (1997) X-linkage, Lyonization and a female premium in the verbal IQ results of Orkney school children, 1947–1975. *Journal of Biosocial Science* 29: 63–72.

Gordon, H. W. (1990) The neurobiological basis of hemisphericity. In *Brain Circuits and Functions of the Mind*, ed. C. Trevarthen, Cambridge: Cambridge University Press.

Gosden, R. B. et al. (1999) Evolutionary interpretations of the diversity of reproductive health and disease. In *Evolution in Health and Disease*, ed. S. C. Stearns, Oxford: Oxford University Press.

Gould, J. and C. Gould (1994) *The Animal Mind*. New York: Scientific American Library.

Gould, S. J. (1977) *Ontogeny and Phylogeny*. Cambridge, Mass.: Belknap Press.

Gould, S. J. (1990) *Wonderful Life: The Burgess Shale and the Nature of History*. London: Hutchinson Radius.

Gould, S. J. and R. C. Lewontin (1979) The spandrels of San Marco and the Panglossian paradigm: a critique of the adaptationist programme. *Proceedings of the Royal Society of London B* 205: 581–98.

Gouldner, A. (1960) The norm of reciprocity: a preliminary statement. *American Sociological Review* 47: 73–80.

Grafen, A. (1982) How not to measure inclusive fitness. *Nature* 298: 425–6.

Grafen, A. (1992) Of mice and the MHC. *Nature* 360: 530.

Grant, V. J. (1998) *Maternal Personality, Evolution and the Sex Ratio: Do Mothers Control the Sex of the Infant?* London: Routledge.

Green, D. W. and R. Larking, (1995) The locus of facilitation in the abstract selection task. *Thinking and Reasoning* 1(2): 121–200.

Griffiths, M. (1968) *Echidnas*. Oxford: Pergamon Press.

Gur, R. and H. Sacheim (1979) Self-deception: a concept in search of a phenomenon. *Journal of Personality and Social Psychology* 37(2): 147–69.

Hagen, E. H. (1996) *Is Post-partum Depression Functional? An Evolutionary Enquiry*. Evanston, Ill.: Human Behavior and Evolution Society, Northwestern University.

Haig, D. (1993) Genetic conflicts in human pregnancy. *Quarterly Review of Biology* 68(4): 495–523.

Haig, D. (1994) Cohabitation and pregnancy-induced hypertension. *The Lancet* 344: 1633.

Haig, D. (1996) Gestational drive and the green-bearded placenta. *Proceedings of the National Academy of Sciences of the USA* 93: 6547.

Haig, D. (1999) Genetic conflicts of pregnancy and childhood. In *Evolution in Health and Disease*, ed. S. C. Stearns, Oxford: Oxford University Press.

Haig, D. and C. Graham (1991) Genomic imprinting and the strange case of the insulin-like growth factor II receptor. *Cell* 64 (22 Mar.): 1045–6.

Hamilton, J. A. (1962) *Postpartum Psychiatric Problems*. St Louis: C. V. Mosby.

Hamilton, W. D. (1963) The evolution of altruistic behavior. *American Naturalist* 97: 354–6.

Hamilton, W. D. (1964) The genetical evolution of social behaviour. *Journal of Theoretical Biology* 7: 1–16, 17–52.

Hamilton, W. D. (1967) Extraordinary sex ratios. *Science* 156: 477–88.

Hamilton, W. D. (1971) Geometry of the selfish herd. *Journal of Theoretical Biology* 31: 295–311.

Hamilton, W. D. (1996) *Narrow Roads of Gene Land*. Oxford: W. H. Freeman/Spektrum.

Hamilton, W. D. and M. Zuk (1989) Parasites and sexual selection. *Nature* 341: 289–90.

Harrington, A. (1985) Nineteenth-century ideas on hemisphere differences and 'duality of mind'. *Behavioral and Brain Sciences* 8: 617–60.

Harris, C. R. and H. E. Pashler (1995) Evolution and Human Emotions. *Psychological Inquiry* 6(1): 44–6.

Harris, J. R. (1999a) Children don't do things half way. Interview with John Brockman, Third Culture website, Feb., EDGE Foundation, New York, http://www.edge.org

Harris, J. R. (1999b) *The Nurture Assumption: Why Children Turn Out the Way They Do*. New York: Free Press.

Hawkes, K. (1990) Why do men hunt? Benefits for risky choices. In *Risk and Uncertainty in Tribal and Peasant Economies*, ed. E. Cashdan, Boulder, Colo.: Westview Press.

Hawkes, N. (1997) Why boys have to learn what comes naturally to girls. *The Times* (London), 12 June p. 5.

Heller, W. (1990) The neuropsychology of emotion: developmental patterns and implications for psychopathology. In *Psychological and Biological Approaches to Emotion*, ed. N. L. Stein, B. Leventhal and T. Trabasso, Hillsdale, NJ: Lawrence Erlbaum.

Henneberg, M. (1987) Hominid cranial capacity change through time: a darwinian process. *Human Evolution* 2(3): 213–20.

Henneberg, M. and M. Steyn (1993) Trends in cranial capacity and cranial index in Subsaharan Africa during the Holocene. *American Journal of Human Biology* 5: 473–9.

Herz, R. S. and E. D. Cahill (1997) Differential use of sensory information in sexual behavior as a function of gender. *Human Nature* 8(3): 275–86.

Heyer, E. et al. (1997) Estimating Y chromosome specific microsatellite mutation frequencies using deep rooting pedigrees. *Human Molecular Genetics* 6: 799–803.

Hill, K. and H. Kaplan (1988) Tradeoffs in male and female reproductive strategies among the Ache. In *Human Reproductive Behavior*, ed. L. Betzig, M. Borgerhoff Mulder and P. Turke, Cambridge: Cambridge University Press.

Holliday, M. A. (1978) Body composition and energy needs during growth. In vol. 2 of *Human Growth*, ed. F. Falker and J. M. Tanner, New York: Plenum.

Holm, V. A. et al. (1993) Prader-Willi syndrome: consensus diagnostic criteria. *Pediatrics* 91(2): 398–402.

Horgan, J. (1995) The new Social Darwinists. *Scientific American.* 273: 152.

Horrobin, D. F. (1998) Schizophrenia: the illness that made us human. *Medical Hypotheses* 50: 269–88.

Howell, N. (1979) *A Demography of the Dobe !Kung.* New York: Academic Press.

Hrdy, S. B. (1979) Infanticide among animals: a review, classification, and examination of the implications for reproductive strategies of females. *Ethology and Sociobiology* 1: 13–40.

Imperato-McGinley, J., R. Petersen, T. Gautier and E. Sturla (1979) Androgens and the evolution of male-gender identity among male pseudohermaphrodites with a 5α-reductase deficiency. *New England Journal of Medicine* 300(22): 1233–7.

Imperato-McGinley, J. et al. (1991) A cluster of male pseudohermaphrodites with 5α-reductase deficiency in Papua New Guinea. *Clinical Endocrinology* 34: 293–8.

Irons, W. (1998) Adaptively relevant environments versus the environment of evolutionary adaptedness. *Evolutionary Anthropology* 6(6): 194–204.

Iverson, J. M. and S. Goldin-Meadow (1998) Why people gesture when they speak. *Nature* 396: 228.

Jablonka, E. and M. Lamb (1995) *Epigenetic Inheritance and Evolution.* Oxford: Oxford University Press.

Jacob, F. (1976) *The Logic of Life: A History of Heredity.* New York: Random House.

Jaenisch, R. (1997) DNA methylation and imprinting: why bother? *Trends in Genetics* 13(8): 323–9.

James, W. H. (1986) Hormonal control of sex ratio. *Journal of Theoretical Biology* 118: 427–41.

Jarvis, J. U. M., M. J. O'Riain, N. C. Bennett and P. W. Sherman (1994) Mammalian eusociality: a family affair. *Trends in Ecology and Evolution* 9(2): 47–51.

Joffe, T. H. (1997) Social pressures have selected for an extended juvenile period in primates. *Journal of Human Evolution* 32: 593–605.

John, R. and M. Surani (1996) Imprinted genes and regulation of gene expression by epigenetic inheritance. *Current Opinion in Cell Biology* 8: 348–53.

Johnson, A. M. et al. (1992) Sexual lifestyles and HIV risk. *Nature* 360: 410–12.

Jolly, C. (1970) The seed-eaters: a new model of hominid differentiations based on a baboon analogy. *Man* 5(1): 1–66.

Jones, S. (1993) *The Language of the Genes: Biology, History and the Evolutionary Future*. London: HarperCollins.

Kavaliers, M. and D. D. Colwell (1995) Discrimination by female mice between the odours of parasitized and non-parasitized males. *Proceedings of the Royal Society of London B* 261: 31–5.

Kelly, M. P. et al. (1991) Human chorionic gonadotropin rise in normal and vanishing twin pregnancies. *Fertility and Sterility* 56: 221–9.

Kemp, M. (1998) Haeckel's hierarchies. *Nature* 395: 447.

Kendrick, K. M., M. R. Hinton and K. Atkins (1998) Mothers determine sexual preferences. *Nature* 395: 229–30.

Kenrick, D. and R. Keefe (1992) Age preferences in mates reflect differences in reproductive strategies. *Behavioral and Brain Sciences* 15: 75–133.

Keverne, E. B. (1992) Primate social relationships: their determinants and consequences. *Advances in the Study of Behavior* 21: 1–35.

Keverne, E. B., F. L. Martel, and C. M. Nevison (1996a) Primate brain evolution: genetic and functional considerations. *Proceedings of the Royal Society of London B* 262: 689–96.

Keverne, E. B. et al. (1996b) Genomic imprinting and the differential roles of parental genomes in brain development. *Developmental Brain Research* 92: 91–100.

Killingback, T. and M. Doebeli (1999) 'Raise the stakes' evolves into a defector. *Nature* 400: 518.

King, R. C. and W. D. Stansfield (1997) *A Dictionary of Genetics*. Oxford: Oxford University Press.

Knight, J. (1998) Upwardly mobile. *New Scientist*. (London), 7 Nov., p. 6.

Koepp, M. J. et al. (1998) Evidence for striatal dopamine release during a video game. *Nature* 393: 266–8.

Kolb, C. R. and J. Brain (1995) Blindsight in normal observers. *Nature* 377 (28 Sept.) 336–8.

Konotey-Ahulu, F. (1980) Male procreative superiority index (MPSI): the missing coefficient in African anthropogenetics. *British Medical Journal* 281: 1700–2.

Krebs, D. (1970) Altruism: an examination of the concept and a review of the literature. *Psychological Bulletin* 73: 258–302.

Kroeber, A. L. (1917) The Superorganic. *American Anthropologist* 19: 163–213.

Kuhn, T. (1970) *The Structure of Scientific Revolutions*. Chicago: University of

Chicago Press.

Kumar, R. and K. M. Robson (1984) A prospective study of emotional disorders in childbearing women. *British Journal of Psychiatry* 144: 35–47.

Lamb, M. (ed.) (1981) *The Role of the Father in Child Development.* New York: Wiley.

Lampert, A. and J. Yassour (1992) Parental investment and risk taking in simulated family situations. *Journal of Economic Psychology* 13(3): 499–507.

Lancaster, J. B. and C. S. Lancaster (1983) Parental investment: the hominid adaptation. In *How Humans Adapt: A Biocultural Odyssey* ed. D. J. Ornter, Washington DC: Smithsonian Institution Press.

Landy, H. J. et al. (1986) The 'vanishing twin': ultrasonographic assessment of fetal disappearance in the first trimester. *American Journal of Obstetrics and Gynecology* 155: 14–19.

LeDoux, J. (1996) *The Emotional Brain: The Mysterious Underpinnings of Emotional Life.* New York: Simon and Schuster.

LeDoux, J. (1997) Parallel memories: putting emotions back into the brain. Interview with John Brockman, Third Culture website, Feb., EDGE Foundation, New York, http://www.edge.org

Lefebvre, L. et al. (1998) Abnormal maternal behaviour and growth retardation associated with loss of the imprinted gene *Mest. Nature Genetics* 20: 163–9.

LeVay, S. (1993) *The Sexual Brain.* Cambridge, Mass.: MIT Press.

Lévi-Strauss, C. (1969) *The Elementary Structures of Kinship.* Boston: Beacon Press.

Lewin, R. (1993) *Human Evolution.* Boston: Blackwell Scientific.

Lewontin, R. C. (1978) Adaptation. *Scientific American* 239 (3): 156–69.

Lewontin, R. C. (1979a) Fitness, survival and optimality. In *Analysis of Ecological Systems*, ed. D. J. Horn, G. R. Stairs and R. D. Mitchell, Columbus: Ohio State University Press.

Lewontin, R. C. (1979b) Sociobiology as an adaptationist program. *Behavioral Science* 24: 5–14.

Liberman, N. and Y. Klar (1996) Hypothesis testing in Wason's selection task: social exchange cheating detection or task understanding. *Cognition* 58: 127–56.

Libet, B. (1985) Unconscious cerebral initiative and the role of conscious will in voluntary action. *The Behavioral and Brain Sciences* 8: 529–66.

Lindström, L. et al. (1984) CSF and plasma b-casomorphin-like opioid peptides in postpartum psychosis. *American Journal of Psychiatry* 141: 1059–66.

Lloyd, A. and R. Nesse (1992) The evolution of dynamic mechanisms. In *The Adapted Mind: Evolutionary Psychology and the Generation of Culture*, ed. J. Barkow, L. Cosmides and J. Tooby, Oxford: Oxford University Press.

Lloyd, E. A. (1999) Evolutionary psychology: the burden of proof. *Biology and Philosophy* 14: 211–33.

Lopreato, J. and T. Crippen (1999) *Crisis in Sociology: The Need for Darwin.* New Brunswick and London: Transaction.

Lorberbaum, J. (1992) No strategy is evolutionarily stable in the repeated prisoner's dilemma. *Journal of Theoretical Biology* 168: 117–30.

Lotem, A., M. A. Fishman and L. Stone (1999) Evolution of cooperation between individuals. *Nature* 400: 226–7.

Love, R. E. and C. M. Kessler (1995) Focusing in Wason's selection task: content and instruction effects. *Thinking and Reasoning* 1(2): 153–82.

Lucotte, G. et al. (1994) Reduced variability in Y-chromosome-specific haplotypes for some Central African populations. *Human Biology* 66(3): 519–26.

Lummaa, V., J. Merilä, and A. Kause (1998) Adaptive sex ratio variation in pre-industrial human *(Homo sapiens)* populations? *Proceedings of the Royal Society of London B* 265: 563–8.

Lumsden, C. J. and E. O. Wilson (1981) *Genes, Mind, and Culture: The Coevolutionary Process.* Cambridge, Mass.: Harvard University Press.

Lyon, B., J. Eadie and L. Hamilton (1994) Parental choice selects for ornamental plumage in American coot chicks. *Nature* 371 (15 Sept.): 240–3.

McCullogh, J. M. and E. York Barton (1991) Relatedness and mortality risk during a crisis year: Plymouth Colony, 1620–1621. *Ethology and Sociobiology* 12: 195–209.

McGrew, W. C. (1998) Culture in non-human primates? *Annual Review of Anthropology* 27: 301–28.

MacLean, P. D. (1949) Psychosomatic disease and the 'visceral brain'. *Psychosomatic Medicine* 11: 338–53.

MacLean, P. D. (1986) Culminating developments in the evolution of the limbic system: the thalamocingulate division. In *The Limbic System: Functional Organization and Clinical Disorders,* ed. B. K. Doane and K. E. Livingston, New York: Raven Press.

MacLean, P. D. (1990) *The Triune Brain in Evolution.* New York: Plenum Press.

Magrath, R. D. (1989) Hatching asynchrony and reproductive success in the blackbird. *Nature* 339: 536–8.

Malthus, T. R. (1982) *An Essay on the Principle of Population.* London: Penguin.

Manning, J. T., R. Anderton and S. M. Washington (1996) Women's waists and the sex ratio of their progeny: evolutionary aspects of the ideal female body shape. *Journal of Human Evolution* 31: 41–7.

Marshall Graves, J. A. (1995a) The evolution of mammalian sex chromosomes and the origin of sex determining genes. *Philosophical Transactions of the Royal Society London B* 350: 305–12.

Marshall Graves, J. A. (1995b) The origin and function of the mammalian Y chromosome and Y-borne genes – an evolving understanding. *BioEssays* 17(4): 311–21.

Marslen-Wilson, W. D. and L. K. Tyler (1997) Dissociating types of mental computation. *Nature* 387: 592–4.

Martin, P. (1997) *The Sickening Mind: Brain, Behaviour, Immunity and Disease.* London: HarperCollins.

Martin, R. D. (1983) *Human Brain Evolution in an Ecological Context.* New York: American Museum of Natural History.

Martin, R. D. (1996) Scaling of the mammalian brain: the maternal energy hypothesis. *News in Physiological Sciences* 11 (Aug.): 149–56.

Mathers, K. and M. Henneberg (1996) Were we ever that big? Gradual increase in hominid body size over time. *Homo* 46(2): 141–73.

May, R. M. (1978) Human reproduction reconsidered. *Nature* 272(6/4): 491–5.

Maynard Smith, J. (1982) *Evolution and the Theory of Games.* Cambridge:

Cambridge University Press.

Maynard Smith, J. (1988) *Games, Sex and Evolution.* London: Harvester-Wheatsheaf.

Maynard Smith, J. and E. Szathmáry (1995) *The Major Transitions in Evolution.* Oxford: W. H. Freeman/Spektrum.

Maynard Smith, J. and F. Szathmáry (1999) *The Origins of Life.* Oxford: Oxford University Press.

Mead, M. (1928) *Coming of Age in Samoa: A Psychological Study of Primitive Youth for Western Civilisation.* London: Jonathan Cape.

Mealey, L. and W. Mackey (1990) Variation in offspring sex ratio in women of differing social status. *Ethology and Sociobiology* 11: 83–95.

Michiels, N. K. and L. J. Newman (1998). Sex and violence in hermaphrodites. *Nature* 391: 647–8.

Miller, L. (1991) *Freud's Brain: Neuropsychodynamic Foundations of Psychoanalysis.* New York: The Guilford Press.

Mlot, C. (1998) Unmasking the emotional unconscious. *Science* 280: 1006.

Mock, D. W. and G. A. Parker (1997) *The Evolution of Sibling Rivalry.* Oxford: Oxford University Press.

Moore, T. and D. Haig (1991) Genomic imprinting in mammalian development: a parental tug-of-war. *Trends in Genetics* 7(2): 45–9.

Morris, J. S. et al. (1996) A differential neural response in the human amygdala to fearful and happy facial expressions. *Nature* 383 (31 Oct.): 812–15.

Motluk, A. (1998) Body talk. *New Scientist* (London), 14 Nov., p. 11.

Murdock, P. (1967) *Ethnographic Atlas.* Pittsburgh: University of Pittsburgh Press.

Nathanielsz, P. W. (1996) The timing of birth. *American Scientist* 84: 562–9.

Nesse, R. M. and K. C. Berridge (1997) Psychoactive drug use in evolutionary perspective. *Science* 278: 63–6.

Newman, J. (1995). How breast milk protects newborns. *Scientific American*, no. 6: 58–61.

Nicholls, R. D., S. Saitoh and B. Horsthemke (1998) Imprinting in Prader-Willi and Angelman syndromes. *Trends in Genetics* 14(5): 194–200.

Nichols, M. J. and W. T. Newsome (1999) Monkeys play the odds. *Nature* 400: 217–18.

Nimmon, D. (1994) Sex and the brain. *Discover* (Mar.): 6–71.

Nowak, M. A. and K. Sigmund (1998) Evolution of indirect reciprocity by image scoring. *Nature* 393: 573–7.

Nyberg, F., L. Lindström and L. Terenius (1988) Reduced beta-casein levels in milk samples from patients with postpartum psychosis. *Biological Psychiatry* 23: 115–22.

Office of National Statistics (1996) *Social Trends.* London: HMSO.

Ohlsson, R., K. Hall and M. Ritzen (eds) (1995) *Genomic Imprinting: Causes and Consequences.* Cambridge: Cambridge University Press.

Orans, M. (1999) Mead misrepresented. *Science* 283: 1649–50.

Owens, I. P. F., C. Rowe and A. L. R. Thomas (1999) Sexual selection, speciation and imprinting: separating the sheep from the goats. *Trends in Ecology and Evolution* 14: 131–2.

Packer, C., M. Tatar and A. Collins (1998) Reproductive cessation in female mammals. *Nature* 392: 807–11.

Pagel, M. (1998) Darwin's fixed course. *Nature* 393: 752.

Paley, W. (1986) *Natural Theology, or Evidences of the Existence and Attributes of the Deity*. Charlottesville, Va.: Lincoln-Rembrandt/Ibis.

Pawlowski, B. (1999) Loss of oestrus and concealed ovulation in human evolution. *Current Anthropology* 40(3): 257–75.

Penton-Voak, I. et al. (1999) Menstrual cycle alters face preference. *Nature* 399: 741–2.

Perrett, D. I. et al. (1998) Effects of sexual dimorphism on facial attractiveness. *Nature* 394: 884–7.

Phillips, M. L. et al. (1997) A specific neural substrate for perceiving facial expressions of disgust. *Nature* 389: 495–8.

Pinker, S. (1994) *The Language Instinct: The New Science of Language and Mind*. London: Allen Lane.

Pinker, S. (1997) *How the Mind Works*. London: Allen Lane.

Pinto-Correia, C. (1997) *The Ovary of Eve: Egg and Sperm and Preformation*. Chicago: University of Chicago Press.

Pitt, B. (1973) Maternity blues. *British Journal of Psychiatry* 122: 431–5.

Platt, M. L. and P. W. Glimcher (1999) Neural correlates of decision variables in parietal cortex. *Nature* 400: 233–8.

Plomin, R., J. C. DeFries and G. E. McClearn (1997) *Behavioral Genetics*. New York: W. H. Freeman.

Potts, R. (1997) Comments on reverse engineering. EDGE Foundation, New York, http://www.edge.org

Povinelli, D. J. and T. M. Preuss (1995) Theory of mind: evolutionary history of a cognitive specialization. *Trends in Neuroscience* 18(9): 418–24.

Premack, D. and G. Woodruff (1978) Does the chimpanzee have a theory of mind? *Behavioral and Brain Sciences* 1(4): 515–26.

Profet, M. (1992) Pregnancy sickness as adaptation: a deterrent to maternal ingestion of teratogens. In *The Adapted Mind: Evolutionary Psychology and the Generation of Culture*, ed. J. H. Barkow, L. Cosmides and J. Tooby, Oxford: Oxford University Press.

Pruitt, D. G. (1968) Reciprocity and credit building in a laboratory dyad. *Journal of Personality and Social Psychology* 8: 143–7.

Puccetti, R. (1973) Brain bisection and personal identity. *British Journal of Philosophy of Science* 24: 339–55.

Puccetti, R. (1981) The case for mental duality: evidence from split-brain data and other considerations. *The Behavioral and Brain Sciences* 4: 93–123.

Ramachandran, V. S. (1994) Phantom limbs, neglect syndromes, repressed memories, and Freudian psychology. In *Selectionism and the Brain*, ed. O. Sporns and G. Tononi, San Diego: Academic Press.

Ramachandran, V. S. (1995) Anosognosia in parietal lobe syndrome. *Consciousness and Cognition* 4: 22–51.

Ramachandran, V. S. (1996) The evolutionary biology of self-deception, laughter, dreaming and depression: some clues from anosognosia. *Medical Hypotheses* 47(5): 347–62.

Ramachandran, V. S. and S. Blakeslee (1998) *Phantoms in the Brain*. London: Fourth Estate.

Ramachandran, V. S. and D. Rogers-Ramachandran (1996) Synaesthesia in phantom limbs induced with mirrors. *Proceedings of the Royal Society of London, B* 263: 377–86.

Ramanamma, A. and U. Bambawale (1980) The mania for sons: an analysis of social values in South Asia. *Sociology and Medicine* 14(B): 107–10.

Reik, W. and E. Maher, R. (1997) Imprinting in clusters: lessons from Beckwith–Wiedemann syndrome. *Trends in Genetics* 13(8): 330–4.

Reik, W. and A. Surani (1997) *Genomic Imprinting.* Oxford: IRL Press.

Resta, R. (1995) Whispered hints. *American Journal of Medical Genetics* 59: 131–3.

Ridley, M. (1993) *The Red Queen: Sex and the Evolution of Human Nature.* London: Viking.

Ridley, M. (1996) *The Origins of Virtue.* London: Viking.

Ridley, M. (1999) *Genome: The Autobiography of a Species in 23 Chapters.* London: Fourth Estate.

Ritvo, L. (1990) *Darwin's Influence on Freud: A Tale of Two Sciences.* New Haven: Yale University Press.

Roberts, G. and T. N. Sherratt (1998) Development of cooperative relationships through increasing investment. *Nature* 394: 175–9.

Rosenberg, K. and W. Trevathan (1996) Bipedalism and human birth: the obstetrical dilemma revisited. *Evolutionary Anthropology* 4(5): 161–8.

Rudnicki, M., L. O. Vejerslev and J. Junge (1991) The vanishing twin: morphological and cytogenetic evaluation of an ultrasonographic phenomenon. *Gynecologic and Obstetric Investigation* 31: 141–5.

Ruff, C. B., E. Trinkaus and W. Holliday Trenton (1997) Body mass and encephalization in Pleistocene *Homo. Nature* 387: 173–6.

Salem, A.-H., F. M. Badr, M. F. Gaballah and S. Pääbo (1996) The genetics of traditional living: Y-chromosomal and mitochondrial lineages in the Sinai Peninsula. *American Journal of Human Genetics* 59: 741–3.

Sapir, E. (1921) *Language.* New York: Harcourt, Brace and World.

Sasse, G., H. Müller, R. Chakraborty and J. Ott (1994) Estimating the frequency of nonpaternity in Switzerland. *Human Heredity* 44: 337–43.

Sawyer, J. (1966) The altruism scale: a measure of cooperative, individualistic, and competitive orientation. *American Journal of Sociology* 7: 407–16.

Segal, N. L. (1995) The genetics of olfactory perception. In *Handbook of Olfaction and Gustation*, ed. R. L. Doty, New York: Marcel Dekker.

Shavit, Y., C. S. Fischer and Y. Koresh (1994) Kin and nonkin under collective threat: Israeli networks during the Gulf War. *Social Forces* 72: 1197–215.

Short, R. V. (1976) The evolution of human reproduction. *Proceedings of the Royal Society of London B* 195: 3–24.

Short, R. V. (1979) Sexual selection and its component parts: somatic and genital selection as illustrated by man and the great apes. *Advances in the Study of Behaviour* 9.

Short, R. V. (1980) Sexual selection: the meeting point of endocrinology and sociobiology. In *Endocrinology 1980*, ed. I. A. Cumming, Canberra: Australian Academy of Science.

Short, R. V. (1987) The biological basis for the contraceptive effects of breast feeding. *International Journal of Gynaecology and Obstetrics* 25 (Supplement): 207–17.

Sillén-Tullberg, B. and A. P. Møller (1993) The relationship between concealed ovulation and mating systems in anthropoid primates: a phylogenetic analysis. *American Naturalist* 141(1): 1–25.

Singh, D. (1993) Body shape and women's attractiveness: the critical role of waist-to-hip ratio. *Human Nature* 4(3): 297–321.

Skinner, B. F. (1969) *Contingencies of Reinforcement: A Theoretical Analysis.* Englewood Cliffs, N.J.: Prentice Hall.

Skuse, D. (1998) Genetic fractionation of perception and memory: evidence from Turner syndrome of oppositely imprinted loci on the X-chromosome affecting neurodevelopment. Paper, Institute of Cognitive Neuroscience.

Skuse, D. (1999) Genomic imprinting of the X chromosome: a novel mechanism for the evolution of sexual dimorphism. *Journal of Laboratory and Clinical Medicine* 133(1): 23–32.

Skuse, D. H. et al. (1997) Evidence from Turner's syndrome of an imprinted X-linked locus affecting cognitive function. *Nature* 387: 705–8.

Smith, R. (1999) The timing of birth. *Scientific American* 280(3): 50–7.

Spencer, H. (1878) *The Principles of Psychology.* London: Williams and Norgate.

Spencer, H. (1884) *First Principles.* London: Williams and Norgate.

Spencer, H. (1885) *The Principles of Sociology.* London: Williams and Norgate.

Sperber, D., F. Cara and V. Girotto (1995) Relevance theory explains the selection task. *Cognition* 57: 31–95.

Sperry, R. W. (1977) Forebrain commissurotomy and conscious awareness. *Journal of Medicine and Philosophy* 2(2).

Springer, S. P. and G. Deutsch (1998) *Left Brain Right Brain: Perspectives from Cognitive Neuroscience.* New York: W. H. Freeman.

Stevens, A. and J. Price (1996) *Evolutionary Psychiatry: A New Beginning.* London: Routledge.

Stoddart, D. M. (1990) *The Scented Ape: The Biology and Culture of Human Odour.* Cambridge: Cambridge University Press.

Strassmann, B. I. (1996) The evolution of endometrial cycles and menstruation. *Quarterly Review of Biology* 71(2): 181–220.

Strassmann, B. I. and R. I. M. Dunbar (1999) Human evolution and disease: putting the Stone Age in perspective. In *Evolution in Health and Disease*, ed. S. C. Stearns, Oxford: Oxford University Press.

Sun, F.-L. et al. (1997) Transactivation of *Igf2* in a mouse model of Beckwith–Wiedemann syndrome. *Nature* 389: 809–15.

Symons, D. (1979) *The Evolution of Human Sexuality.* New York: Oxford University Press.

Tager-Flusberg, H. (1993) What language reveals about the understanding of mind in children with autism. In *Understanding Other Minds*, ed. S. Baron-Cohen, H. Tager-Flusberg and D. J. Cohen, Oxford: Oxford University Press.

Taylor, A. et al. (1994) Serum cortisol levels are related to moods of elation and dysphoria in new mothers. *Psychiatry Research* 54: 241–7.

Taylor, T. (1996) *The Prehistory of Sex: Four Million Years of Human Sexual Culture.* London: Fourth Estate.

Tesser, A., R. Gatewood and M. Driver (1968) Some determinants of gratitude. *Journal of Personality and Social Psychology* 9: 232–6.

Thapa, S., R. V. Short and M. Potts (1988) Breast feeding, birth spacing and their effects on child survival. *Nature* 335: 679.

Thomson, R. F. (1985) *The Brain: An Introduction to Neuroscience*. New York: W. H. Freeman.

Tooby, J. and L. Cosmides (1992) The psychological foundations of culture. In *The Adapted Mind: Evolutionary Psychology and the Generation of Culture*, ed. J. Barkow, L. Cosmides and J. Tooby, Oxford: Oxford University Press.

Tooby, J. and L. Cosmides (1997) Think again. In *Human Nature: A Critical Reader*, ed. L. Betzig, Oxford: Oxford University Press.

Tranel, D. and A. R. Damasio (1985) Knowledge without awareness: an autonomic index of facial recognition by prosopagnosics. *Science* 228: 1453–5.

Trevarthen, C. (ed.) (1990a) *Brain Circuits and Functions of the Mind: Essays in Honor of Roger W. Sperry*. Cambridge: Cambridge University Press.

Trevarthen, C. (1990b) Growth and education of the hemispheres. In *Brain Circuits and Functions of the Mind*, ed. C. Trevarthen, Cambridge: Cambridge University Press.

Trivers, R. L. (1971) The evolution of reciprocal altruism. *Quarterly Review of Biology* 46: 35–57.

Trivers, R. L. (1972) Parental investment and sexual selection. In *Sexual Selection and the Descent of Man 1871–1971*, ed. B. Campbell, London: Heinemann.

Trivers, R. L. (1974) Parent–offspring conflict. *American Zoologist* 14: 249–64.

Trivers, R. L. (1981) Sociobiology and politics. In *Sociobiology and Human Politics*, ed. E. White, Lexington, Mass.: Lexington Books.

Trivers, R. L. (1985) *Social Evolution*. Menlo Park, Calif.: Benjamin/Cummings.

Trivers, R. L. and A. Burt (1999) Kinship and genomic imprinting. In *Genomic Imprinting*, ed. R. Ohlsson. New York: Springer Verlag.

Trivers, R. L. and D. Willard (1973) Natural selection of parental ability to vary the sex ratio of offspring. *Science* 179: 90–2.

Tucker, D. M. and S. L. Frederick (1989) Emotion and brain lateralization. In *Handbook of Social Psychophysiology*, ed. H. Wagner and A. Manstead, New York: Wiley.

Turner, G. (1996a) Finding genes on the X chromosome by which *Homo* may have become *sapiens*. *American Journal of Human Genetics* 58: 1109–10.

Turner, G. (1996b) Intelligence and the X chromosome. *Lancet* 347: 1814–15.

Turner, P. E. and L. Chao (1999) Prisoner's dilemma in an RNA virus. *Nature* 398: 441–3.

Vogel, S. A. (1990) Gender differences in intelligence, language, visual-motor abilities, and academic achievement in students with learning disabilities: a review of the literature. *Journal of Learning Disabilities* 23(1): 44–52.

Voland, E. (1988) Differential infant and child mortality in evolutionary perspective: data from the late seventeenth to nineteenth century Ostfriesland. In *Human Reproductive Behavior*, ed. L. Betzig, M. Borgerhoff Hulder and P. Turke, Cambridge: Cambridge University Press.

Voland, E. and R. Voland (1989) Evolutionary biology and psychiatry: the case of anorexia nervosa. *Ethology and Sociobiology* 10: 223–40.

Wallace, J. and E. Sadalla (1966) Behavioral consequences of transgression: the effects of social recognition. *Journal of Experimental Research in Personality* 1: 187–94.

Watson, G. (1985) *The Idea of Liberalism*. London: Macmillan.

Watson, J. (1970) *Behaviorism*. New York: Norton.

Wauters, L. A., S. A. de Crombrugghe, N. Nour and E. Matthysen (1995) Do female roe deer in good condition produce more sons that daughters? *Behavioral Ecology and Sociobiology* 37: 189–93.

Wedekind, C. and S. Füri (1997) Body odour preferences in men and women: do they aim for specific MHC combinations or simple heterozygosity? *Proceedings of the Royal Society of London B* 264: 1471–9.

Wedekind, C., J. Seebeck, F. Bettens and A. Paepke (1995) MHC-dependent mate preferences in humans. *Proceedings of the Royal Society of London B* 260: 245–9.

Weiskrantz, L. (1986) *Blindsight: A Case Study and Implications*. Oxford: Clarendon Press.

Weiskrantz, L. (1997) *Consciousness Lost and Found*. Oxford: Oxford University Press.

Wells, A. (1998) Evolutionary psychology and theories of cognitive architecture. *Handbook of Evolutionary Psychology: Ideas, Issues and Applications*, ed. C. Crawford and D. Krebs, Hillsdale, N.J.: Lawrence Erlbaum.

Wenk, R. A., T. Houtz, M. Brooks and F. A. Chiafari (1992) How frequent is heteropaternal superfecundation? *Acta Geneticae Medicae et Gemellologiae* 41: 43–7.

White, D. R. (1988) Rethinking polygyny. *Current Anthropology* 29(4): 529–58.

Whiten, A. et al. (1999) Culture in chimpanzees. *Nature* 399: 682–5.

Whitmeyer, J. M. (1998) On the relationship between memes and genes: a critique of Dennett. *Biology and Philosophy* 13: 187–204.

Wickelgren, I. (1998) Tracking insulin to the mind. *Science*. 280: 517–18.

Wickler, W. (1986) On intra-uterine mother–offspring conflict and a possible case in the pig. *Ethology* 72: 250–3.

Williams, G. C. (1966) *Adaptation and Natural Selection: A Critique of Some Current Evolutionary Thought*. Princeton, N.J.: Princeton University Press.

Williams, G. C. (1985) A defense of reductionism in evolutionary biology. In *Oxford Surveys in Evolutionary Biology*, ed. R. Dawkins and M. Ridley, Oxford: Oxford University Press.

Williams, G. C. (1996) *Plan and Purpose in Nature*. London: Weidenfeld and Nicolson.

Winson, J. (1985) *Brain and Psyche*. New York: Anchor Press/Doubleday.

Wolpert, L. (1991) *The Triumph of the Embryo*. Oxford: Oxford University Press.

World Health Organization (1996) *The World Health Report 1996: Fighting Disease, Fostering Development*. Geneva: WHO.

Wright, B. (1942) Altruism in children and the perceived conduct of others. *Journal of Abnormal Psychology* 37: 218–33.

Wright, R. (1994) *The Moral Animal: The New Science of Evolutionary Psychology*. New York: Pantheon Books.

Wynne-Edwards, V. C. (1986) *Evolution through Group Selection*. Oxford: Blackwell Scientific.

Yalom, I. D., D. T. Lunde and R. H. Moos (1968) 'Postpartum blues' syndrome. *Archives of General Psychiatry* 18: 16–27.

Index

spite 89
split-brain research 137–40, 147
spontaneous abortion 200
Sry 63
Standard Social Science Model
    (SSSM) 228–34, 266
step-parents 87–8
sterility 80–2
suboptimal design 19–21, 35
sucking 216–17
superego 223–4
super-organic/super-organism
    72–3
survival 5
survival of the fittest 6–9
Swiss army knife model 22–4
sympathy 104

talking cure 131
testes 166–7
testosterone 8–9, 161–2, 181
theory of mind 113–15
throat 21
thymus gland 57
Tibet 157
Tinbergen, Niko 112
TIT-FOR-TAT 92–102, 105
Tooby, John 17, 19, 22, 123
triune brain 24–9
Trivers, Robert L. 76, 102–6,
    132–3, 143, 145–6, 218, 162
Trivers–Willard rule 179–87, 219
Turner's syndrome 253–60, 267
turtles 63–5
twins 164, 200

unconscious 134–48, 268

variance of reproductive success 14,
    152–5, 177, 266
variation 5
verbal representations 147–8
Vervet monkeys 171–2
vestibular system 140–3
violence 87, 165–6, 258–9
voice recognition 143–4
volition 136, 265

waist-to-hip ratio 162–3
Wason selection task 106–10
Watson, James 49
Watson, John B. 239
weaning conflicts 212–19
Wedekind, Claus 177
Weismann, August 49
wildebeest 76–8
Williams, George 18, 19, 22, 112
Williams syndrome 251–2
word brain 27
World War I 99–100
wug-test 246–7
Wynne-Edwards, V. C. 74

X chromosome 48–52, 83–4, 250,
    255–60
X^m/X^p 255–60

Y chromosome 48–52, 63, 83–4,
    153, 250, 258
Yanomamö 166, 258

Zebra finch 180–2